AMPLIFY

GRAPHIC NARRATIVES OF FEMINIST RESISTANCE

AMPLIFY

GRAPHIC NARRATIVES OF FEMINIST RESISTANCE

NORAH BOWMAN
MEG BRAEM

Art by
DOMINIQUE HUI

UNIVERSITY OF TORONTO PRESS
Toronto Buffalo London

© University of Toronto Press 2019
Toronto Buffalo London
utorontopress.com
Printed in Canada

All rights reserved. The use of any part of this publication reproduced, transmitted
in any form or by any means, electronic, mechanical, photocopying, recording,
or otherwise, or stored in a retrieval system, without prior written consent of the
publisher – or in the case of photocopying, a license from Access Copyright (the
Canadian Copyright Licensing Agency) 320–56 Wellesley Street West, Toronto,
Ontario, M5S 2S3 – is an infringement of the copyright law.

Library and Archives Canada Cataloguing in Publication

Title: Amplify : graphic narratives of feminist resistance / Norah Bowman, Meg
    Braem ; art by Dominique Hui.
Names: Bowman, Norah, author. | Braem, Meg, author.
Description: Includes bibliographical references.
Identifiers: Canadiana 20190091649 | ISBN 9781487593636 (cloth) |
    ISBN 9781487593629 (paper)
Subjects: LCSH: Feminists—Political activity—Case studies. | LCSH: Women
    political activists—Case studies. | LCSH: Social justice—Case studies. | LCSH:
    Feminism—Case studies. | LCGFT: Case studies.
Classification: LCC HQ1155 .B69 2019 | DDC 305.42—dc23

We welcome comments and suggestions regarding any aspect of our publications –
please feel free to contact us at news@utorontopress.com or visit our internet site at
utorontopress.com.

North America
5201 Dufferin Street
North York, Ontario, Canada, M3H 5T8
2250 Military Road
Tonawanda, New York, USA, 14150
ORDERS PHONE: 1-800-565-9523
ORDERS FAX: 1-800-221-9985
ORDERS E-MAIL: utpbooks@utpress.
utoronto.ca

UK, Ireland, and continental Europe
NBN International
Estover Road, Plymouth, PL6 7PY, UK
ORDERS PHONE: 44 (0) 1752 202301
ORDERS FAX: 44 (0) 1752 202333
ORDERS E-MAIL: enquiries@
nbninternational.com

Every effort has been made to contact copyright holders; in the event of an error or
omission, please notify the publisher.

This book is printed on acid-free paper.

University of Toronto Press acknowledges the financial assistance to its publishing
program of the Canada Council for the Arts and the Ontario Arts Council, an agency
of the Government of Ontario.

 Canada Council Conseil des Arts
for the Arts du Canada

 ONTARIO ARTS COUNCIL
CONSEIL DES ARTS DE L'ONTARIO
an Ontario government agency
un organisme du gouvernement de l'Ontario

Funded by the Financé par le
Government gouvernement
of Canada du Canada

 Canada

 MIX
Paper from
responsible sources
FSC FSC® C016245

Dedicated to Heather and Janet

In memory of Wu Chien-Shiung, an inspirational woman physicist

CONTENTS

PREFACE

The stories presented in this book are based on historical information drawn from books, newspapers, and interviews. College professor Norah Bowman, who has studied intersectional feminist resistance movements around the world, researched the historical narratives, and developed the feminist analysis. Norah shared the historical narratives with playwright Meg Braem. Meg and Norah developed a script together, with Meg in charge of storytelling and drama. Artist Dominique Hui turned the story into a graphic narrative, using historical images that Norah collected from archives and news sources. Together the authors cooperated to amplify feminist resistance stories.

The representations are influenced by the authors' own narrative styles and affinities. Others might tell these stories differently, at different times, for different reasons. Here these stories are shared humbly, in a spirit of solidarity, with anyone anywhere who wishes for a freer, more just world.

ACKNOWLEDGMENTS

We acknowledge the support, guidance, and friendship of Ruthann Lee, Will Pratt, Ismael Traore, Texas Constantine, Mo Sadeghi-Esfahlani, Okanagan College, Anne Brackenbury, Anne Laughlin, Jacinda Mack, and Vanessa Blake. Norah Bowman in particular acknowledges the support of Okanagan College.

AMPLIFY

GRAPHIC NARRATIVES OF FEMINIST RESISTANCE

INTRODUCTION

Norah Bowman

Feminist, queer, and antiracist histories can be thought of as histories of those who are willing to be willful, who are willing to turn a diagnosis into an act of self-description. Let's go back: let's listen to what and to who is behind us.

(Sara Ahmed, *Willful Subjects*, 134)

The willful taking-on of a feminist political identity is an act of *resistance*. Feminism resists stagnant gender roles; feminism demands a better, fairer world; feminism amplifies voices that the powerful prefer to ignore. Feminist resistance anticipates risk. Claiming feminism means proclaiming resistance to a global politic in which gender is unequally assigned, performed, and policed. Claiming feminism means stepping up to learn from other feminists about social justice, racialization, mobility, class, sexuality, ability, and citizenship. This feminist book serves as a megaphone for feminist voices, calling out with courage and calling you in to the resistance.

In this book, as in much contemporary feminist writing and activism, the authors take an *intersectional feminist* approach. Pioneers of this approach include the Combahee River Collective, formed in 1977 by a group of black American women who were civil rights advocates, feminists, and advocates for lesbian rights. The Combahee River Collective Statement declared that to be a feminist one must combat multiple oppressions. Until the most vulnerable person is free, no one is free; this explicitly political, activist, feminist, anti-racist, anti-capitalist, and lesbian rights document laid the ground for what later became intersectional feminism. In 1989, American legal and critical race scholar Kimberlé Crenshaw introduced intersectionality as an academic term to describe and evaluate how multiple privileges and oppressions operate on any given individual experience. Feminist analysis and feminist activism must therefore be cautious about ascribing singular causes to oppressive experiences; an intersectional analysis asks questions about race, class, disability, citizenship, sexual orientation, gender, and religion. Black feminists in the United States knew that their struggle for liberation was not accurately represented by either white feminist or black civil rights organizing; intersectional analysis is a sophisticated tool for making sure our social justice work is more inclusive and ultimately more effective across all segments of society.

Whether or not you read intersectional feminist theory (we suggest you read some, and we include a reading list at the end of each chapter), you likely recognize that an Indigenous Canadian woman's experience of oppression is different from that of a Latina woman living in the United States or of a transgender man living in Russia. A white heterosexual woman's experience of sexist oppression is different from that of a black lesbian friend who, in addition, also faces racism and homophobia. We share some experiences, but not all, and it is only with humility and an eagerness to learn that we can be feminists who struggle to make the world better for everyone (not just for ourselves). White, monied, straight, cisgender privileged feminists who don't examine their own privilege end up contributing to the oppressive structures of *white supremacy*, *heteronormativity*, and *capitalism*. Intersectional feminism takes the position that our different experiences of oppression and privilege must be acknowledged, dismantled, and reimagined if we are to bring about a better world. The authors of this book believe that feminism is most powerful when it takes into account all our social relations.

Social justice organizers know from practice that oppressions are experienced in clusters. Poverty and racism are often experienced together. In Canada, Indigenous children and women live in disproportionate poverty. In the United States, black men and women are overrepresented in prisons. This is because white supremacy and racism are mutually reinforcing forces of oppression. They work together to delegitimize poor, queer, immigrant, and single-parent families. They deem white elite families more credible and more moral, and refuse to hear the wisdom of diverse families.

We expect that our readers will be diverse: male, female, trans, racialized, white, well-off, poor, middle-class, disabled, able-bodied, queer, straight, newcomer, refugee, young, and old. We believe that every person is deserving of liberation. Feminist activist writer Harsha Walia writes that, because "oppression is relational and contextual," we can't always know how people experience oppression, and our arguments over who is more oppressed are counterproductive (189). We experience privilege and oppression differently. We are beholden to one another's stories; the first practice of social justice is listening.

And there is infinite wisdom in the lives of resisters. The survival story of a single-parent immigrant family reveals indomitable strength and resistance to sexism, white-supremacy, *colonialism*, classism, and heteronormativity. People are drawn to freedom, and women have always known how to share wisdom and strength under conditions of oppression. It is through these resistance stories that our book hopes to inspire a new generation of intersectional feminists.

We believe that feminist resistance stories are stories about connection, compassion, determination, and love. Love of nation, love of family, love of art, or love of self; in every story there is a passion that keeps the woman and her community going.

A Book of Grassroots Feminist Resistance Stories

This book, then, is an amplification of stories to feed your community conversations about feminism. Of course, we tell only seven stories, and there are forms of feminist resistance that we aren't representing. We haven't told stories of women running for public office, or working from within economic and political institutions.

Our stories are mostly about grassroots organizing, working from positions of relative disempowerment. By *grassroots* we mean organizing that is led by people experiencing oppression, working without official institutional support.

Feminist resistance comes from inside and outside social institutions; in a future publication we could tell the stories of intersectional feminist work from inside power structures. For now, our focus is on the stories of change from the ground up, and we hope that you are inspired to look for more stories of intersectional feminism in your world.

Media and politics play parts in the story of Nadya, Masha, and Kat in Pussy Riot. International media attention on their art and their imprisonment brought worldwide attention to human rights abuses of LGBTQIIA people in Russia. The story of Pussy Riot is also a personal story about women with young children who willingly risk jail time for their political beliefs. Our vignette about Pussy Riot might motivate you to look further into Russian feminist performance art. As well, it might propel you to wonder what it means for mothers to engage in dangerous direct action.

Not all the organizations and individuals in this book identify primarily as feminist activists. Vancouver activist and organizer Harsha Walia's writing and activism call forward the stories of migrant people. Walia, author of *Beyond Border Imperialism*, is an anti-racist border imperialism activist whose leadership is recognized globally. So, while Walia's work is not only, or centrally, feminist, her intersectional social justice framework is exactly the practice of courage most needed – and often practiced – by feminist movements in the twenty-first century. State forces around the world, in recent years, have increasingly militarized borders and criminalized movement of people seeking better, safer lives. Border violence often replicates white supremacist structural oppression, allowing white people greater border mobility than racialized people. Resistance to border violence demands an intersectional approach, as many people seeking greater mobility are fleeing a range of gender, ethnic, and political oppressions.

What Harsha Walia and Pussy Riot share is a strong connection to community. For the women we write about in this book, feminist practice includes being attentive to women's social networks, thinking about women's material survival, and being willing to engage in vulnerable relationships. The resistance these women undertake is a process of relation-building. We propose that resistance to gendered oppression is measured not by absolute demolition of the oppressive structures but by the solidarity, survival, and creativity of the resisters.

Angela Davis is an American feminist, activist, and writer. For Davis, feminism is a worldview and a practice:

> The tradition of feminism with which I have always identified ... is linked to all the important social movements – against racism, against imperialism, for labor rights, and so forth. This tradition of feminism emphasizes certain habits of perception, certain habits of imagination. Just as it was once important to imagine a world in which women were not assumed to be inherently inferior to men, it is now important to imagine a world without xenophobia and the fenced borders designed to make us think of people in and from a southern region outside the USA as the enemy. (20)

Davis's feminism imagines a world without fear of difference, a world in which borders do not create enemies and gender is not a hierarchy. She sets forth intersectional feminism as a visionary practice. Davis's "radical feminism" eschews a movement limited to individual gain; it rejects war and accepts risk (20). Radical feminism, then, moves beyond asking for a better day or a better life for one woman, or even for one group of women. Radical feminism asks for a better society. Radical feminism works to unsettle the status quo, because it realizes that intersecting oppressive frameworks (economic, border, race) must be resisted in order to ensure lasting social change.

Feminist resistance is the process of taking a radically imaginative feminist vision and working to put it into action in contemporary society. While resistance calls for an interruption to systemic oppression, and is inherently troublesome to *someone*, feminist resistance is also always visionary. It is radically inclusive, it challenges status quo organizing practices, and it asks all people involved to challenge their own biases and ways of thinking that may contribute to oppression. Two examples of radical resistance organizing are the creation of non-hierarchical change groups and the development of social visions that benefit people unlike and even unknown to the organizers. A group without a rigid hierarchy creates resistance as it works, because it challenges members to take on roles of leadership and action they might otherwise avoid. And by building radically inclusive visions, feminist resistance movements avoid the pitfalls of single-issue liberal feminism. Intersectional feminist resistance is a liberating process.

Interrupting "Business as Usual": Doing Direct Action

For writer and activist Judy Rohrer, Davis's call to imagine a freer world, without oppressive divisions, is at the heart of feminist direct action. *Direct action* activism seeks to change a specific target, like oppressive border practices or restrictions to birth control; it is organized, specific, and visionary. Feminist direct action flows from a critique of oppressive structures as they exist, and a belief that "by interrupting 'business as usual,'" positive change can result (225). And what is the change that might result? The goals of direct action "are often multiple and can include: arousing public awareness of an issue (via the media, the Internet, bystanders, and so forth); applying pressure to a target (be it government agency, corporation, university, media outlet, etc.); disabling a target (for example, missile silos, logging equipment, military recruitment offices, factory farms); modeling the world we want to live in; and building community" (225).

Rohrer tells us about the Women in Black (WIB) movement in the United States, an international peace network action group in which women dress in black and stand in public places in silent vigil (227). WIB started in Israel in 1998, protesting Israel's occupation of the West Bank and Gaza. WIB states, on its website, that the organization has "a feminist understanding: that male violence against women in domestic life and in the community, in times of peace and in times of war, are interrelated. Violence is used as a means of controlling women" (cited in Rohrer 228). By protesting war publicly Women in Black takes direct action against institutional violence.

Rohrer takes her own experience of direct action and academic training to respond to the "jaded response to direct action" that criticizes actions that do not "stop injustice or change public opinion" (229). We've heard these critics – saying that rallies are not clever enough, or protests are not informed enough, and that they are therefore a waste of time at best, or damaging to social change at worst.

Rohrer's response to such cynicism is to ask for feminists and social justice thinkers to pose intellectually generous questions. Instead of asking "Did your rally stop the oppression?" Rohrer suggests we ask:

> What are the goals of the organizers? Is there more than one constituency being organized and how is that managed? What do the participants identify as their reasons for joining an action and how do they match up with the organizer's goals? How much has to do with conscience? How much has to do with process? How might we think about these actions as acts of cultural transformation? (230)

We would add other questions, inspired by Rohrer's critique: Does this action interrupt "business as usual" (230)? Does the action ask participants to move from a passive critique of injustice to an active participation in that critique? Does the action push private worries into the public sphere? Does this action push the private gender oppression that men, women, queer folk, children, immigrants, refugees, and Indigenous people face every day into a public discussion? Does this action create critical conversations among viewers, passersby, media, and politicians? Does this action employ a vision of a more equitable, peaceful, just world, and is this vision fundamental to the action?

What are your questions? By what measure do you hold your municipal, state, provincial, or federal representatives accountable for creating a better world? Do you hold your teachers and parents accountable for creating freer classrooms and families? And if you are a feminist yourself, how do you measure your own daily actions to build a less oppressive society?

None of the questions should lead to a pass or fail; just as legislation to create a more equitable nation is never definitive, direct action is not about seeking a lasting solution to intersecting oppressions. The expectation for rallies, protests, performances, or activist literature to quickly overcome white supremacist, capitalist, colonial patriarchy is unrealistic and damaging. Every march for transgender rights in the United States and Canada contributes to the democratic dialogue about gender expression; legislative change, when it comes, will seem fast and dramatic, but it will only come after significant and multifarious social discussion.

Intersectional feminist movements, then, include discussion as well as direct action, and ideally work with a principle of radical inclusion. *Radical inclusion* means that a multitude of direct actions, some of which include people with disabilities, some of which include artists, some of which include babies, and some of which include incarcerated people, come together, over time, to contribute to social change.

The Feminist Collectives

This book sets forth narrative vignettes of resistance practice that are either explicitly gender rights- and feminist-based or more broadly human rights-based; all can be studied as examples of intersectional feminist resistance activism. These stories are intended to represent just a few of the many forms of feminist resistance, not *all* feminist resistance. We write about feminist resistance in collective movements to show how women working together to fight oppression and create a better world can have creative, progressive impact. These collectives should inform and inspire our readers to look for similar collectives in their own communities, or to start them if they don't exist. In these narratives, we offer a small glimpse into complex actions taking place in the presence of powerful geo-political forces; some chapters provide a great deal of personal bio-graphical detail, while others pan out for a broader social narrative. In this way, we offer learners and teachers micro and macro studies of resistance and social change for study and discussion. We believe this approach draws in more learners, allowing for different kinds of narrative enjoyment, and encouraging sociological and/or liter-ary analysis.

The collectives we narrate are Pussy Riot, Idle No More, and Rote Zora. Pussy Riot, a performance art collective, uses art, theater, and music to stand up against homophobia, police violence, and patri-archal oppression in Russia. Idle No More is an Indigenous ally or-ganization started by three Canadian women that continues to fight for Indigenous sovereignty and against racist colonial oppression in North America. In the 1980s, Rote Zora grew out of Revolution-ary Cells, an anti-capitalist European group, to become an under-ground network of women who took direct action for reproductive freedom, women's security, and women's sexual autonomy in Ger-many. These groups organized to resist racism, homophobia, misog-yny, colonialism, and white supremacy. Their feminist direct action was motivated by a vision of a world in which every girl, woman, and queer person, and every black, Indigenous, and otherwise ra-cialized or marginalized person could live in security and dignity.

Direct action has always been an aspect of feminist resistance. Some of the original members of Rote Zora had experience with the urban guerrilla movement, the Revolutionary Cells, a radical leftist group responsible for 185 anti-capitalist actions in Germany during that period. Like Pussy Riot, Rote Zora grew out of a mixed-gender activist group in order to focus on social issues related to gender and feminism. Their targets of direct action included factories, shops that sold pornography, and medical research facilities and these actions were often violent, angry, and uncompromising. In the history of feminist resistance we often find women refusing to conform to expectations of femininity, such as a pacifist orientation. Women taking part in violent activism are sometimes criticized for engaging in patriarchal, dominant behavior, yet they are also sometimes heralded for courageous rejection of female stereotypes of submissiveness. Coming out of a tradition of nineteenth-century anarchist action, radical attacks such as the bombing of buildings and destruction of elite property are called *propaganda of the deed*, and are meant to be insurrectionary practices to inspire widespread revolt. In this way, the actions of Rote Zora and Pussy Riot could be seen as calls for feminist revolution. As you read the chapters in this book, consider how their actions built momentum for other types of actions.

We in North America live in a time when a commitment to inter-sectional feminism means taking into account struggles for Indigenous rights. In this book, we introduce readers to the Indigenous rights movement Idle No More. In Canada, in March 2012, Sylvia McAdams, Nina Wilson, Jessica Gordon, and Sheelah McLean held a conference in Saskatoon they called Idle No More. The women gathered in opposition to Bill C-45, an omnibus bill that moved to take away rights and protection for lands and waters guaranteed to First Nations in Canada through historic treaties. At the same time, news media began to cover poverty in northern First Nations communities in Canada, including the community of Attawapiskat, which lacked potable water and adequate shelter for its Indigenous residents. By the end of 2012, the Idle No More movement, led and supported by Indigenous men and women across Canada and the United States, had organized a number of conferences and public events.

The women of Idle No More and Chief Theresa Spence, the chief of Attawapiskat, called for a day of action in December 2012, and Chief Spence began a hunger strike to demand justice for her people. Idle No More has always been a grassroots direct-action movement with a vision for a world in which Indigenous men, women, and children are free from poverty and violence. When you read the story of Idle No More, you meet the kind of visionary activism Angela Davis has in mind when she advocates for social movements that disrupt the status quo. Idle No More has led political demands for an inquiry into the more than 1000 murdered and missing Indigenous women in Canada. Women have led the Idle No More movement in academic, legal, political, and activist circles around North America; it is a social justice movement organized and led by women of all ages and backgrounds and is integral to an understanding of contemporary feminist and women's resistance movements. Canada has far to go to redress more than 150 years of oppression of Indigenous people, and the leadership of Idle No More continues to guide Canadians, Indigenous and non-Indigenous, in the hard work of reconciliation.

Individuals in Resistance

As well as stories about feminist and women-led resistance collectives, we tell the stories of some individual women: No One Is Illegal activist and writer Harsha Walia, peace activist Leymah Gbowee, and transgender rights activist Laxmi Narayan Tripathi. We also focus on Kathleen Cleaver's role in the Black Panther Party.

Each of these women's stories reflects ongoing, collective activism for a world in which people are free from sexist, racist, homophobic, transphobic, and militaristic oppression. Gbowee's peace activism comes from her experience as a single mother and a women's trauma counselor in a time of war. Walia works for human dignity for migrant populations; she is inspired by the people in her community and her family. Tripathi's activism comes from the women she worked alongside and her own experiences as a woman, dancer, and hijra. Each woman has a moving and inspiring personal story, and each woman is connected to broader, global movements for a more equitable world.

When I asked activist and writer Harsha Walia to let us feature her in this book, Walia answered that she favored collective resistance narratives and was wary of hero stories. Her thoughtful answer shows her dedication to collective, grassroots activism. Walia, as a writer, speaker, and organizer, has advocated for the dignity of the many unknown, unnamed, and often undocumented men and women who move across national borders. Her activism might be inspired by her own life – her father was a migrant worker and her mother's family was divided by the 1947 border partition of India and Pakistan. Walia herself lived with precarious legal status for years – but her vision is for all humanity. In our book we tell the story of Walia's work with No One Is Illegal, a migrant justice movement that mobilizes support for refugees, undocumented migrants, and workers, and works within an anti-colonial, anti-capitalist, ecological justice, Indigenous ally, and anti-oppression framework. We recommend to readers Walia's book *Undoing Border Imperialism*, an influential social justice book that has found its way into social justice meetings, rallies, and classrooms across North America.

Theories of intersectional feminism are inherently practical and evolutionary. Readers might ask how their own developing feminist knowledge reflects, or fails to reflect, the complexities of oppression and freedom around them, in their own communities. Who might be excluded from your feminist thinking? To what extent does your feminist practice contribute to anti-colonial, anti-racist activism? Can you develop a feminist perspective that allows for influence from the marginalized communities around you?

The story of Liberian peace activist Leymah Gbowee is a story of a woman risking her own safety for her community and her nation. It is also an example of solidarity and direct action. When Leymah Gbowee was seventeen years old, the Liberian civil war started, an event that upended her life with her family. During the war, Gbowee became a single mother, a social worker, and a trauma counselor. She worked with community members and with ex–child soldiers, and led the women's movement to restore peace. In 2003, Gbowee organized the Women of Liberia Mass Action for Peace in a protest that lasted weeks and included thousands of women.

Gbowee went on to hold important roles in Liberia, across Africa, and with the United Nations. In 2011, for her work as a peace activist, Gbowee was awarded the Nobel Peace Prize. When you read the story of Leymah Gbowee, you might think of women throughout history who have suffered from the trauma of war and who have advocated for peace. *Transnational feminism* is feminist practice based on solidarity; it assumes that feminists from Western nations can learn from feminists from non-Western nations. By rejecting the hegemonic white feminist philanthropy model in which Western feminists call the shots, transnational feminism offers learning, solidarity, and global strength among communities.

What, then, can Gbowee's courage and leadership offer feminists in North America? How can we learn from her indefatigable spirit, her willingness to stand up to a violent dictator, and her ability to transform empathy into leadership? In your home country, what roles do women take in military negotiations? How often are women's stories heard? What is the role of feminism in times of war, and can men also take on advocacy for feminism and peace? Is feminism always a peace-building movement, and if so, why? We hope that you go on to learn more about pacifist and anti-war movements led by women throughout history and today, such as the Revolutionary Association of the Women of Afghanistan (RAWA), or the Swiss Feminist Peace Organization (cfd), and in so doing learn more about transnational feminism.

In the area of feminist resistance, transgender activist Laxmi Narayan Tripathi is an example of an individual drawing on culture and direct action to challenge gender norms. Tripathi combines a love for music and dance with a dedication to rights activism. Her story shows us how activism can move from a local level to a national and an international level. Tripathi's advocacy for transgender rights is one of ongoing struggle, as most nations do not recognize the right to gender expression or allow for a third gender on official identity documents. After you read Tripathi's story, research *gender expression* rights in your own country. Are people protected from discrimination based on gender expression? How prevalent is rights activism? How does the discourse around that activism intersect with class, gender, sexuality, and race? And how can diverse cultural gender practices inform Eurocentric binary gender norms?

In the 1960s in the United States, the Black Panther Party (BPP) represented organized action against systemic racism and white supremacy. The BPP coordinated community support as well as direct resistance; they fed people, provided medical care to black communities, and took families to visit incarcerated loved ones. Kathleen Cleaver, secretary of the BPP in the 1960s, highlights the importance of cultural community support alongside direct action resistance – stronger, nurturing communities are more likely to be resilient and creative. Women of the BPP brought a feminist ideology to the black civil rights movement in the United States, challenging their own partners, sisters, and brothers to value gender equality. And as social activist and former BPP leader Angela Davis articulates, a vision for a strong community, and the knowledge to sustain communities, is central to any revolutionary vision. In this book, when you read the stories of the women of the BPP, you might want to consider the extent to which social justice struggles are intersectional. Can sexism and racism be fought separately, or are we more effective when we put forward an anti-racist feminist vision?

The African-American feminist bell hooks coined the phrase "white supremacist capitalist patriarchy": her vision for a better world is one in which people live in comfort, in equality, with freedom from oppression regardless of their race, gender, or sexuality, and she welcomes men to the movement (1–12). Her feminism is always intersectional, both in resistance and in vision. The BPP brought together black men and women to fight white supremacy, capitalism, and imperialism. Today, the Black Lives Matter movement, led by the passionate anti-racist organizers Patrisse Khan-Cullors, Alicia Garza, and Opal Tometi, calls for radical inclusion. These three women call on the United States and Canada to dismantle, once and for all, oppressive criminal justice, policing, and incarceration practices. We hope that readers of this book will find their own ways to be advocates for an inclusive and just world.

Just Another Bleeding Heart

When I was a college student, I had a button that said "just another bleeding heart for peace and justice." Since then I have run for political office, I have become a professor of gender studies, and I have organized and taken part in many direct actions. Some of the actions

I participated in were inspiring, inclusive, and life-changing for those of us involved. Some were less so – we would pack up our signs and go home glum. Or worse, we would go home divided and angry. Social change isn't easy, and the best way forward isn't always clear. But at a certain point, one must stand up for the freedom, security, and well-being of vulnerable people. I encourage you to find a way to amplify the voices that are least heard, and I encourage you to forgive yourself and others for sometimes getting it wrong.

We should, at least, strive to always learn from one another, and bring our individual experiences of gender, race, class, ability, and citizenship to our activism. Since feminist resistance entails a vision in which all people are respected as creative, rights-bearing, and community-contributing, we need to listen to one another. We need to share our weaknesses and build our strengths together. Gbowee's vulnerability and fortitude as a single mother gave her courage to stand in front of warlord Charles Taylor. After their time in a Russian prison, the women of Pussy Riot fought for LGBTQIIA rights *and* prisoners' rights. And with No One Is Illegal, Harsha Walia has brought solidarity to the Black Lives Matter movement while continuing to fight for dignity for migrant workers.

This book contributes to feminist activist scholarship by collecting real stories of resistance. Not only can you learn about intersectional feminist analysis by reading this introduction and analyzing each chapter, you can compare and consider a range of different feminist actions. You can then go on to read the strong words of Angela Davis's brave radical feminist writing, Sara Ahmed's literary feminist analysis, Leanne Betasamosake Simpson's Indigenous feminist calls to action, and Harsha Walia's anti-colonial, anti-imperialist analysis. We hope that you read their contributions to contemporary intellectual discourse and activist practice as part of a study of historic and ongoing feminist action. With fellow learners, you will be able to envision, write about, speak about, and bring about the world you want to live in.

In the stories in *Amplify* you may find inspiration on how to organize, how to speak up, and how to locate your personal and community resources. Whether you follow the #MeToo movement on social media, attend a Black Lives Matter rally, volunteer for a political candidate, or research social issues in your community, we hope that the stories in this book inspire you to be another bleeding heart for peace and justice, to amplify the call for an end to oppression.

Works Cited

Davis, Angela. *The Angela Davis Reader.* Ed. Joy James. Oxford: Blackwell Publishing, 1998.

hooks, bell. *Feminism Is for Everybody: Passionate Politics.* Cambridge, MA: Southend Press, 2000.

Rohrer, Judy. "'We Say Code Pink': Feminist Direct Action and the 'War on Terror.'" *Feminism and War: Confronting U.S. Imperialism,* Chandra T. Mohanty, Minnie Bruce Pratt, and Robin Riley, eds. London: Zed Press, 2008, 224–31.

Walia, Harsha. *Undoing Border Imperialism.* Washington, DC: AK Press, 2013.

pussy riot!

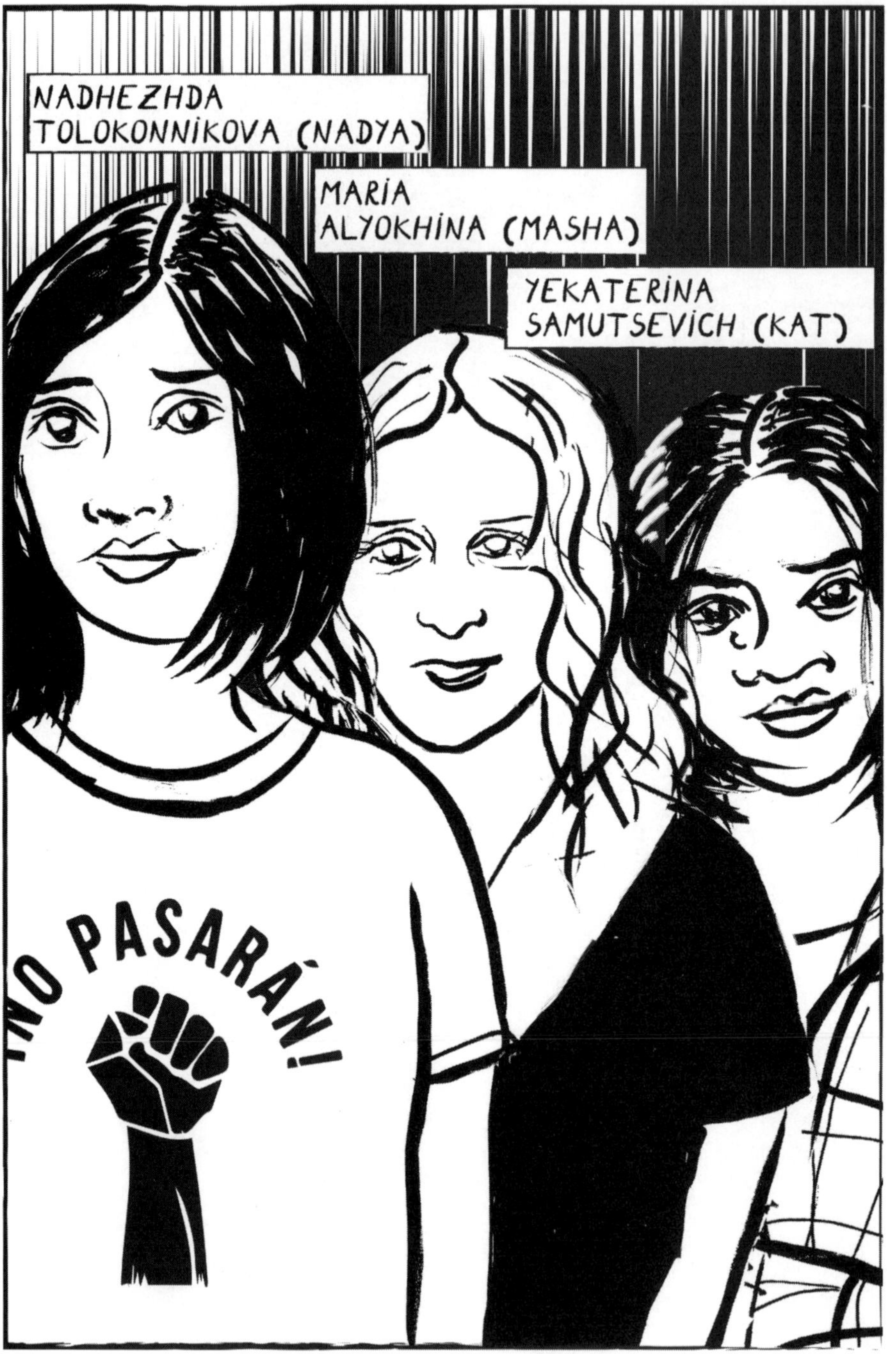
NADHEZHDA TOLOKONNIKOVA (NADYA)
MARIA ALYOKHINA (MASHA)
YEKATERINA SAMUTSEVICH (KAT)
¡NO PASARÁN!

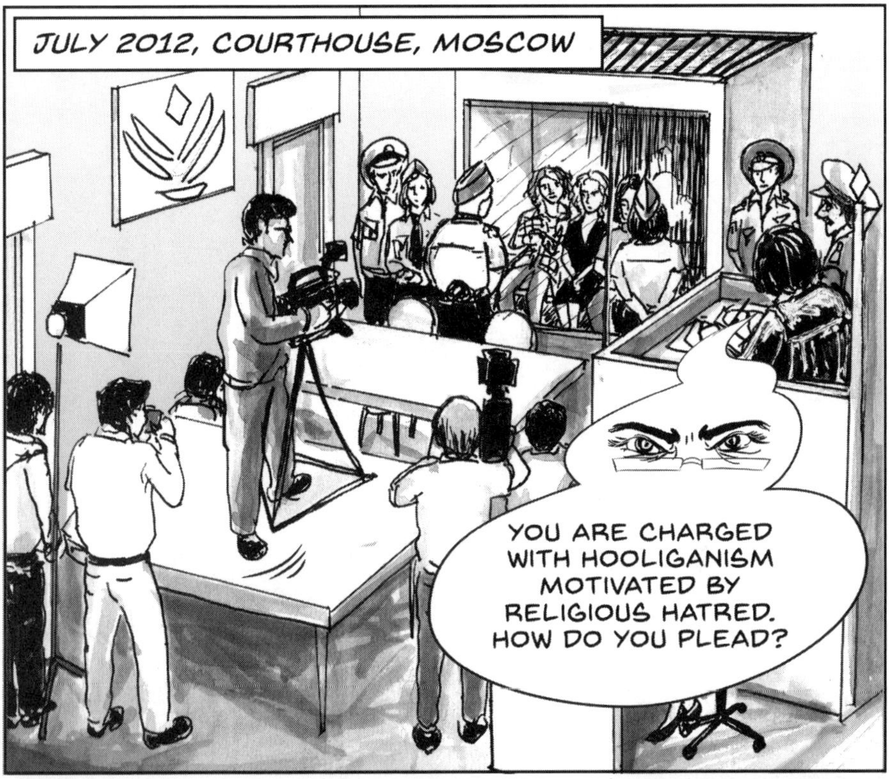
JULY 2012, COURTHOUSE, MOSCOW
YOU ARE CHARGED WITH HOOLIGANISM MOTIVATED BY RELIGIOUS HATRED. HOW DO YOU PLEAD?

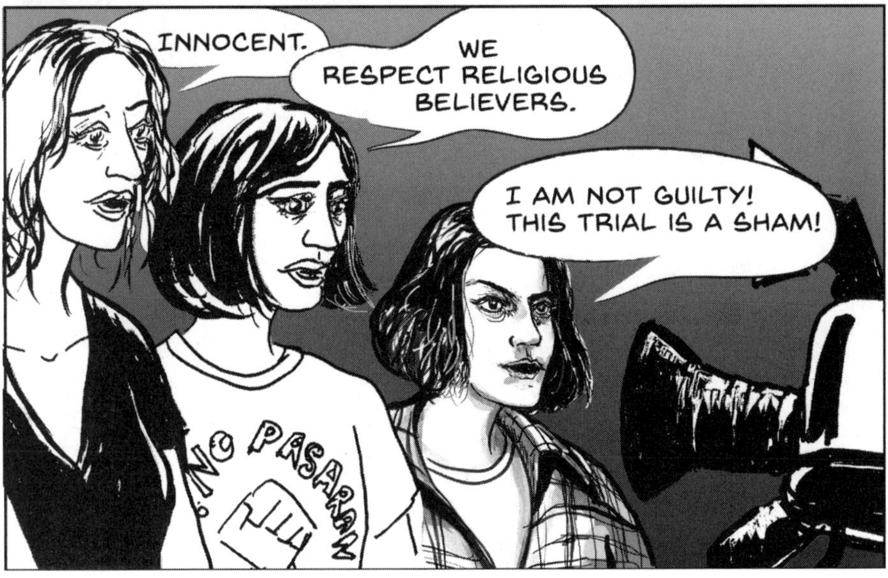
INNOCENT.
WE RESPECT RELIGIOUS BELIEVERS.
I AM NOT GUILTY! THIS TRIAL IS A SHAM!
NO PASARAN

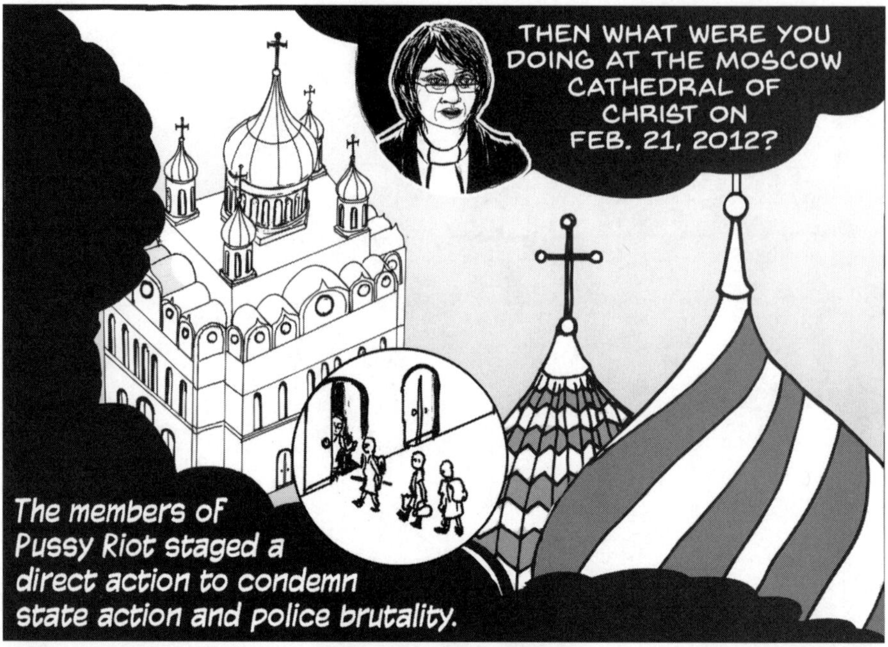
THEN WHAT WERE YOU DOING AT THE MOSCOW CATHEDRAL OF CHRIST ON FEB. 21, 2012?
The members of Pussy Riot staged a direct action to condemn state action and police brutality.

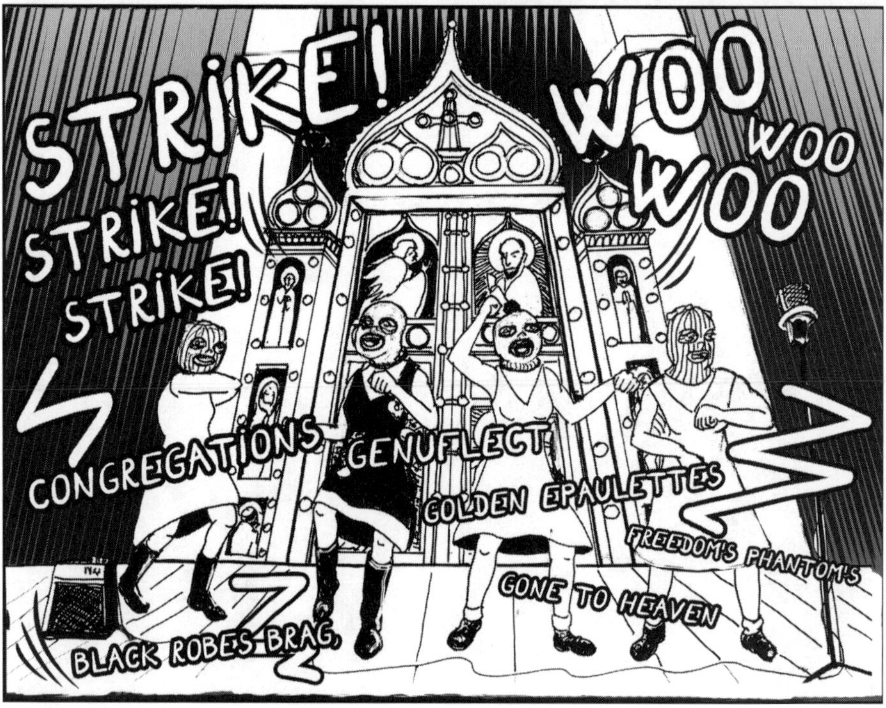
STRIKE!
STRIKE!
STRIKE!
WOO
WOO
WOO
CONGREGATIONS GENUFLECT
BLACK ROBES BRAG,
GOLDEN EPAULETTES
FREEDOM'S PHANTOM'S
GONE TO HEAVEN

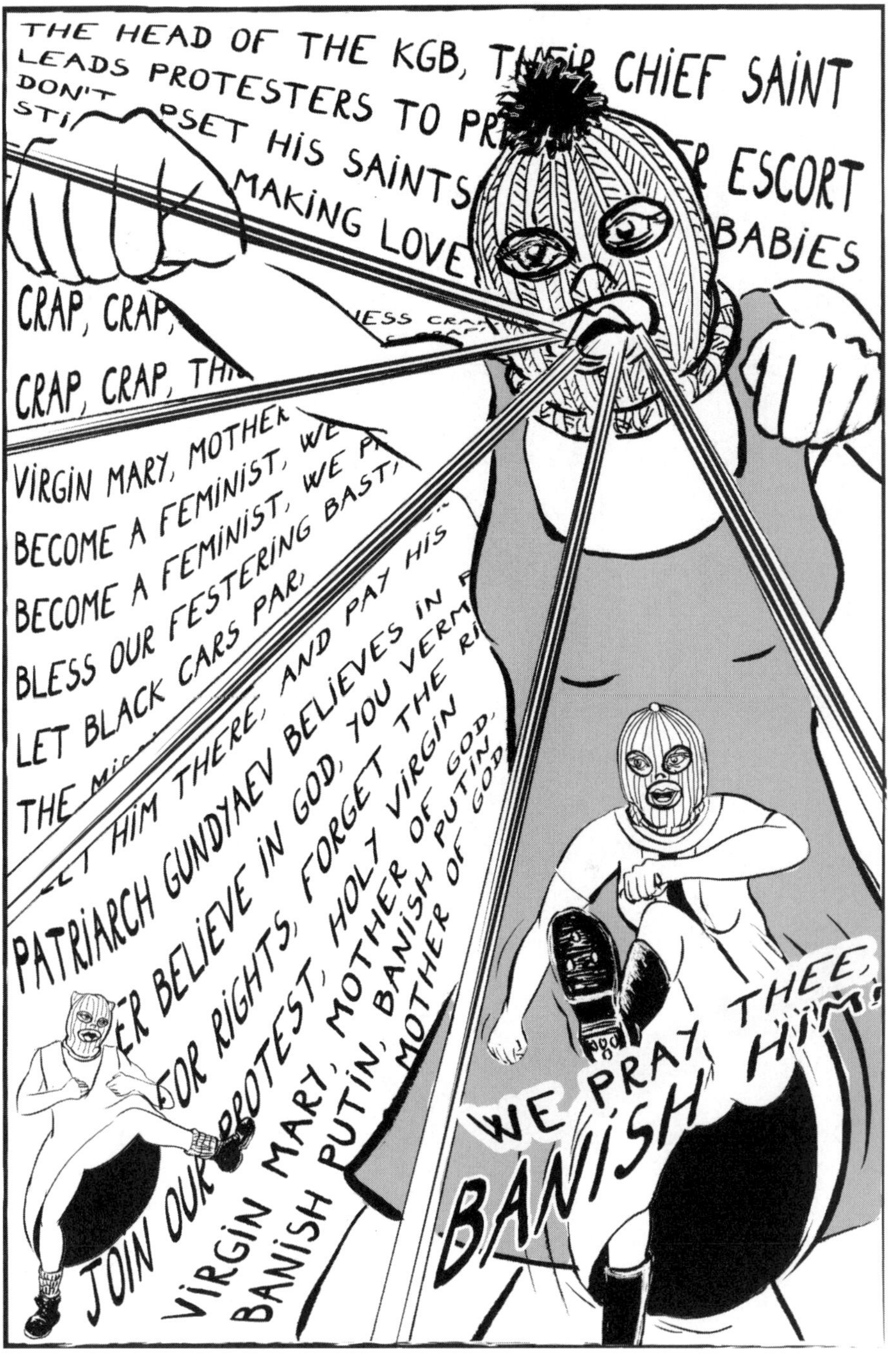
THE HEAD OF THE KGB,
CHIEF SAINT
LEADS PROTESTERS TO PR
ESCORT
DON'T
STI
PSET HIS SAINTS
MAKING LOVE
BABIES
CRAP, CRAP,
CRAP, CRAP, TH
VIRGIN MARY, MOTHER
BECOME A FEMINIST, WE
BECOME A FEMINIST, WE P
BLESS OUR FESTERING BAST
LET BLACK CARS PAR
THE
LET HIM THERE, AND PAY HIS
PATRIARCH GUNDYAEV BELIEVES IN
ER BELIEVE IN GOD, YOU VERM
FOR RIGHTS, FORGET THE
JOIN OUR PROTEST, HOLY VIRGIN
VIRGIN MARY, MOTHER OF GOD,
BANISH PUTIN, BANISH PUTIN,
MOTHER OF GOD
WE PRAY THEE,
BANISH HIM!

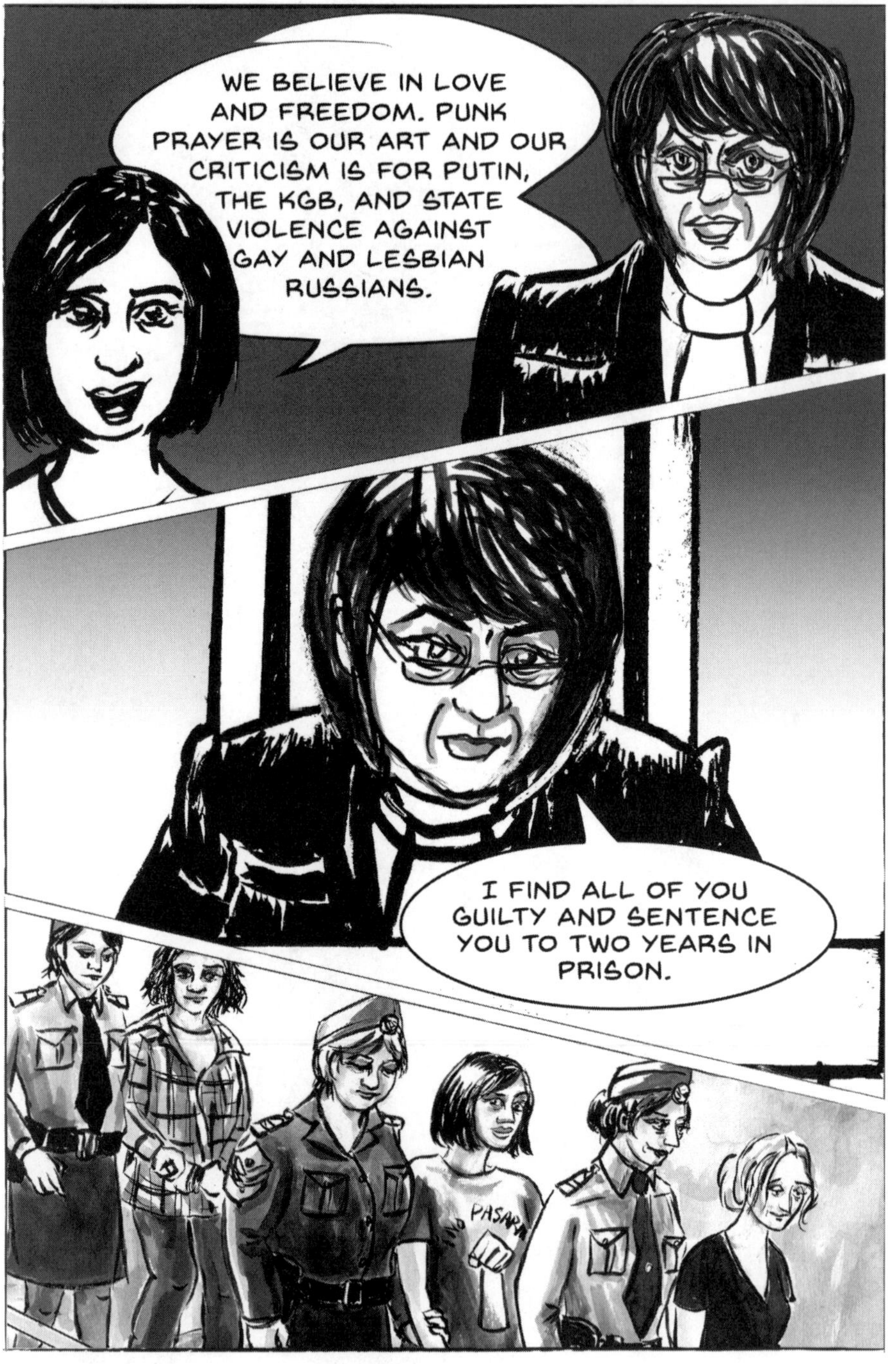
WE BELIEVE IN LOVE AND FREEDOM. PUNK PRAYER IS OUR ART AND OUR CRITICISM IS FOR PUTIN, THE KGB, AND STATE VIOLENCE AGAINST GAY AND LESBIAN RUSSIANS.
I FIND ALL OF YOU GUILTY AND SENTENCE YOU TO TWO YEARS IN PRISON.

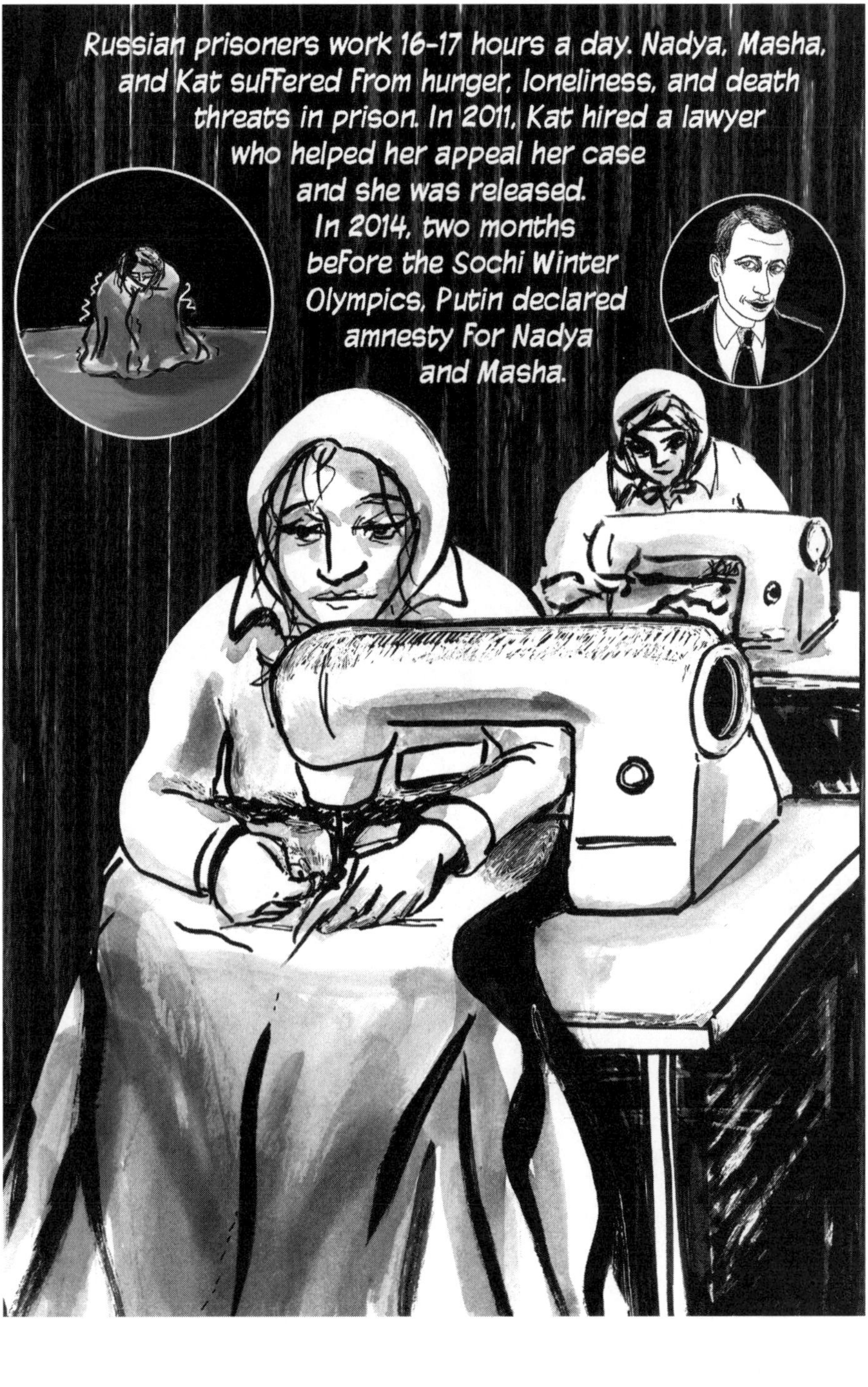
Russian prisoners work 16-17 hours a day. Nadya, Masha, and Kat suffered from hunger, loneliness, and death threats in prison. In 2011, Kat hired a lawyer who helped her appeal her case and she was released. In 2014, two months before the Sochi Winter Olympics, Putin declared amnesty for Nadya and Masha.

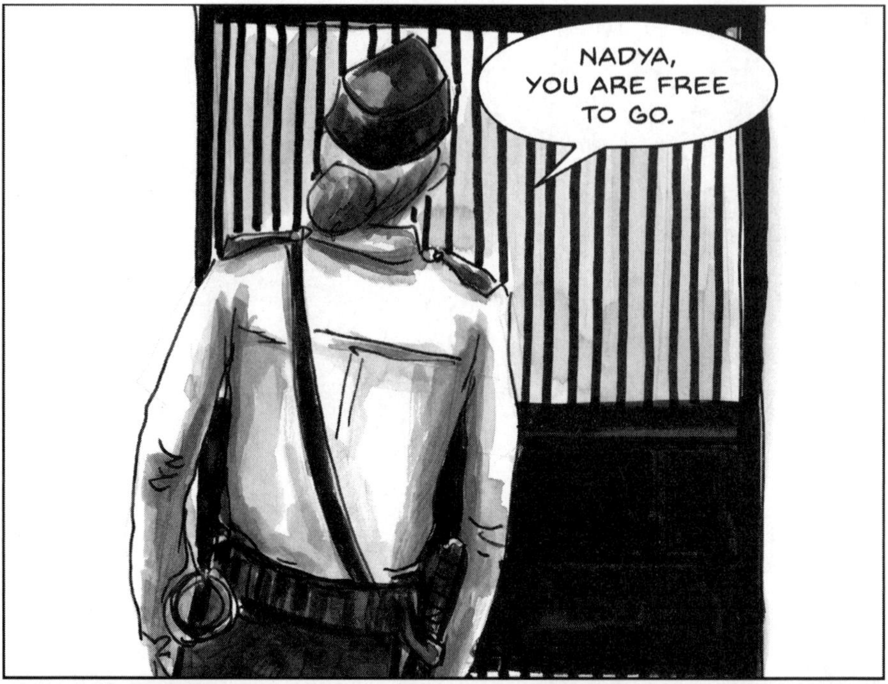
NADYA, YOU ARE FREE TO GO.

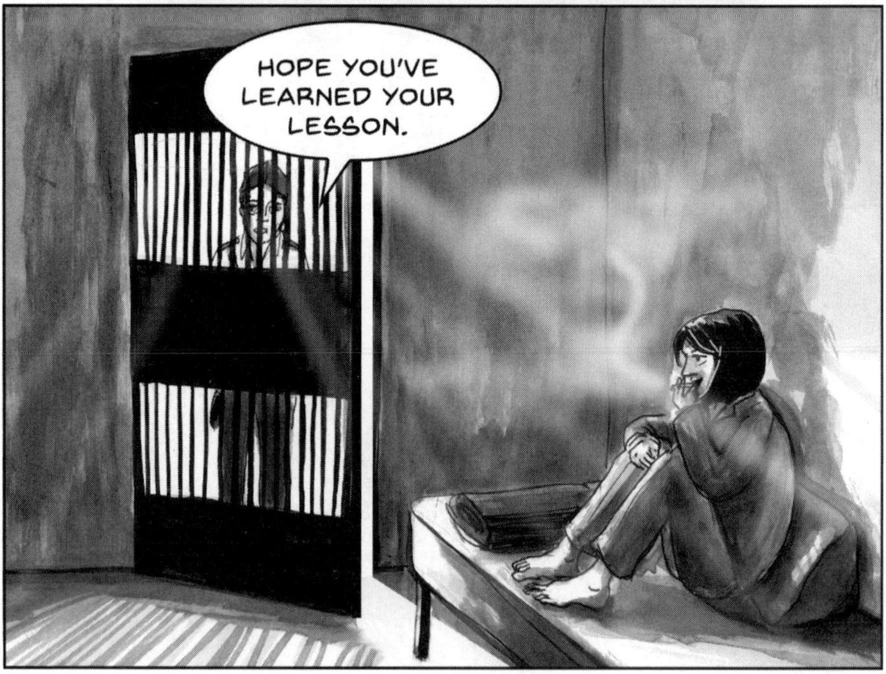
HOPE YOU'VE LEARNED YOUR LESSON.

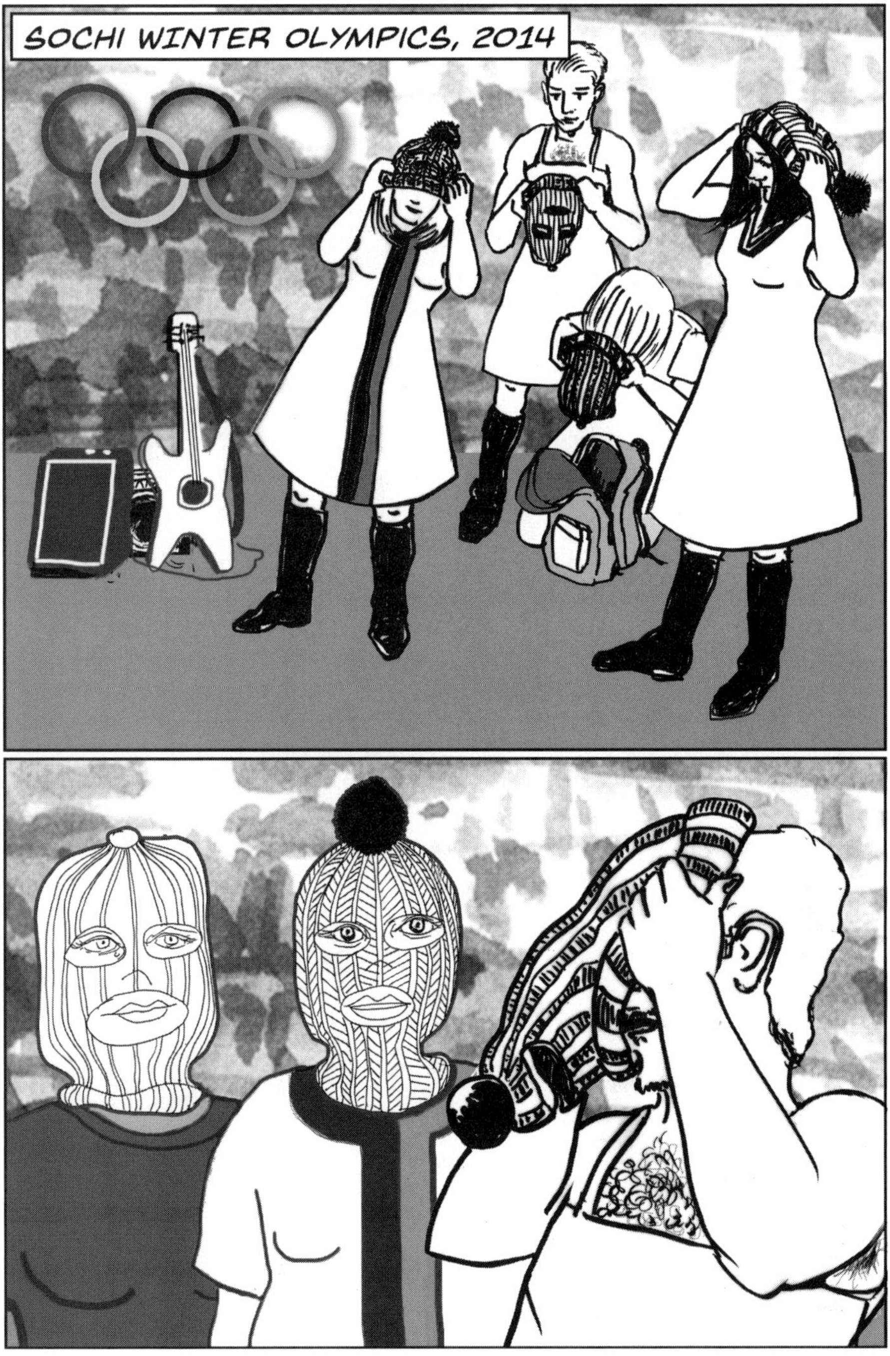
SOCHI WINTER OLYMPICS, 2014

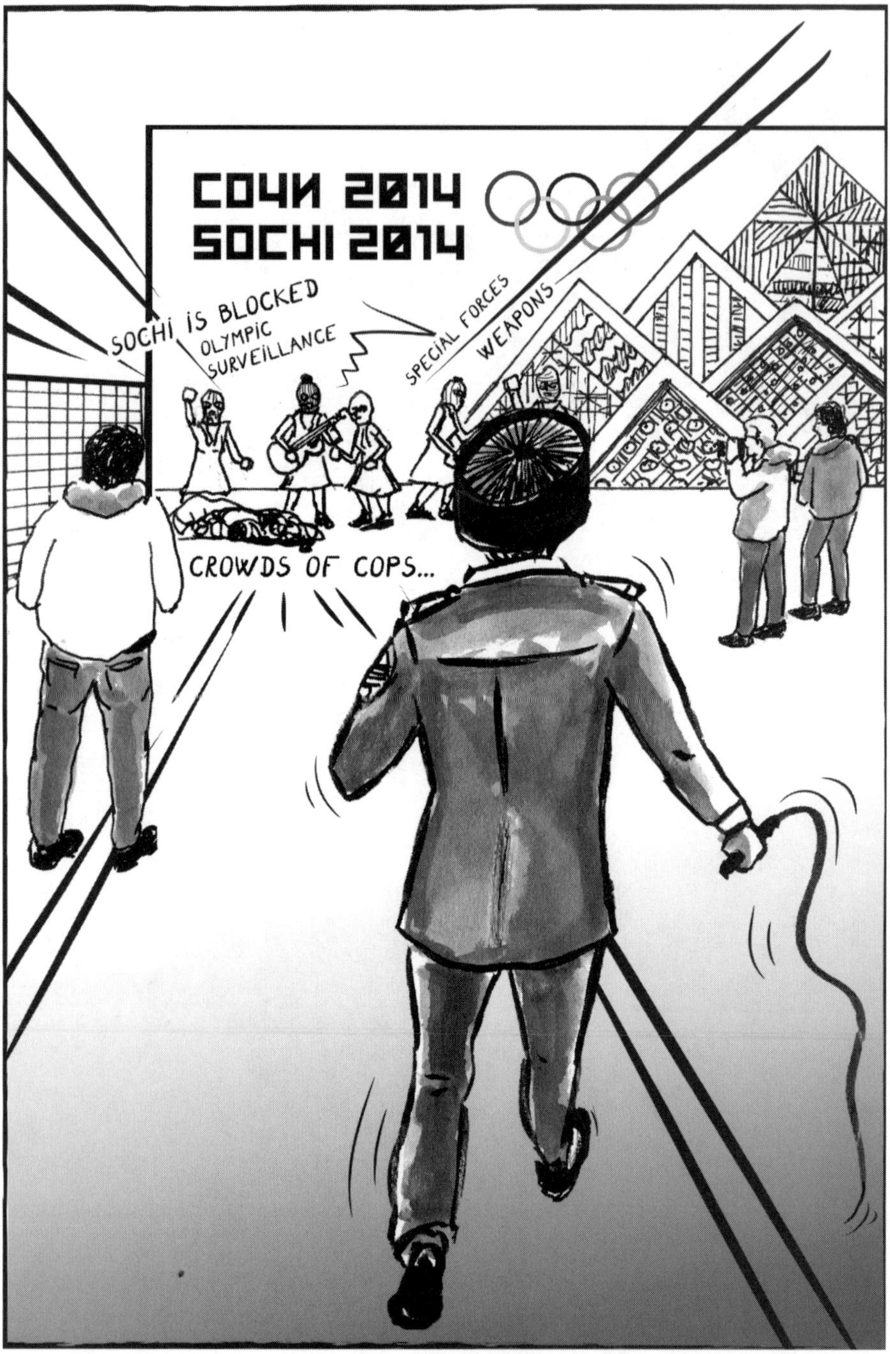
СОЧИ 2014
SOCHI 2014
SOCHI IS BLOCKED
OLYMPIC SURVEILLANCE
SPECIAL FORCES
WEAPONS
CROWDS OF COPS...

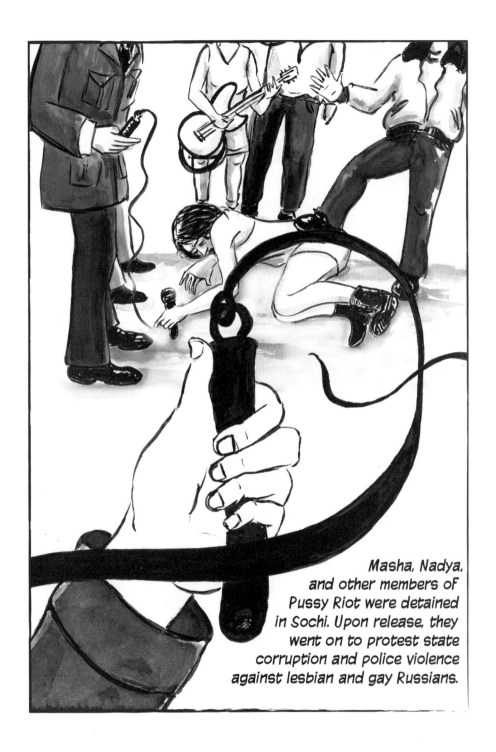

Masha, Nadya, and other members of Pussy Riot were detained in Sochi. Upon release, they went on to protest state corruption and police violence against lesbian and gay Russians.

In the 2000s, in Moscow, a collective of university students, artists, and activists formed a performance art group named Voina. The group (the word *voina* means war in Russian) performed ironic, witty, and clever performances aimed at government corruption, repression of LGBTQIIA communities, and police brutality. Perhaps their most infamous stunt was a large drawing of a penis and testicles on a drawbridge in front of the KGB station in Moscow; when the drawbridge was raised, the penis lifted, pointing in the direction of the KGB. The acts of Voina were recorded and spread through YouTube videos and international social media; the members, however, remained under the radar.

Pussy Riot emerged from a Voina LGBTQIIA rights action. Members of Voina approached police officers, asked for directions, and thanked the police officers with an enthusiastic embrace and kiss on the mouth. These exchanges were coordinated to only be same-sex encounters, but male members of Voina made excuses to avoid involvement. The women of Voina went ahead with the action, and from the women's success came the idea for Pussy Riot, a women-led performance art collective with a focus on gender and sexual orientation rights and freedoms.

The collective first formed in August 2011 with eleven members between the ages of twenty and forty-two. Nadhezhda Tolokonnikova (Nadya), Maria Alyokhina (Masha), and Yekaterina Samutsevich (Kat) were three of the permanent members. Kat, Masha, and Nadya were arrested in 2012 for their participation in the performance of "Punk Prayer, Mother of God Chase Putin Away" in a Russian Orthodox church. In prison the women became activists for their fellow inmates, and once released, Nadya and Masha returned to Pussy Riot activities and performances, enduring violent attacks from Russian police and citizens.

Openly feminist and advocating for queer rights, Pussy Riot uses the lively medium of punk music and original Russian lyrics to express its protest message. Pussy Riot performances are taped by collective members and shared on YouTube; even when three members were imprisoned, the messages of Pussy Riot were shared around the world. Feminists worldwide engage in transnational feminist practice when they learn from Pussy Riot; in recent actions, men and women have worn colored balaclavas and formed their own Pussy Riot collectives to advocate for transgender rights and reproductive freedom in the United States and across Europe. Inspired by Pussy Riot, men and women around the world have come together to fight for the rights of women and LGBTQIIA people and for freedom of expression.

Discussion Questions

1 For what crime were the women of Pussy Riot imprisoned, and how long was their sentence? Under what circumstances were they released?
2 What was the environment in court while the women of Pussy Riot were being tried?
3 Is it ever acceptable to violate laws or religious or social norms for the sake of social or political change? When, and why or why not?

Research Questions and Activities

1 In Russia, Pussy Riot was criticized for showing disrespect to a symbol of religious tradition, an Orthodox church. Does Pussy Riot's criticism of both the state and the church compromise or strengthen their feminist civil rights critique?
2 Pussy Riot's video of their song "Make America Great Again" criticizes American immigration and reproductive rights laws. What is the role of international feminist groups in critiquing Western feminism, and how might this critique relate to transnational feminist practices?
3 Research the history of punk music in feminist activism, and find out which other feminists have been involved with punk music.

Further Reading and Viewing

Denysenko, Nicholas. "An Appeal to Mary: An Analysis of Pussy Riot's Punk Performance in Moscow." *Journal of the American Academy of Religion* 81.4 (2013): 1061–92. Academic Search Complete. Web. 20 Sept. 2015.

Gessen, Masha. *Words Will Break Cement: The Passion of Pussy Riot.* New York: Riverhead Books, 2014.

Pussy Riot: A Punk Prayer. Dir. Mike Lerner. Documentary. British Broadcasting Corporation, 2014.

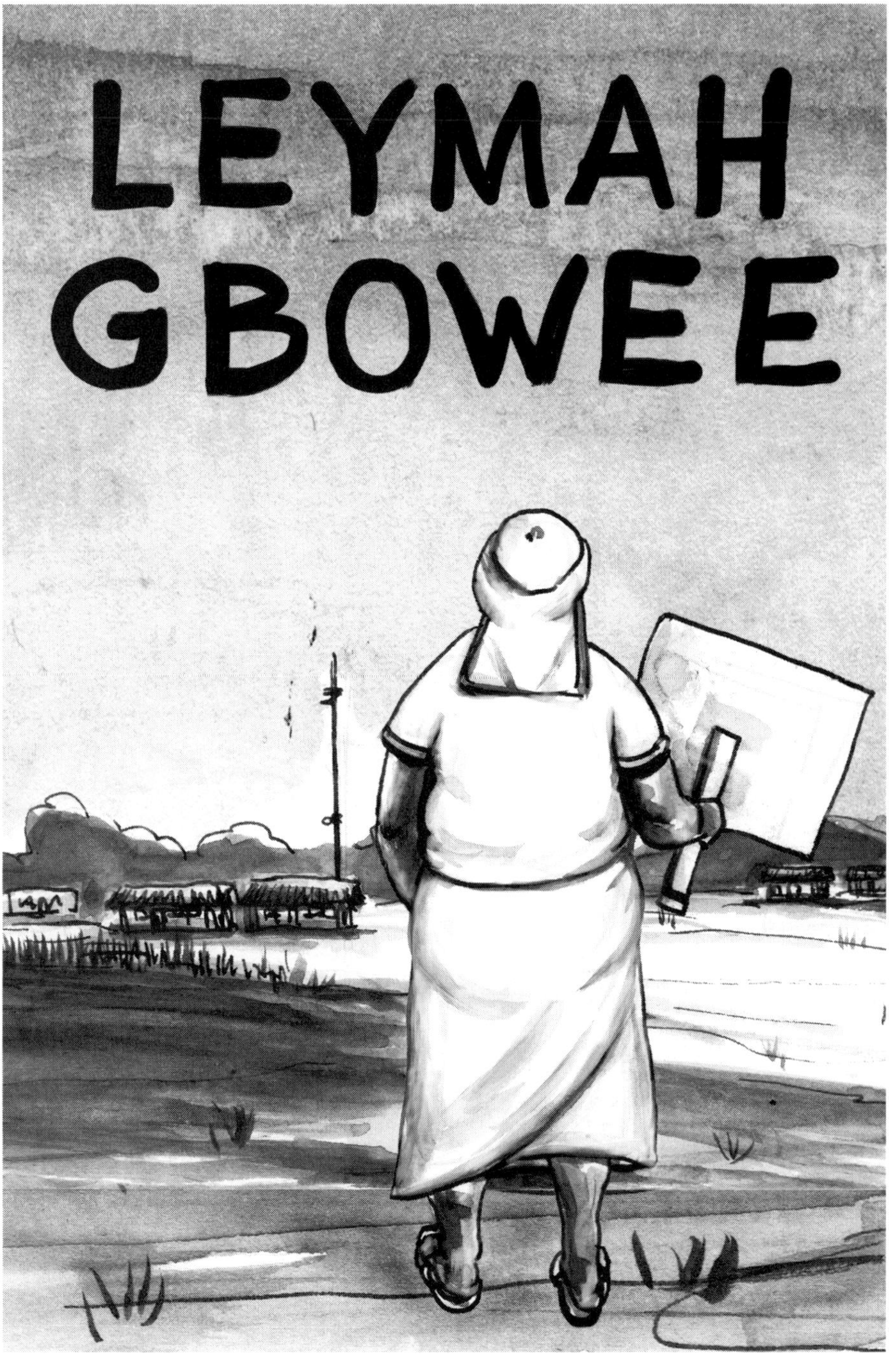
LEYMAH GBOWEE

MONROVIA, CAPITAL CITY OF LIBERIA, APRIL 14, 2003

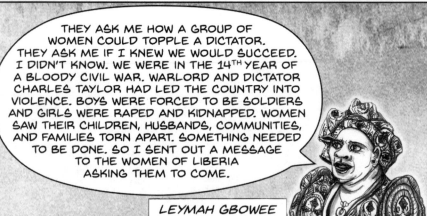

THEY ASK ME HOW A GROUP OF WOMEN COULD TOPPLE A DICTATOR. THEY ASK ME IF I KNEW WE WOULD SUCCEED. I DIDN'T KNOW. WE WERE IN THE 14TH YEAR OF A BLOODY CIVIL WAR. WARLORD AND DICTATOR CHARLES TAYLOR HAD LED THE COUNTRY INTO VIOLENCE. BOYS WERE FORCED TO BE SOLDIERS AND GIRLS WERE RAPED AND KIDNAPPED. WOMEN SAW THEIR CHILDREN, HUSBANDS, COMMUNITIES, AND FAMILIES TORN APART. SOMETHING NEEDED TO BE DONE. SO I SENT OUT A MESSAGE TO THE WOMEN OF LIBERIA ASKING THEM TO COME.

LEYMAH GBOWEE

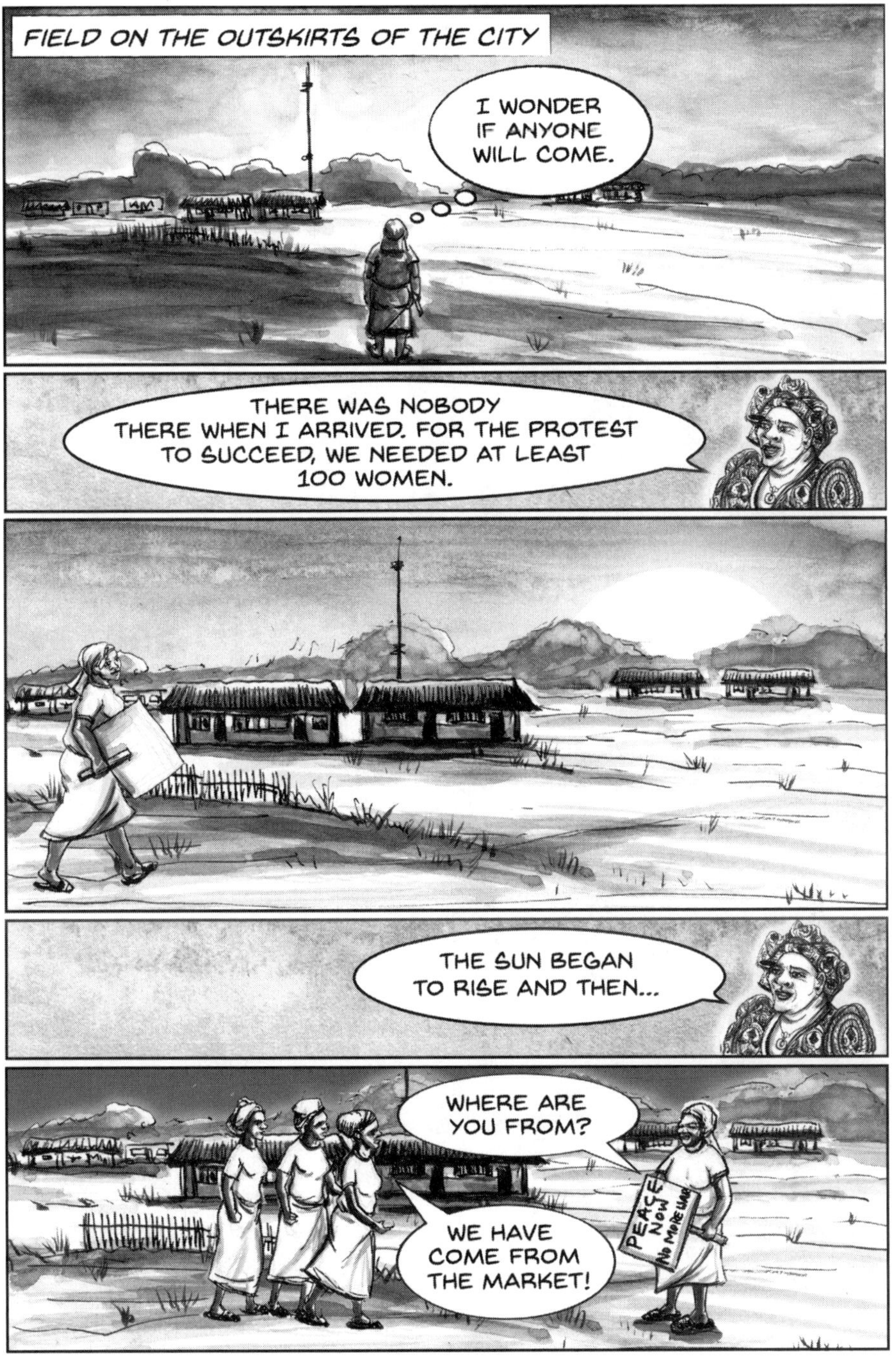
FIELD ON THE OUTSKIRTS OF THE CITY
I WONDER IF ANYONE WILL COME.
THERE WAS NOBODY THERE WHEN I ARRIVED. FOR THE PROTEST TO SUCCEED, WE NEEDED AT LEAST 100 WOMEN.
THE SUN BEGAN TO RISE AND THEN...
WHERE ARE YOU FROM?
PEACE NOW NO MORE WAR
WE HAVE COME FROM THE MARKET!

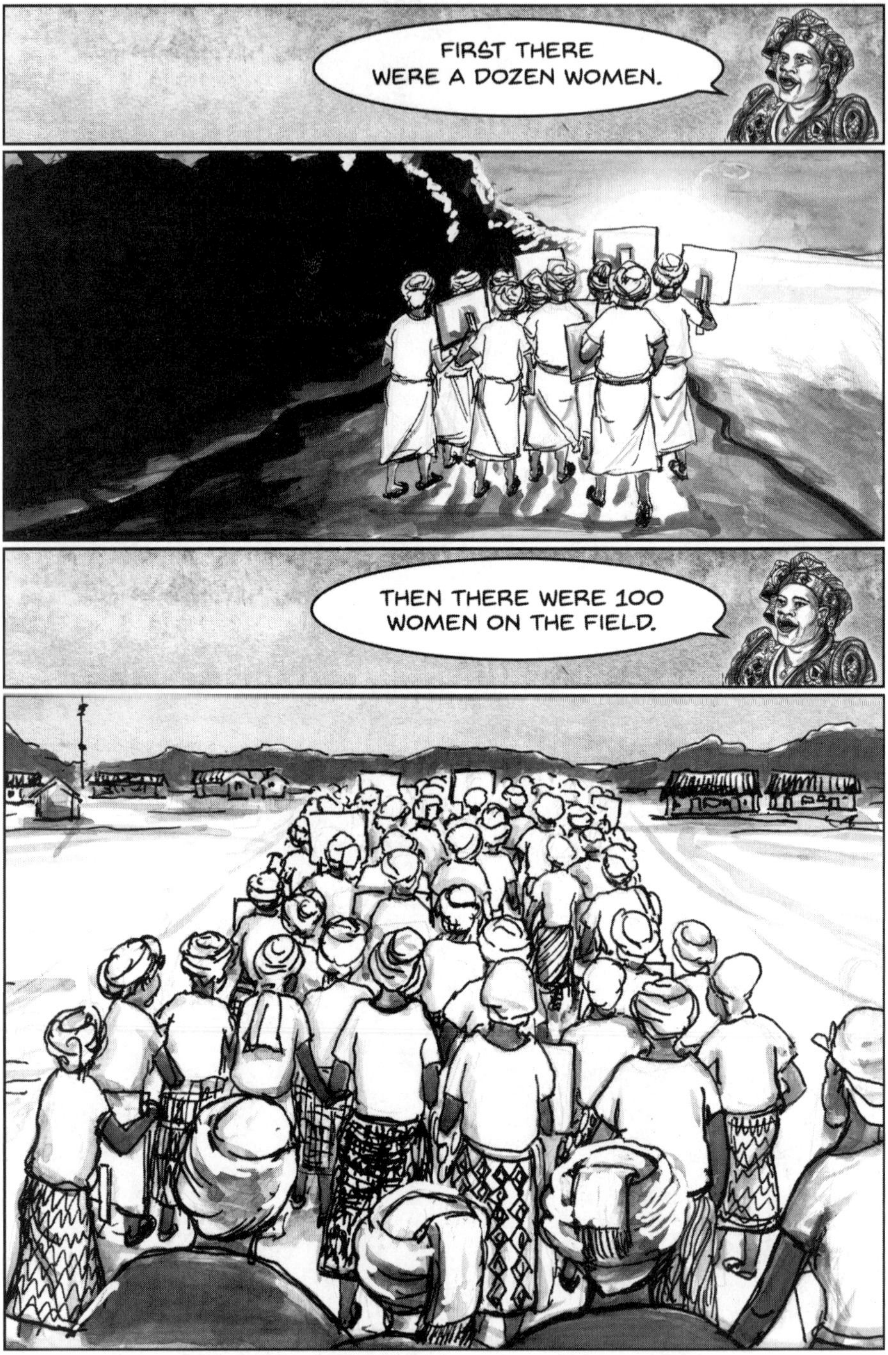
FIRST THERE
WERE A DOZEN WOMEN.
THEN THERE WERE 100
WOMEN ON THE FIELD.

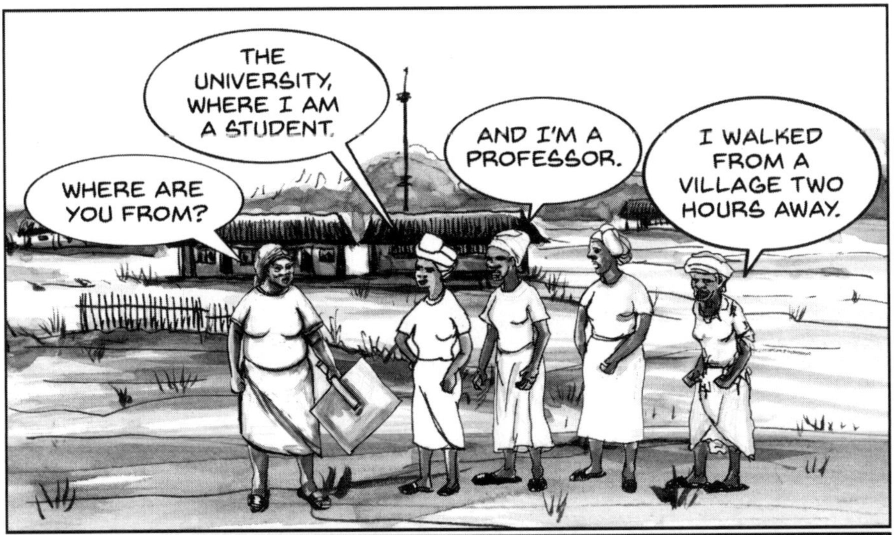
WHERE ARE YOU FROM?
THE UNIVERSITY, WHERE I AM A STUDENT.
AND I'M A PROFESSOR.
I WALKED FROM A VILLAGE TWO HOURS AWAY.

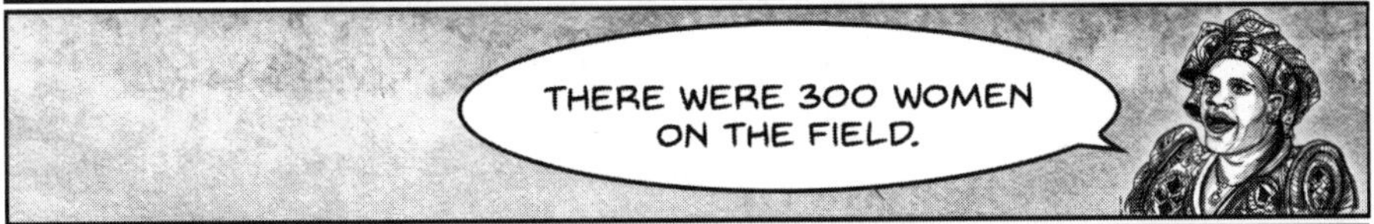
THERE WERE 300 WOMEN ON THE FIELD.

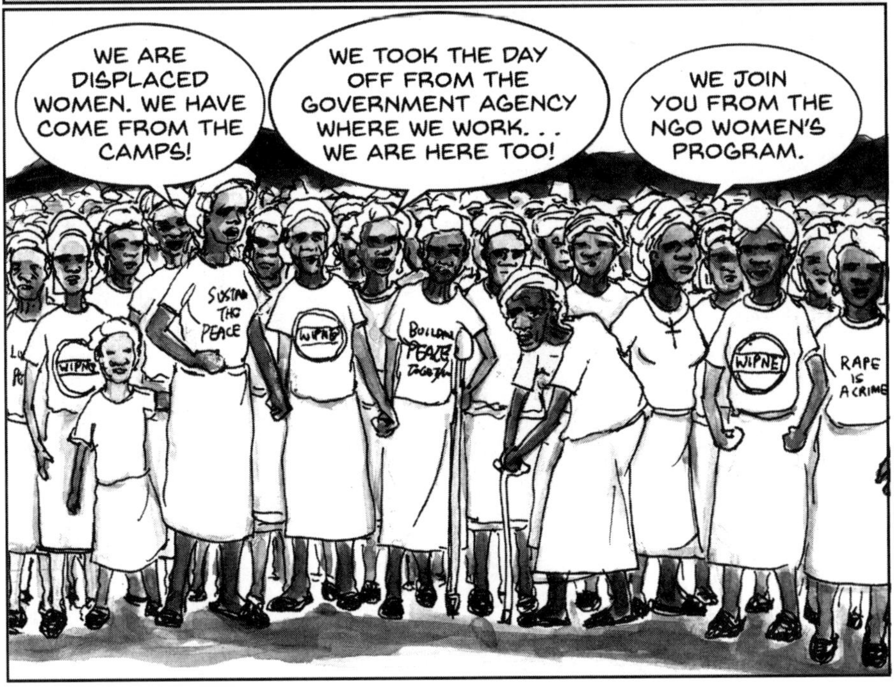
WE ARE DISPLACED WOMEN. WE HAVE COME FROM THE CAMPS!
WE TOOK THE DAY OFF FROM THE GOVERNMENT AGENCY WHERE WE WORK. . . WE ARE HERE TOO!
WE JOIN YOU FROM THE NGO WOMEN'S PROGRAM.
RAPE IS A CRIME

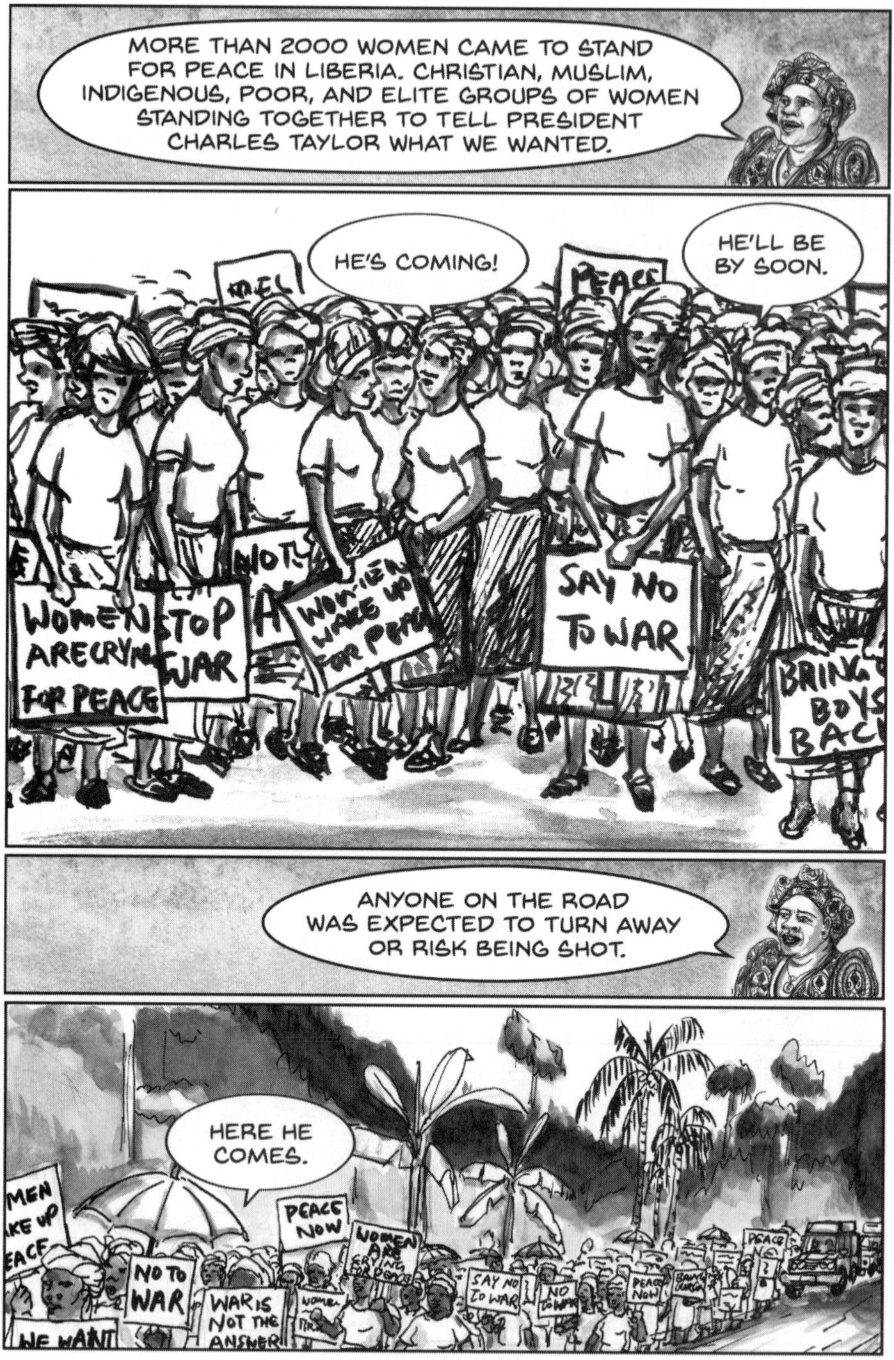
MORE THAN 2000 WOMEN CAME TO STAND FOR PEACE IN LIBERIA. CHRISTIAN, MUSLIM, INDIGENOUS, POOR, AND ELITE GROUPS OF WOMEN STANDING TOGETHER TO TELL PRESIDENT CHARLES TAYLOR WHAT WE WANTED.
HE'S COMING!
HE'LL BE BY SOON.
WOMEN ARECRYING FOR PEACE
STOP WAR
SAY NO TO WAR
ANYONE ON THE ROAD WAS EXPECTED TO TURN AWAY OR RISK BEING SHOT.
HERE HE COMES.
PEACE NOW
NO TO WAR
WAR IS NOT THE ANSWER
SAY NO TO WAR

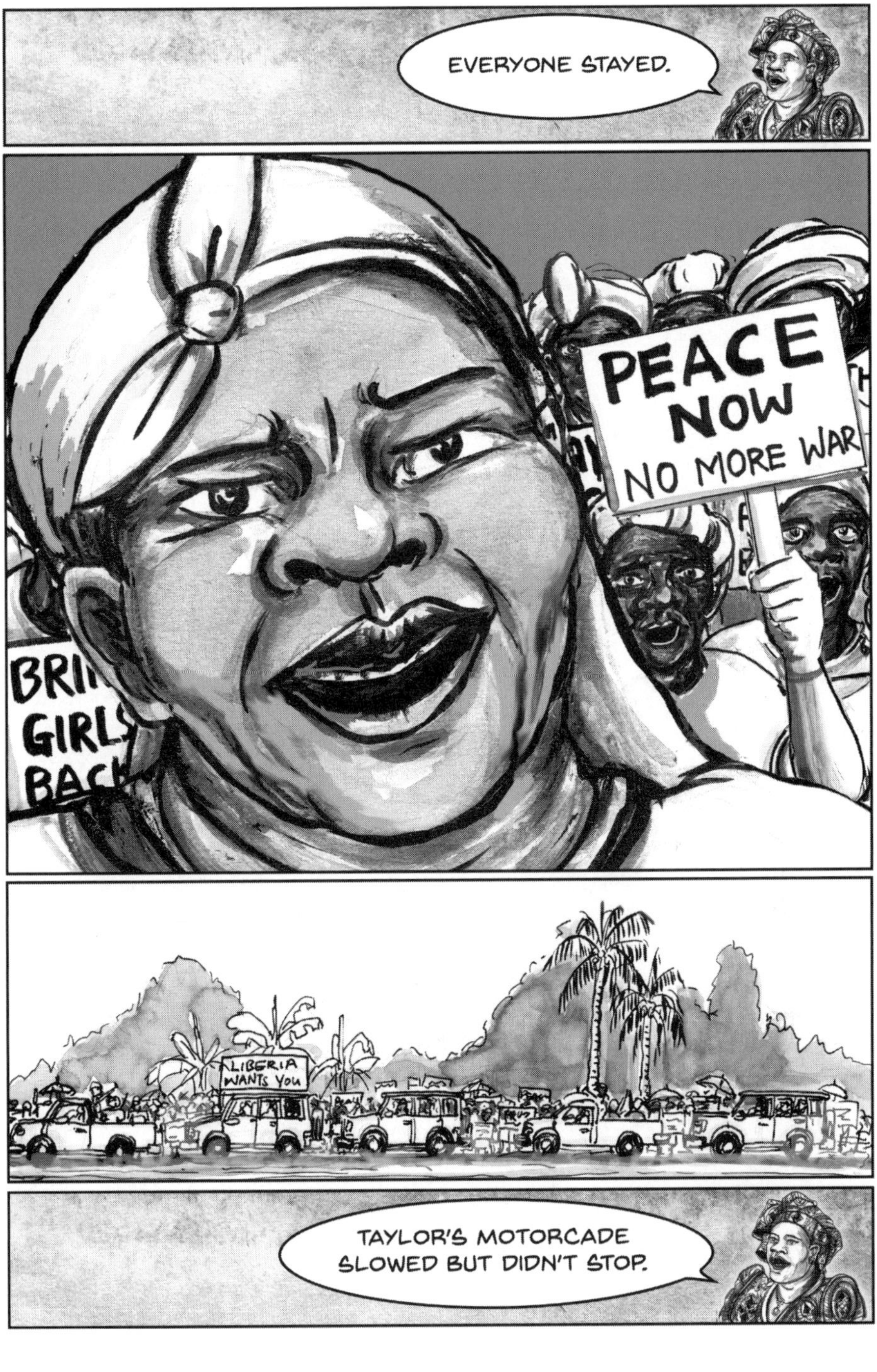
EVERYONE STAYED.
PEACE NOW NO MORE WAR
LIBERIA WANTS YOU
TAYLOR'S MOTORCADE SLOWED BUT DIDN'T STOP.

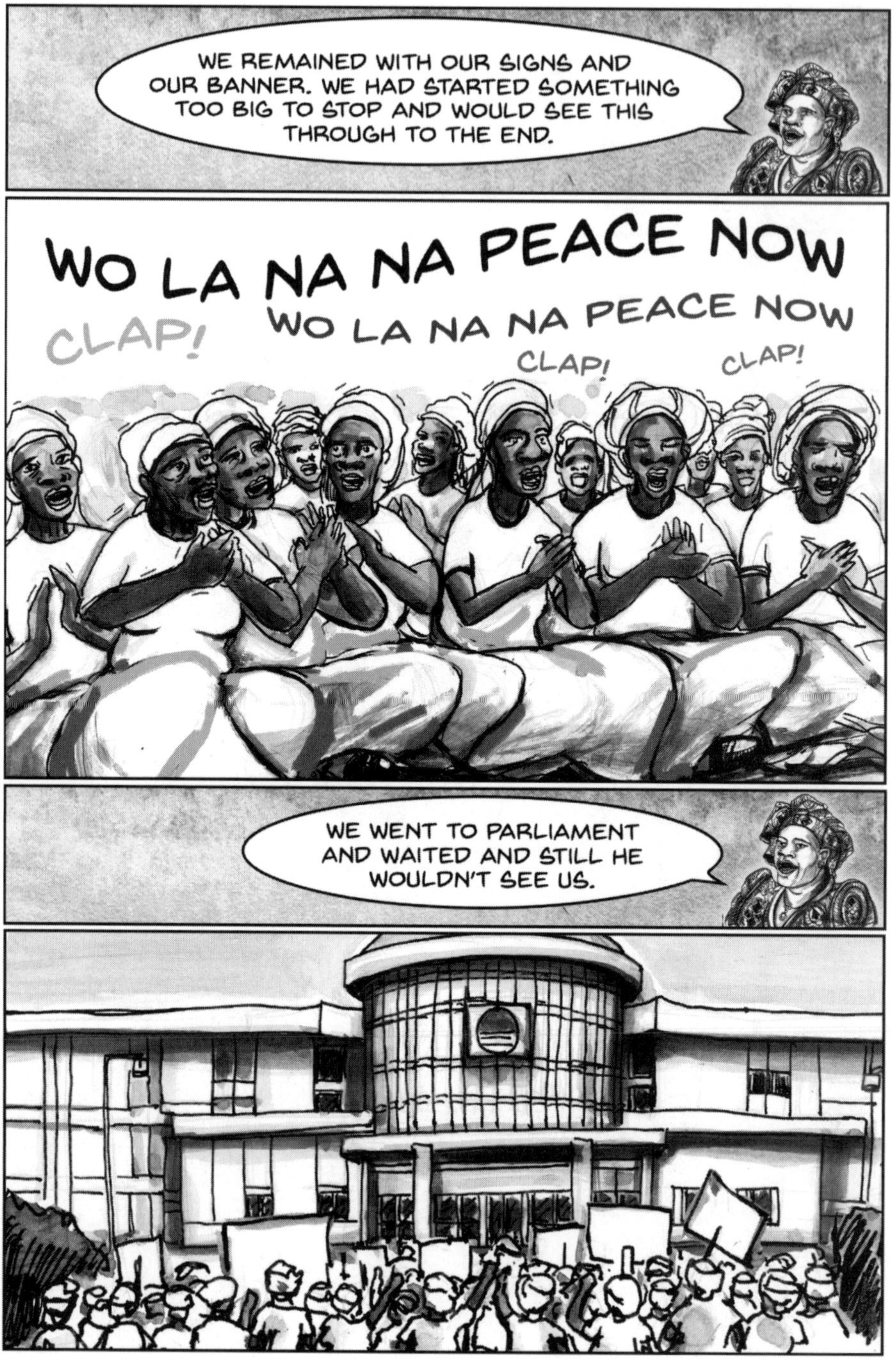
WE REMAINED WITH OUR SIGNS AND OUR BANNER. WE HAD STARTED SOMETHING TOO BIG TO STOP AND WOULD SEE THIS THROUGH TO THE END.
WO LA NA NA PEACE NOW
CLAP!
WO LA NA NA PEACE NOW
CLAP!
CLAP!
WE WENT TO PARLIAMENT AND WAITED AND STILL HE WOULDN'T SEE US.

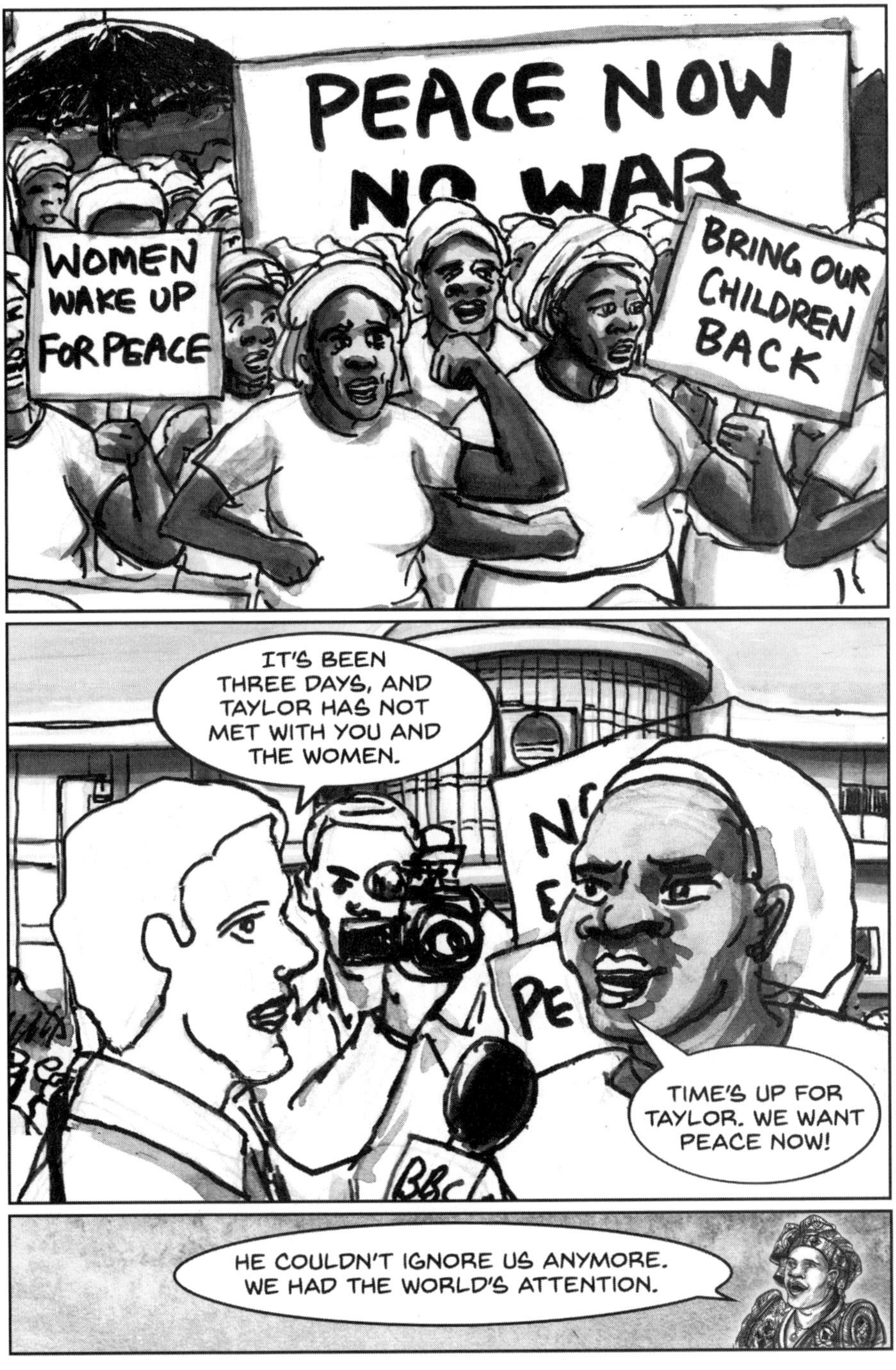
PEACE NOW NO WAR
WOMEN WAKE UP FOR PEACE
BRING OUR CHILDREN BACK
IT'S BEEN THREE DAYS, AND TAYLOR HAS NOT MET WITH YOU AND THE WOMEN.
TIME'S UP FOR TAYLOR. WE WANT PEACE NOW!
HE COULDN'T IGNORE US ANYMORE. WE HAD THE WORLD'S ATTENTION.

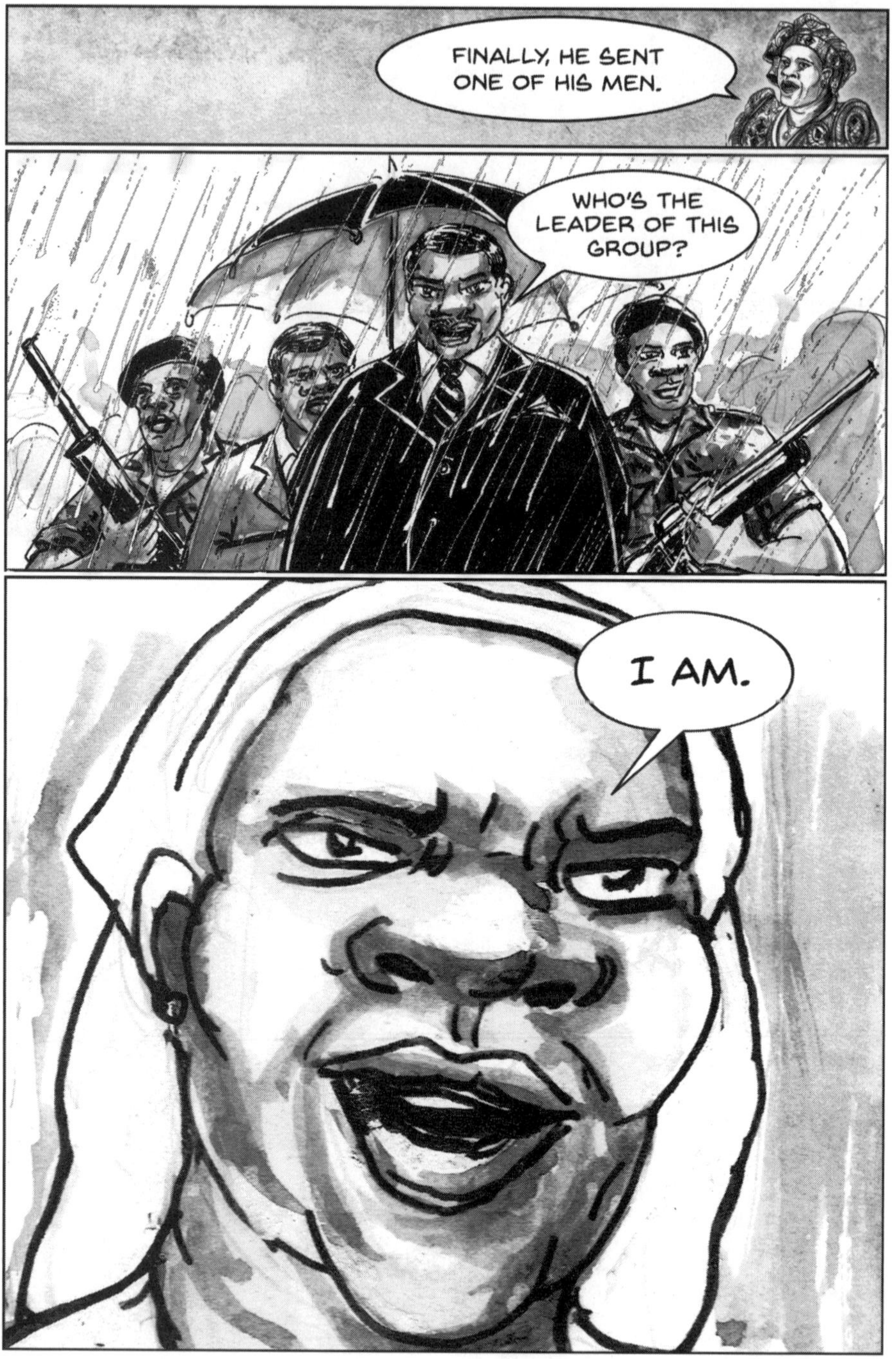
FINALLY, HE SENT ONE OF HIS MEN.
WHO'S THE LEADER OF THIS GROUP?
I AM.

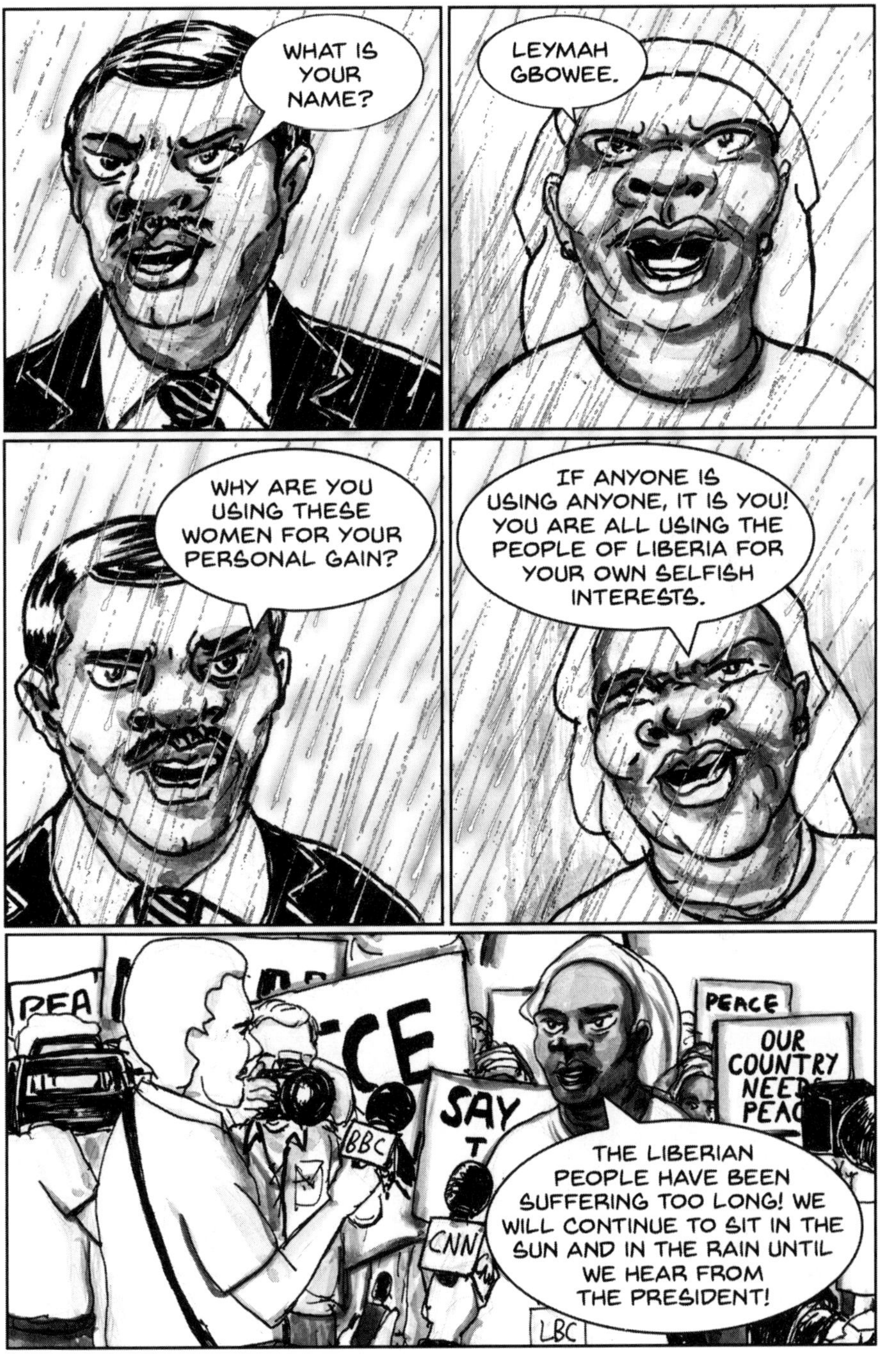
WHAT IS YOUR NAME?
LEYMAH GBOWEE.
WHY ARE YOU USING THESE WOMEN FOR YOUR PERSONAL GAIN?
IF ANYONE IS USING ANYONE, IT IS YOU! YOU ARE ALL USING THE PEOPLE OF LIBERIA FOR YOUR OWN SELFISH INTERESTS.
PEACE
OUR COUNTRY
SAY
BBC
CNN
LBC
THE LIBERIAN PEOPLE HAVE BEEN SUFFERING TOO LONG! WE WILL CONTINUE TO SIT IN THE SUN AND IN THE RAIN UNTIL WE HEAR FROM THE PRESIDENT!

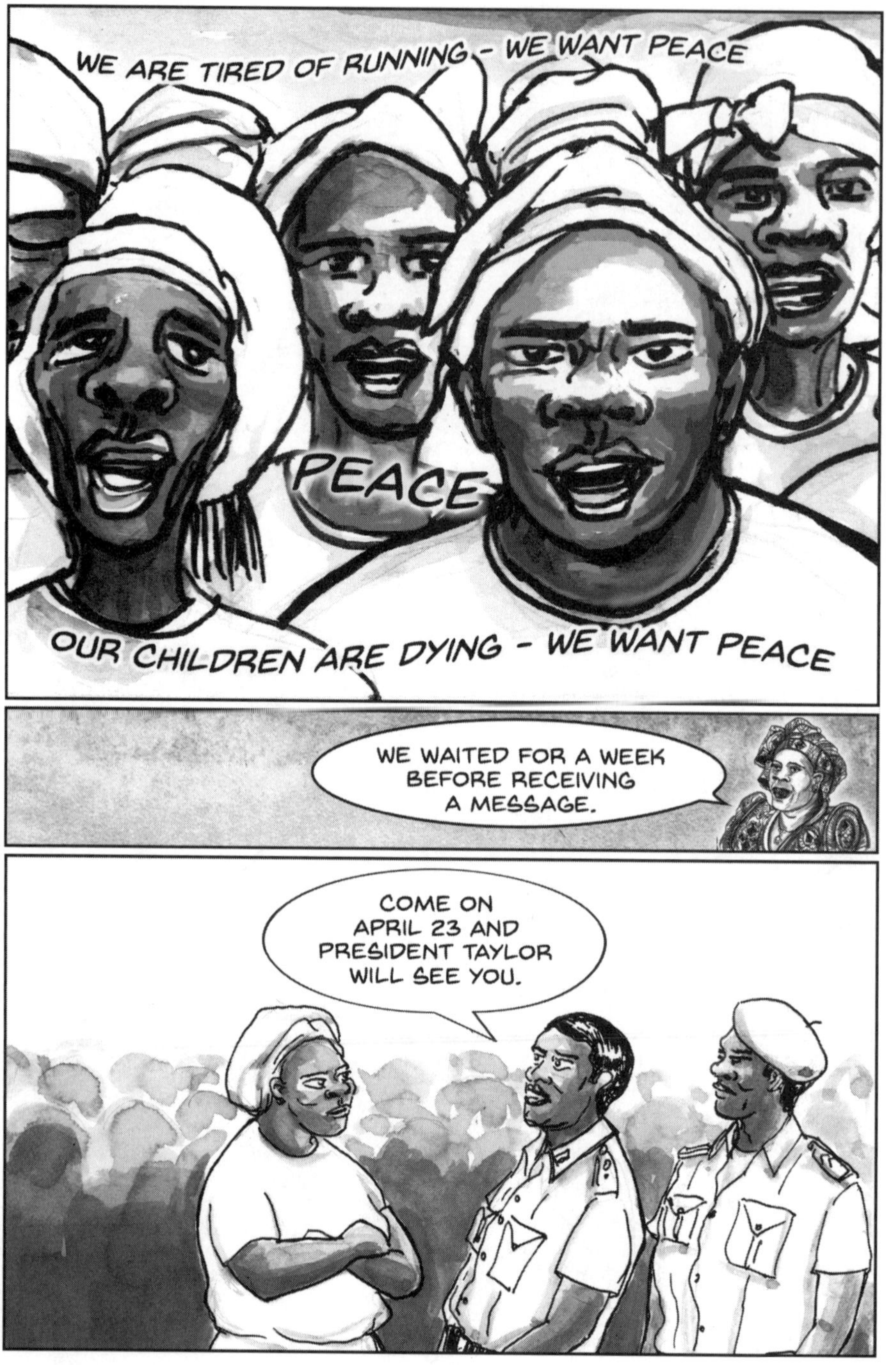
WE ARE TIRED OF RUNNING - WE WANT PEACE
PEACE
OUR CHILDREN ARE DYING - WE WANT PEACE
WE WAITED FOR A WEEK BEFORE RECEIVING A MESSAGE.
COME ON APRIL 23 AND PRESIDENT TAYLOR WILL SEE YOU.

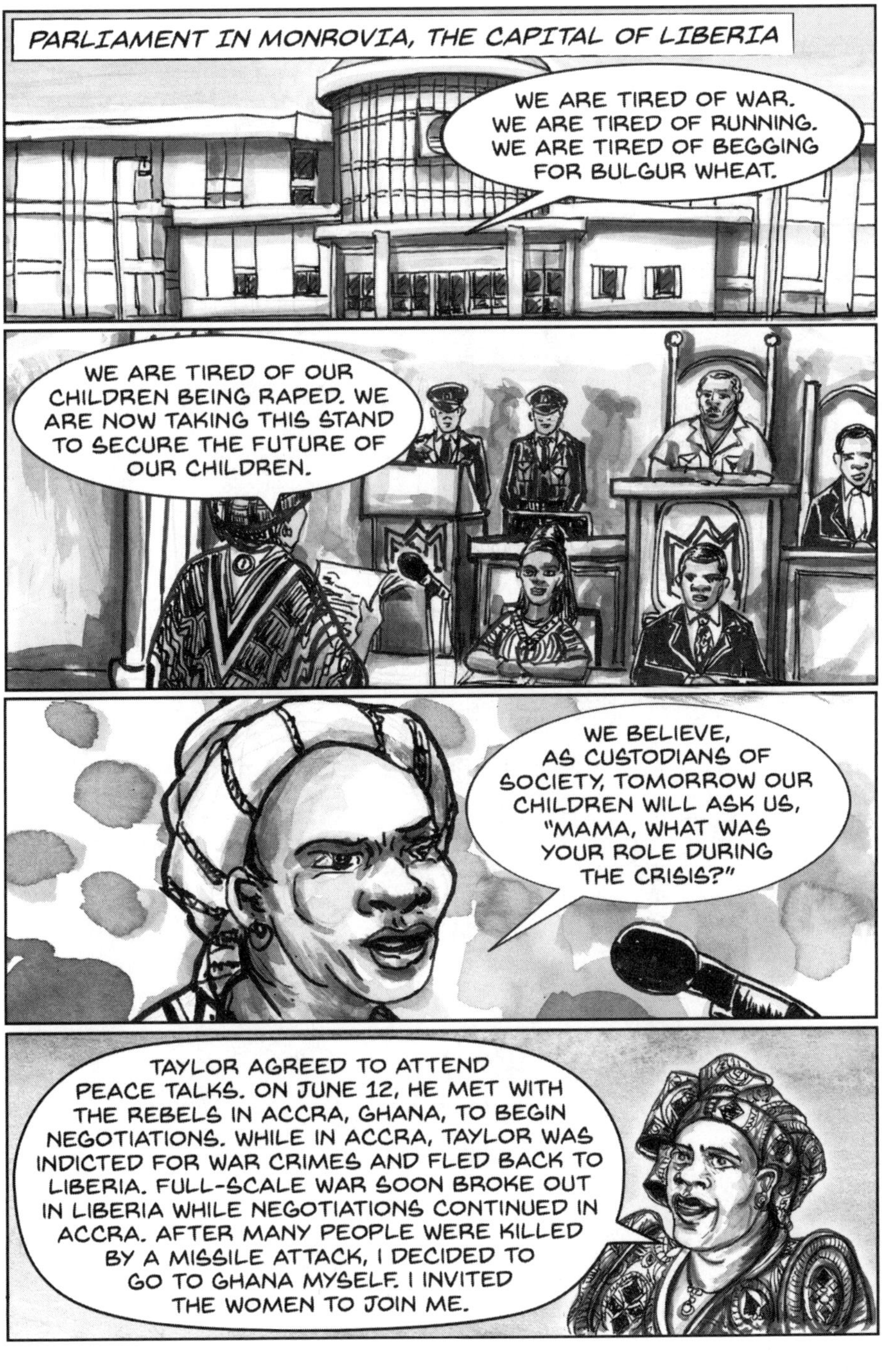
PARLIAMENT IN MONROVIA, THE CAPITAL OF LIBERIA
WE ARE TIRED OF WAR. WE ARE TIRED OF RUNNING. WE ARE TIRED OF BEGGING FOR BULGUR WHEAT.
WE ARE TIRED OF OUR CHILDREN BEING RAPED. WE ARE NOW TAKING THIS STAND TO SECURE THE FUTURE OF OUR CHILDREN.
WE BELIEVE, AS CUSTODIANS OF SOCIETY, TOMORROW OUR CHILDREN WILL ASK US, "MAMA, WHAT WAS YOUR ROLE DURING THE CRISIS?"
TAYLOR AGREED TO ATTEND PEACE TALKS. ON JUNE 12, HE MET WITH THE REBELS IN ACCRA, GHANA, TO BEGIN NEGOTIATIONS. WHILE IN ACCRA, TAYLOR WAS INDICTED FOR WAR CRIMES AND FLED BACK TO LIBERIA. FULL-SCALE WAR SOON BROKE OUT IN LIBERIA WHILE NEGOTIATIONS CONTINUED IN ACCRA. AFTER MANY PEOPLE WERE KILLED BY A MISSILE ATTACK, I DECIDED TO GO TO GHANA MYSELF. I INVITED THE WOMEN TO JOIN ME.

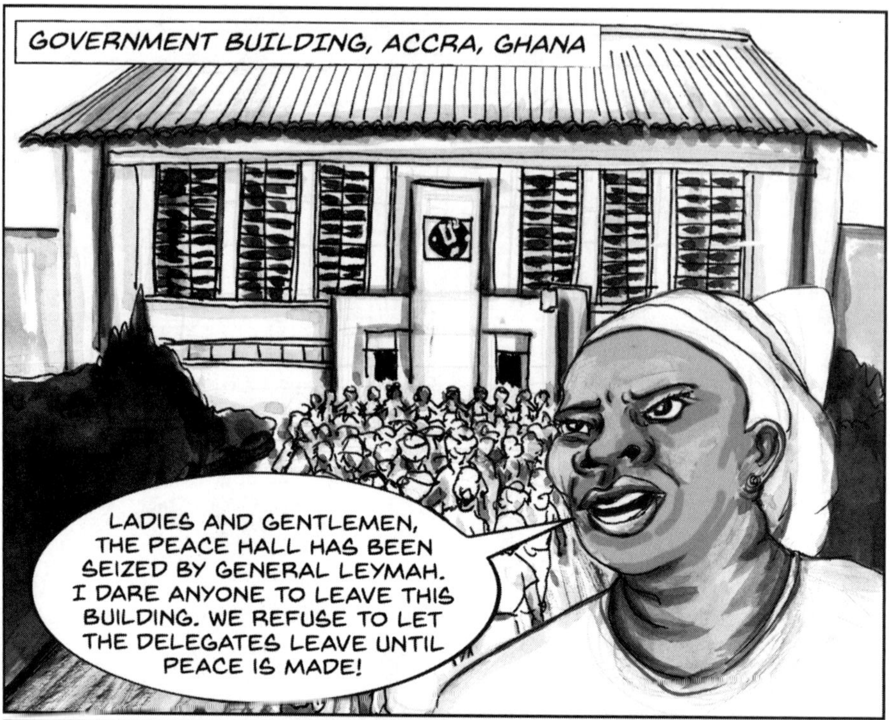
GOVERNMENT BUILDING, ACCRA, GHANA
LADIES AND GENTLEMEN, THE PEACE HALL HAS BEEN SEIZED BY GENERAL LEYMAH. I DARE ANYONE TO LEAVE THIS BUILDING. WE REFUSE TO LET THE DELEGATES LEAVE UNTIL PEACE IS MADE!

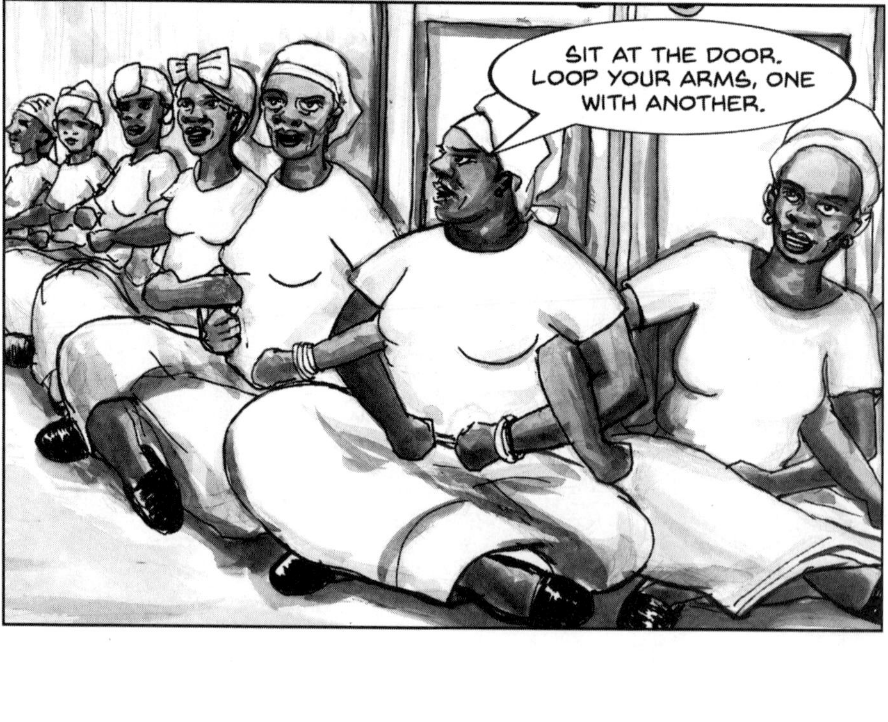
SIT AT THE DOOR. LOOP YOUR ARMS, ONE WITH ANOTHER.

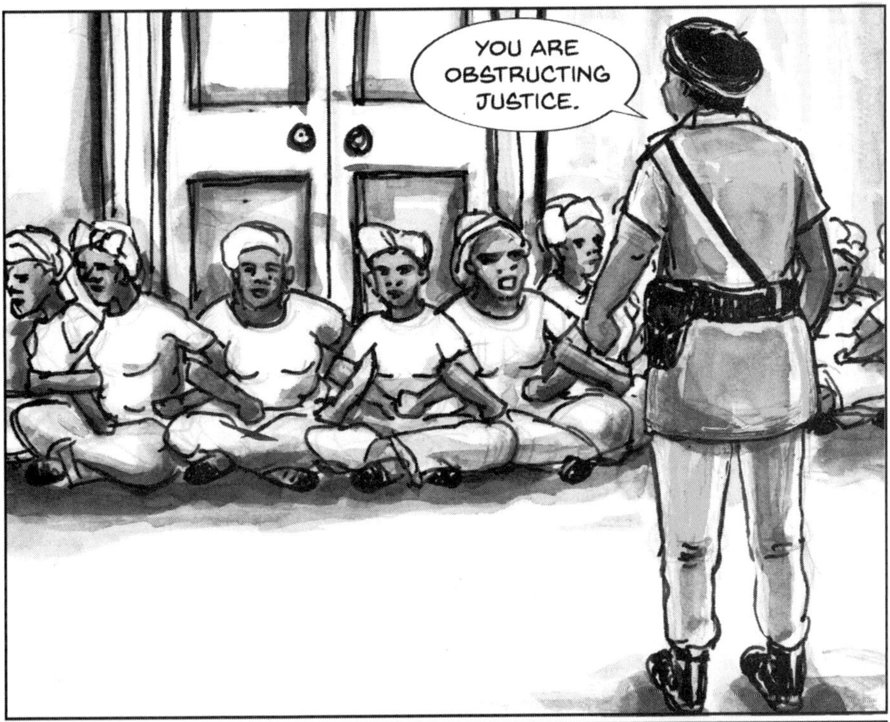
YOU ARE OBSTRUCTING JUSTICE.

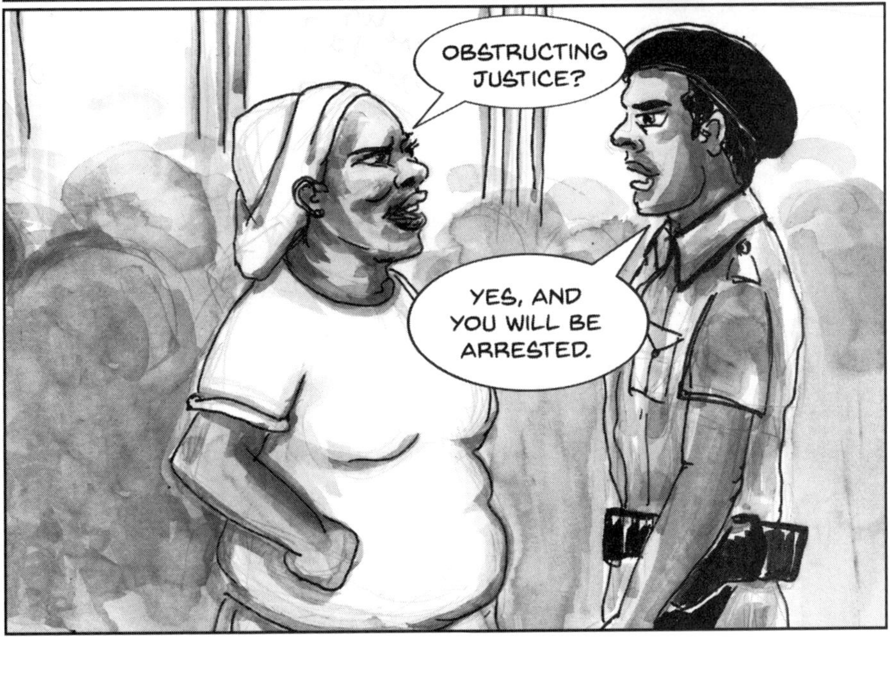
OBSTRUCTING JUSTICE?
YES, AND YOU WILL BE ARRESTED.

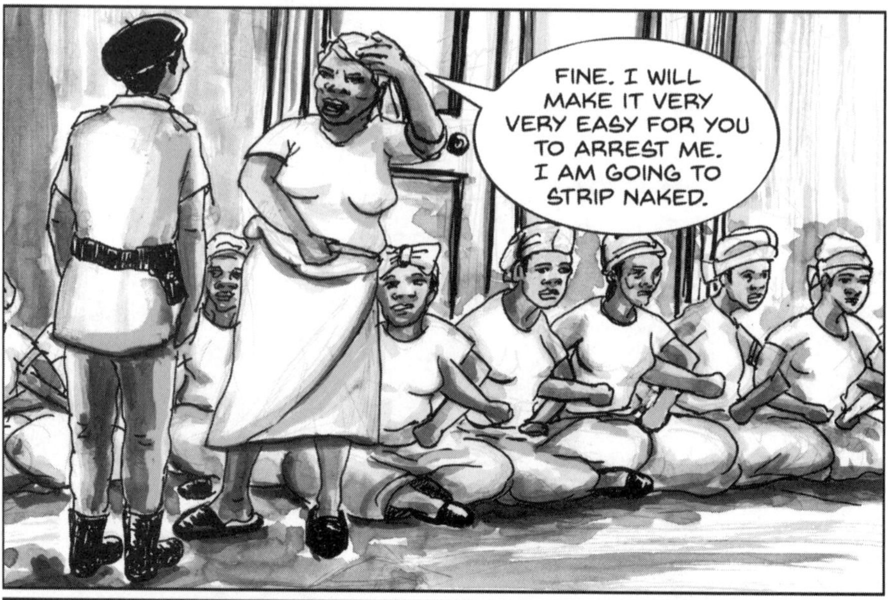
FINE. I WILL MAKE IT VERY VERY EASY FOR YOU TO ARREST ME. I AM GOING TO STRIP NAKED.

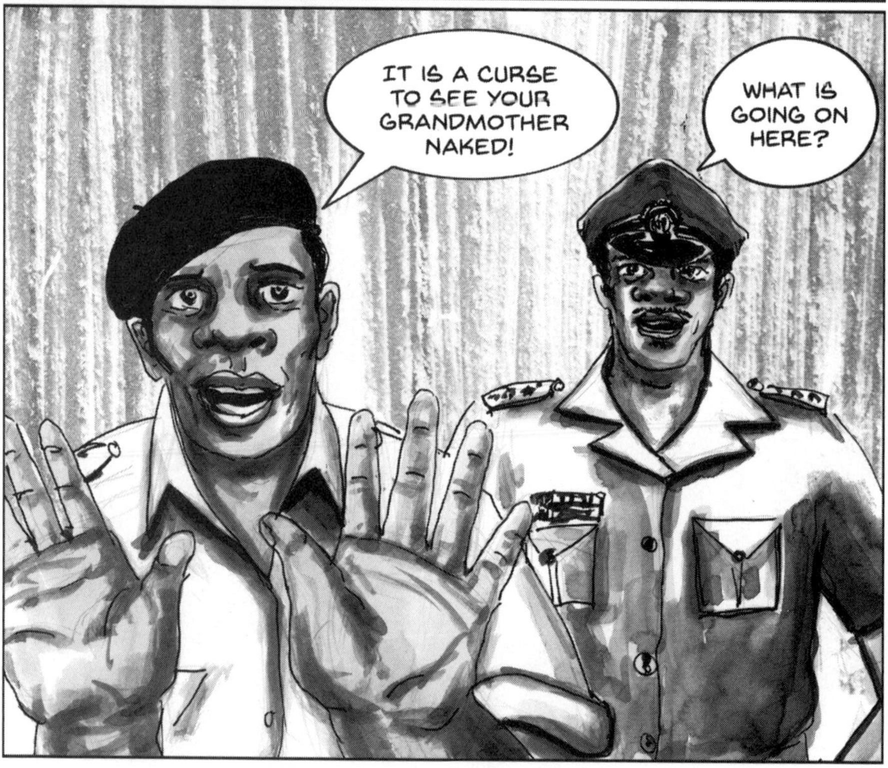
IT IS A CURSE TO SEE YOUR GRANDMOTHER NAKED!
WHAT IS GOING ON HERE?

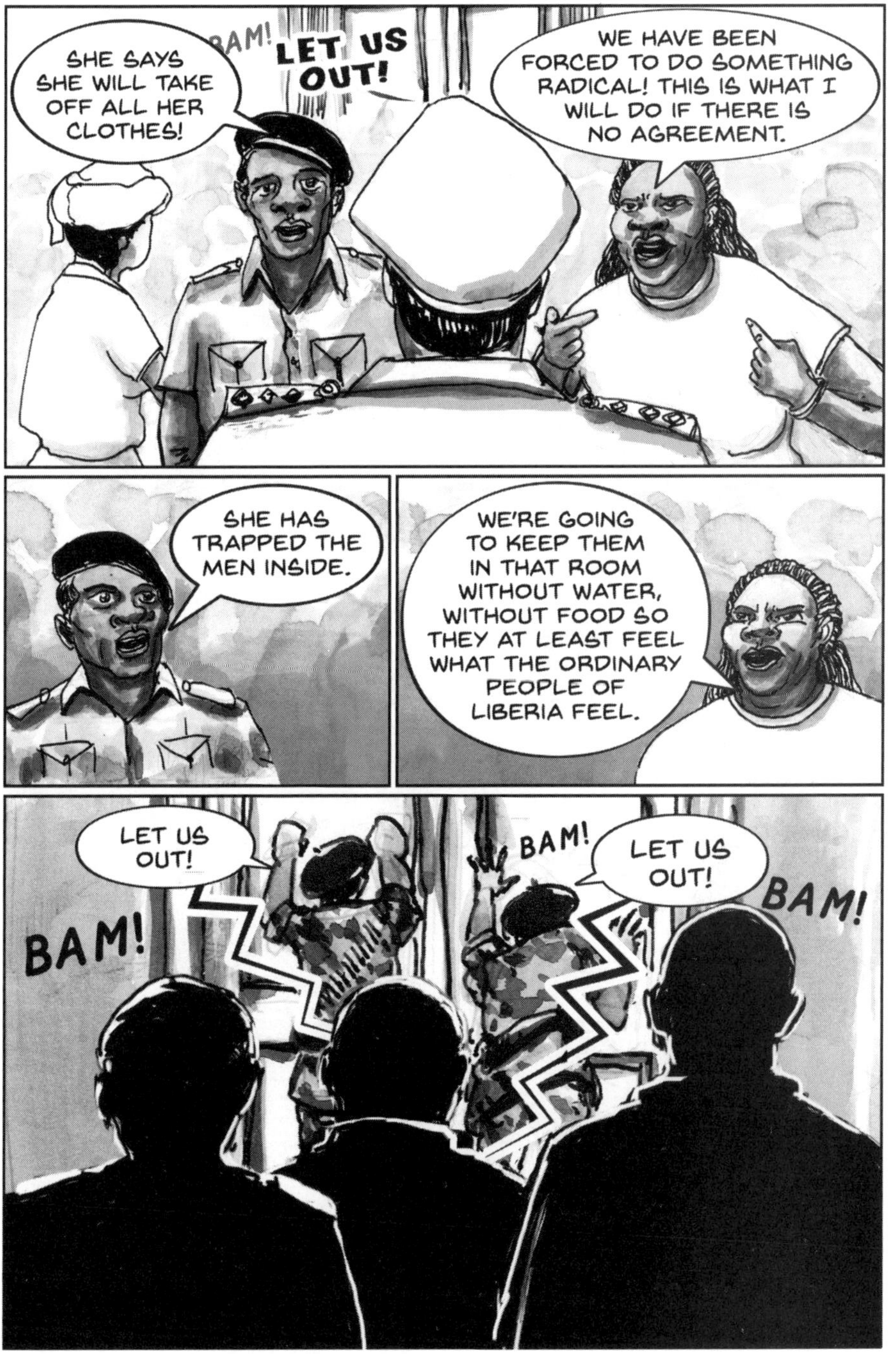
SHE SAYS SHE WILL TAKE OFF ALL HER CLOTHES!
BAM!
LET US OUT!
WE HAVE BEEN FORCED TO DO SOMETHING RADICAL! THIS IS WHAT I WILL DO IF THERE IS NO AGREEMENT.
SHE HAS TRAPPED THE MEN INSIDE.
WE'RE GOING TO KEEP THEM IN THAT ROOM WITHOUT WATER, WITHOUT FOOD SO THEY AT LEAST FEEL WHAT THE ORDINARY PEOPLE OF LIBERIA FEEL.
LET US OUT!
BAM!
LET US OUT!
BAM!
BAM!

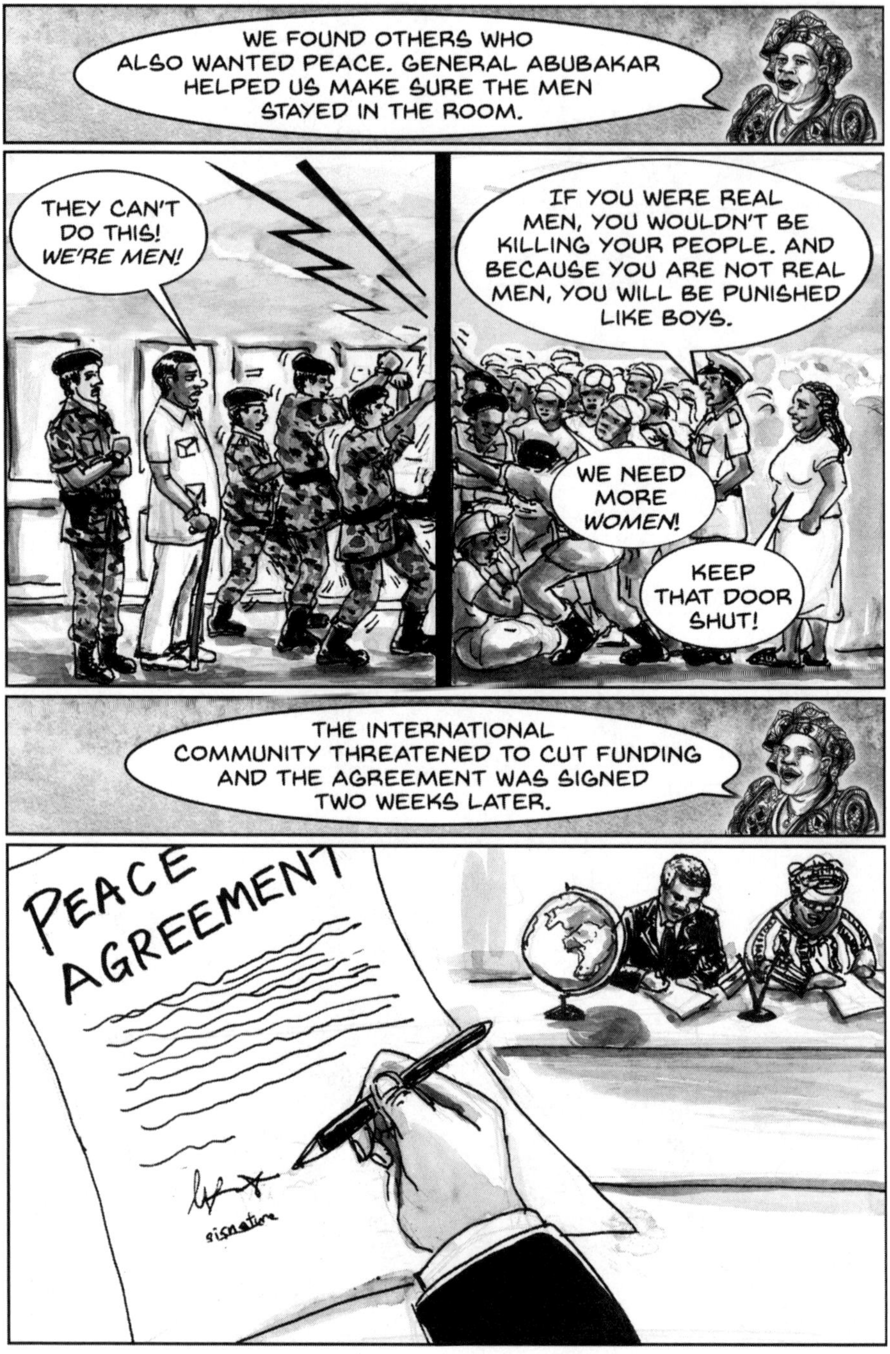
WE FOUND OTHERS WHO ALSO WANTED PEACE. GENERAL ABUBAKAR HELPED US MAKE SURE THE MEN STAYED IN THE ROOM.
THEY CAN'T DO THIS! *WE'RE MEN!*
IF YOU WERE REAL MEN, YOU WOULDN'T BE KILLING YOUR PEOPLE. AND BECAUSE YOU ARE NOT REAL MEN, YOU WILL BE PUNISHED LIKE BOYS.
WE NEED MORE *WOMEN!*
KEEP THAT DOOR SHUT!
THE INTERNATIONAL COMMUNITY THREATENED TO CUT FUNDING AND THE AGREEMENT WAS SIGNED TWO WEEKS LATER.
PEACE AGREEMENT
signature

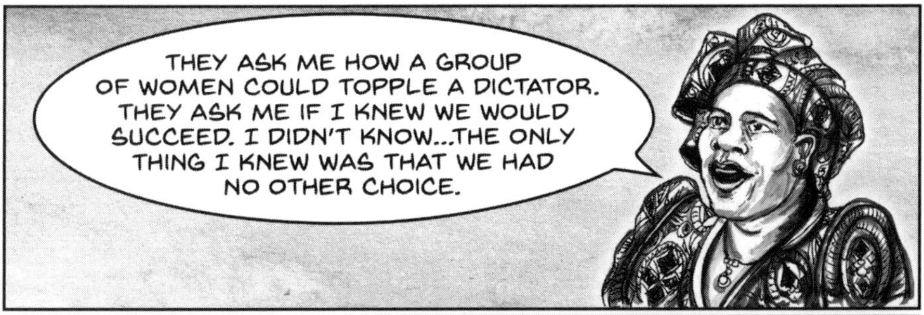
THEY ASK ME HOW A GROUP OF WOMEN COULD TOPPLE A DICTATOR. THEY ASK ME IF I KNEW WE WOULD SUCCEED. I DIDN'T KNOW...THE ONLY THING I KNEW WAS THAT WE HAD NO OTHER CHOICE.

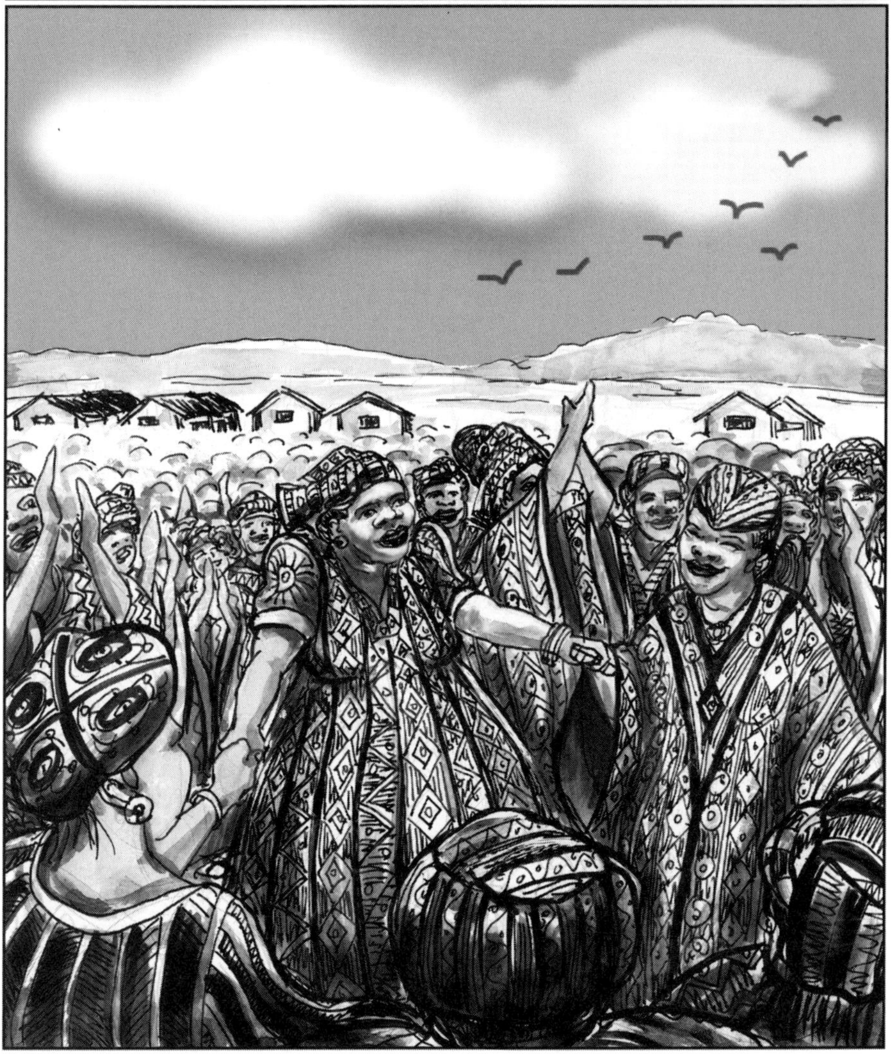

Speaking of the civil wars in Liberia, peace activist Leymah Gbowee said that "the wars in our region are fought on the bodies of women." Affecting individuals, families, and communities, war in Liberia was controlled by men and enacted through the experiences of people of all genders. Gbowee knew this from first-hand experience; Gbowee was seventeen when the first Liberian civil war broke out, and as a result of the war she had to give up her dream of attending medical school. She witnessed the manifold tragic effects of the war on Liberian citizens, and it was during this time that she became a trauma counselor and learned to treat traumatized former child soldiers. In 1999 civil war erupted again, resulting in more systematic rape and brutality. Liberian women saw their sons forced into battle, their daughters being raped, and their husbands murdered.

By 2003, the women of Liberia had had enough. Leymah Gbowee formed the Women of Liberia Mass Action for Peace, a diverse group of women held together by their dedication to peace. The movement quickly grew, bringing together Muslim, Christian, Indigenous, elite, and poor women. They found solidarity in their shared suffering, and their diversity made the movement stronger. Liberian women, having reached their limits of patience, were steadfast in their struggle to establish peace in their country for their families and communities. The actions they organized included nonviolent protests of thousands of women, pray-ins, a sex strike in which they withheld sex from male partners, the threat of a curse, the threat to disrobe publicly, and wearing uniforms of white t-shirts and white hair ties. They demanded reconciliation and an end to war.

At pivotal moments in the peace protests, Gbowee chose to disobey her male political leaders, and to instead act as a political leader herself, speaking out against their decisions and rallying other women to join with her. After years of listening to stories of wartime traumas experienced by women and children, Gbowee was empowered to speak the truth and advocate for peace. Of her confrontation with then-president of Liberia and war criminal Charles Taylor in Accra, Ghana, she recounts the danger she and the other women faced: "We didn't know what to expect. We could be arrested. We could be beaten. If it came to the worst, we could be killed. But we decided we would still go ... when I looked at Taylor sitting there with his dark glasses on, I decided to go with what I was feeling: that there was this exhaustion of war, exhaustion of rape, exhaustion of so many things" (2012). She did not give up, and in a 2003 protest she forced Taylor to meet with the women and to agree to take part in formal peace talks in Accra. Gbowee and her fellow peace activists followed Taylor to Ghana. At a crucial point in the peace talks, Gbowee and nearly 200 women barricaded Taylor, his representatives, and the rebel warlords in their meeting hall to prevent them from leaving until they could come to a peace agreement. Within weeks of the meeting, Taylor resigned and went into exile, and a peace treaty mandating a transitional government was signed. The women of Liberia were tired of years of violence and trauma. Gbowee's courage, leadership, and dedication were what the peace movement in Liberia needed.

Discussion Questions

1 What are three of the ways the Women of Liberia Mass Action created a unified activist identity?
2 The Women of Liberia Mass Action came together across normally divisive class and religious lines. What brought the women together?
3 What is one of the culturally specific actions that the Women of Liberia Mass Action took?
4 How is the Women of Liberia Mass Action an intersectional feminist movement?

Research Questions and Activities

1 Can you think of a culturally specific resistance action that would only be meaningful in your own cultural environment?

2 How did the civil war affect traditional gender roles in Liberia? Research the roles of women and men in families and communities in Liberia before, during, and after the civil wars.

3 Former Liberian president Ellen Johnson Sirleaf is the first woman to have been elected a head of state in Africa. Her work to rebuild Liberia after the civil wars included reforms to improve the lives of women. Do research on Sirleaf to learn more about her life and role as president. What can feminists and other activists in your country learn from the work of Sirleaf? Which of her policies and practices could be implemented in your home country?

Further Reading and Viewing

Gbowee, Leymah. *Mighty Be Our Powers: How Sisterhood, Prayer and Sex Changed a Nation at War*. New York: Perseus Books, 2013.

Kamara-Umunna, Agnes, and Emily Holland. *And Still Peace Did Not Come: A Memoir of Reconciliation*. New York: Hyperion, 2011.

Pal, Amitabh. "Leymah Gbowee." *The Progressive*. 13 Sept. 2012. <progressive.org>

Prasch, Allison M. "Maternal Bodies in Militant Protest: Leymah Gbowee and Rhetorical Agency of African Motherhood." *Women's Studies in Communication* 38.2 (May 2015): 187–205.

Pray the Devil Back to Hell. Dir. Gini Reticker. Prod. Abigail E. Disney. New York: Fork Films, 2008.

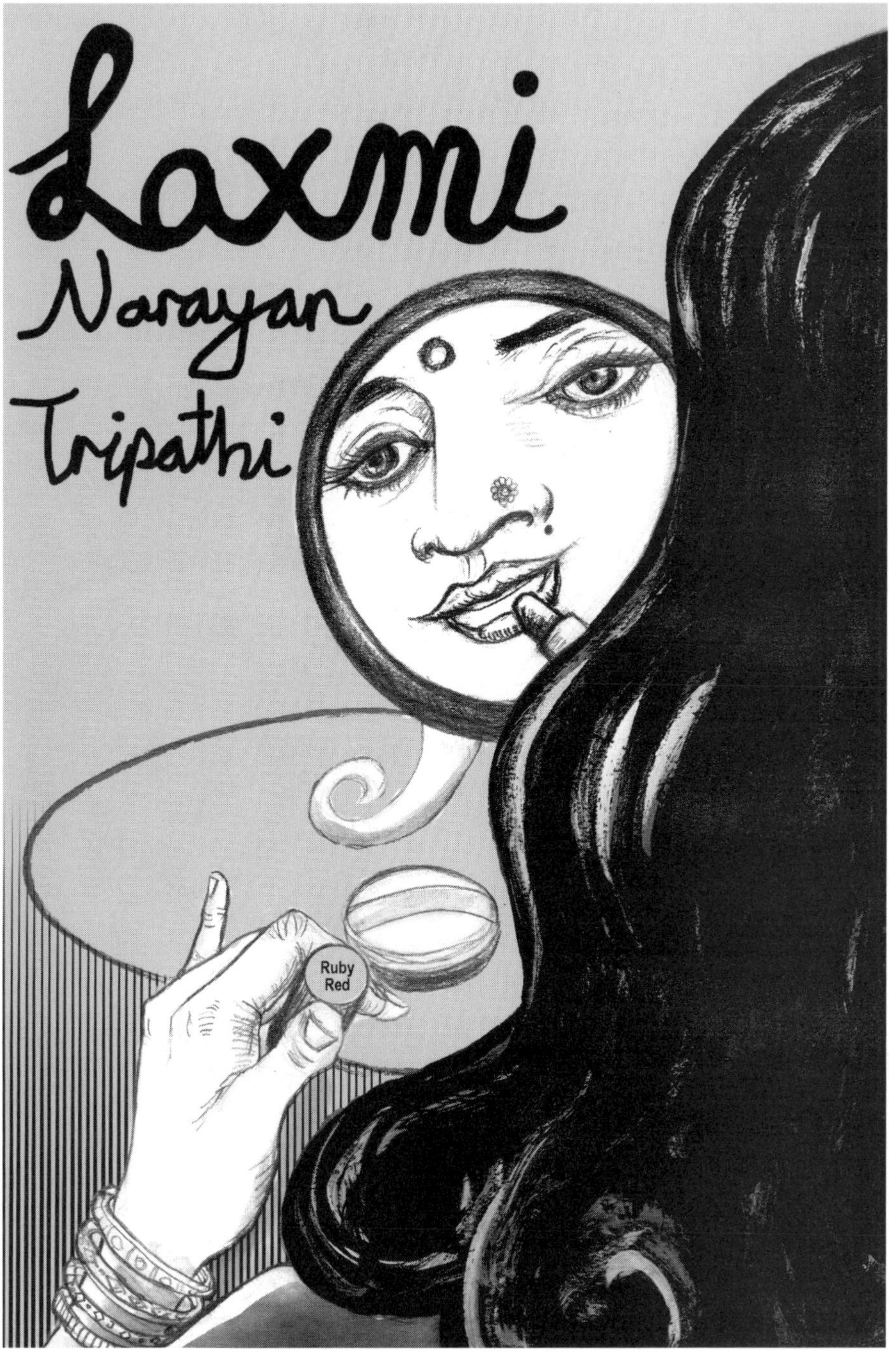
Laxmi
Narayan
Tripathi
Ruby
Red

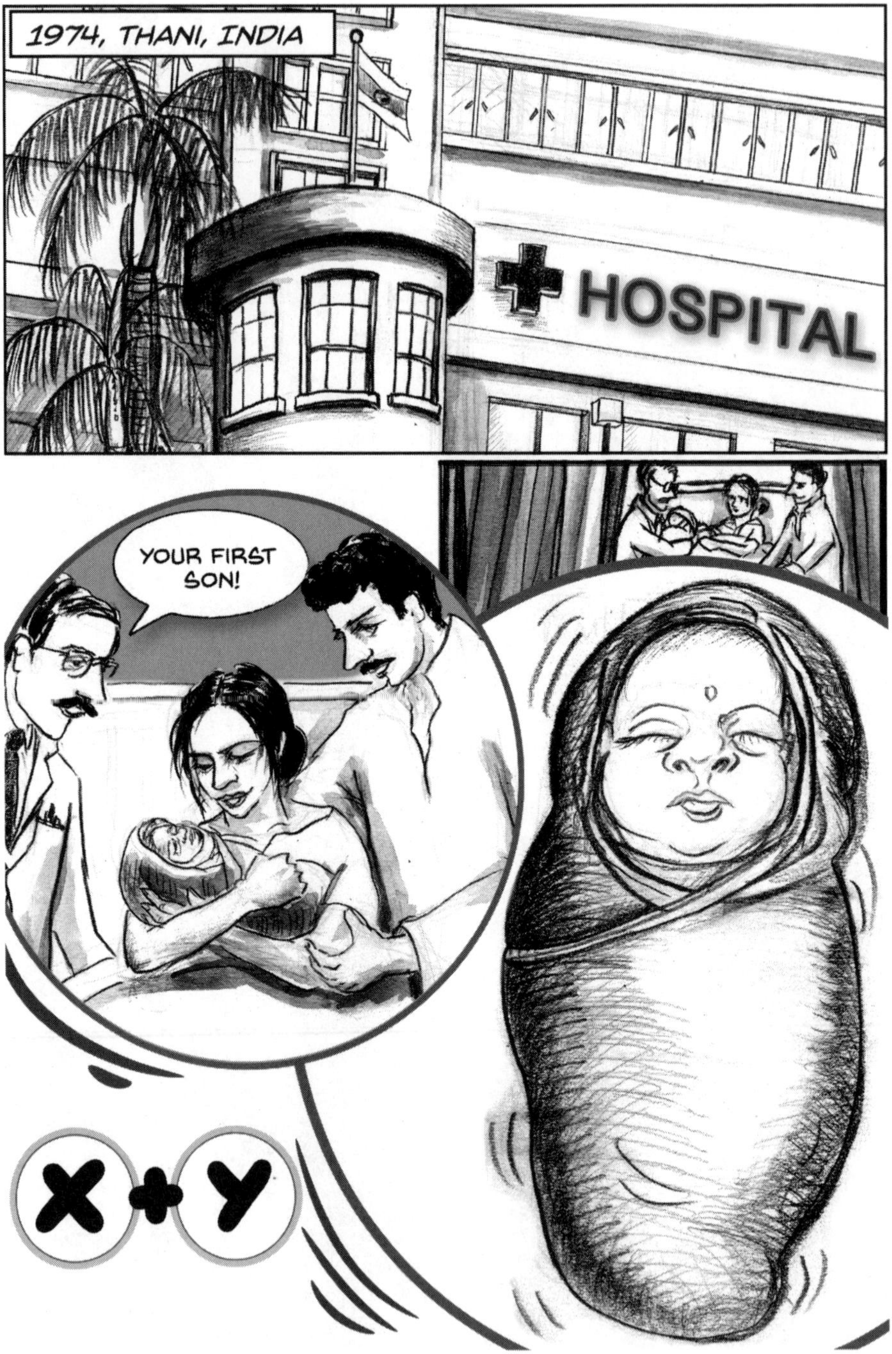
1974, THANI, INDIA
HOSPITAL
YOUR FIRST SON!
X+Y

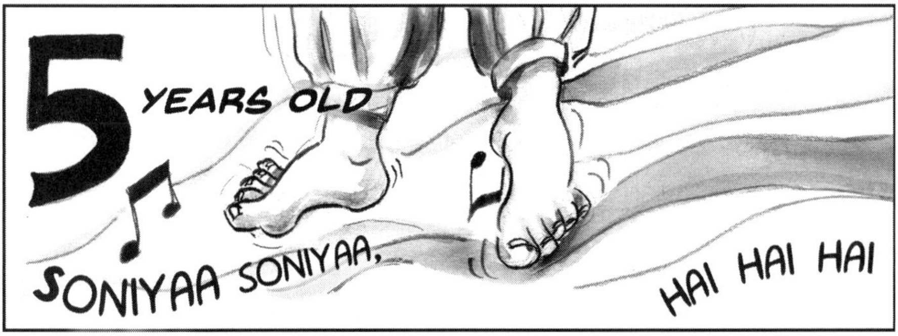
5 YEARS OLD
SONIYAA SONIYAA,
HAI HAI HAI

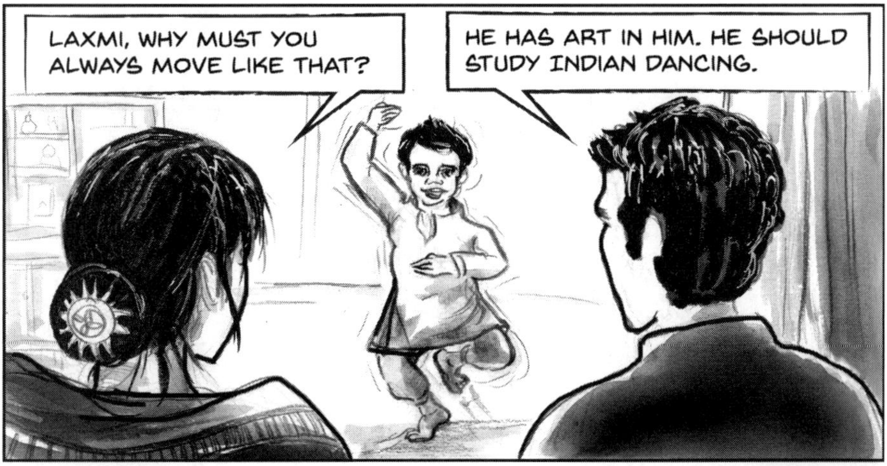
LAXMI, WHY MUST YOU ALWAYS MOVE LIKE THAT?
HE HAS ART IN HIM. HE SHOULD STUDY INDIAN DANCING.

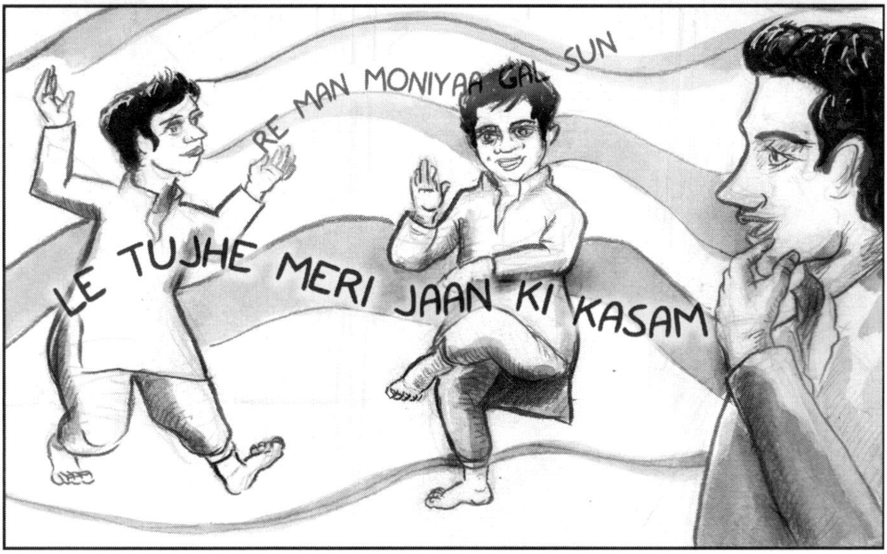
RE MAN MONIYAA GAL SUN
LE TUJHE MERI JAAN KI KASAM

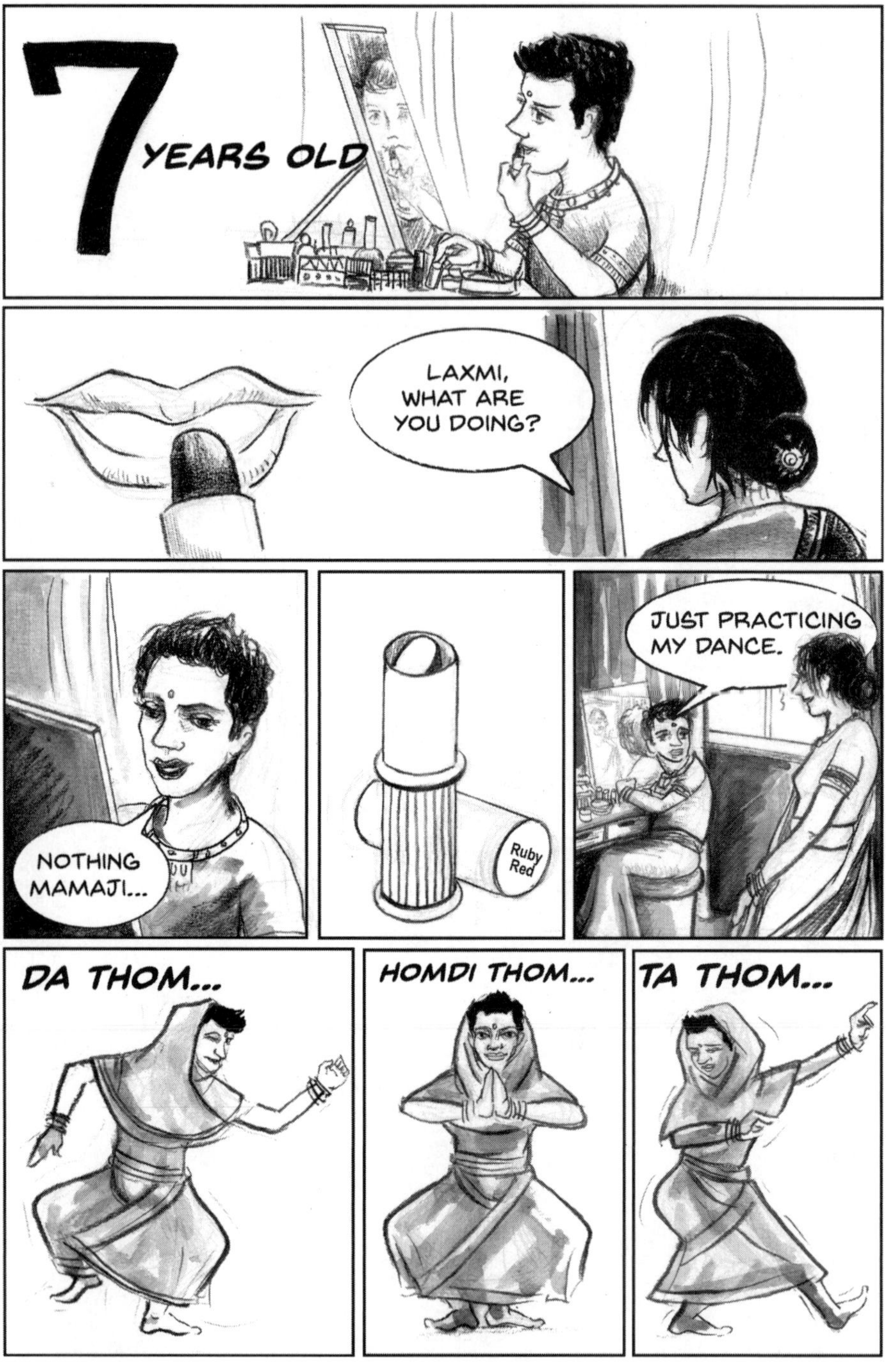
7 YEARS OLD
LAXMI, WHAT ARE YOU DOING?
NOTHING MAMAJI...
Ruby Red
JUST PRACTICING MY DANCE.
DA THOM...
HOMDI THOM...
TA THOM...

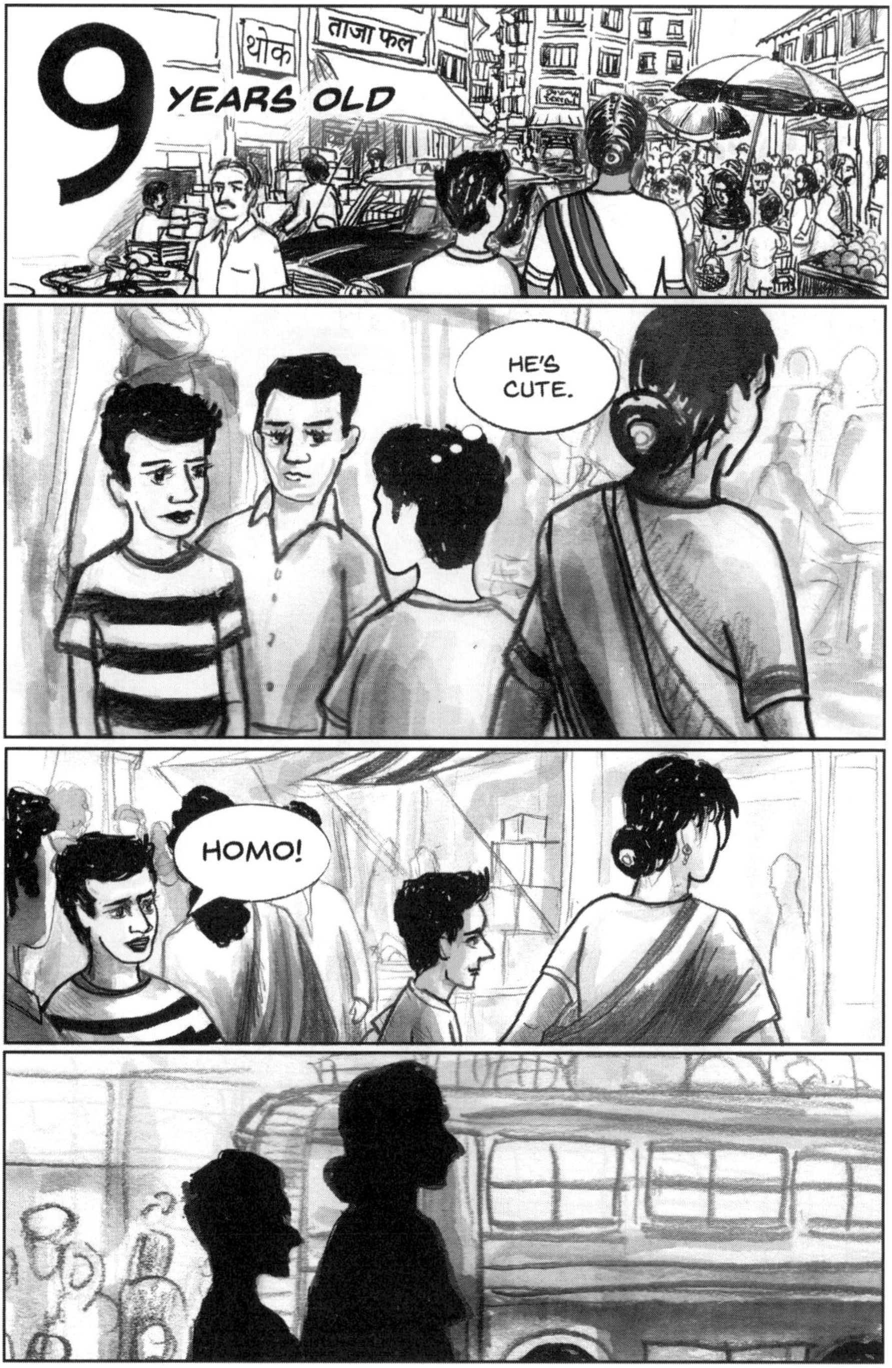
थोक
ताजा फल
9 YEARS OLD
HE'S CUTE.
HOMO!

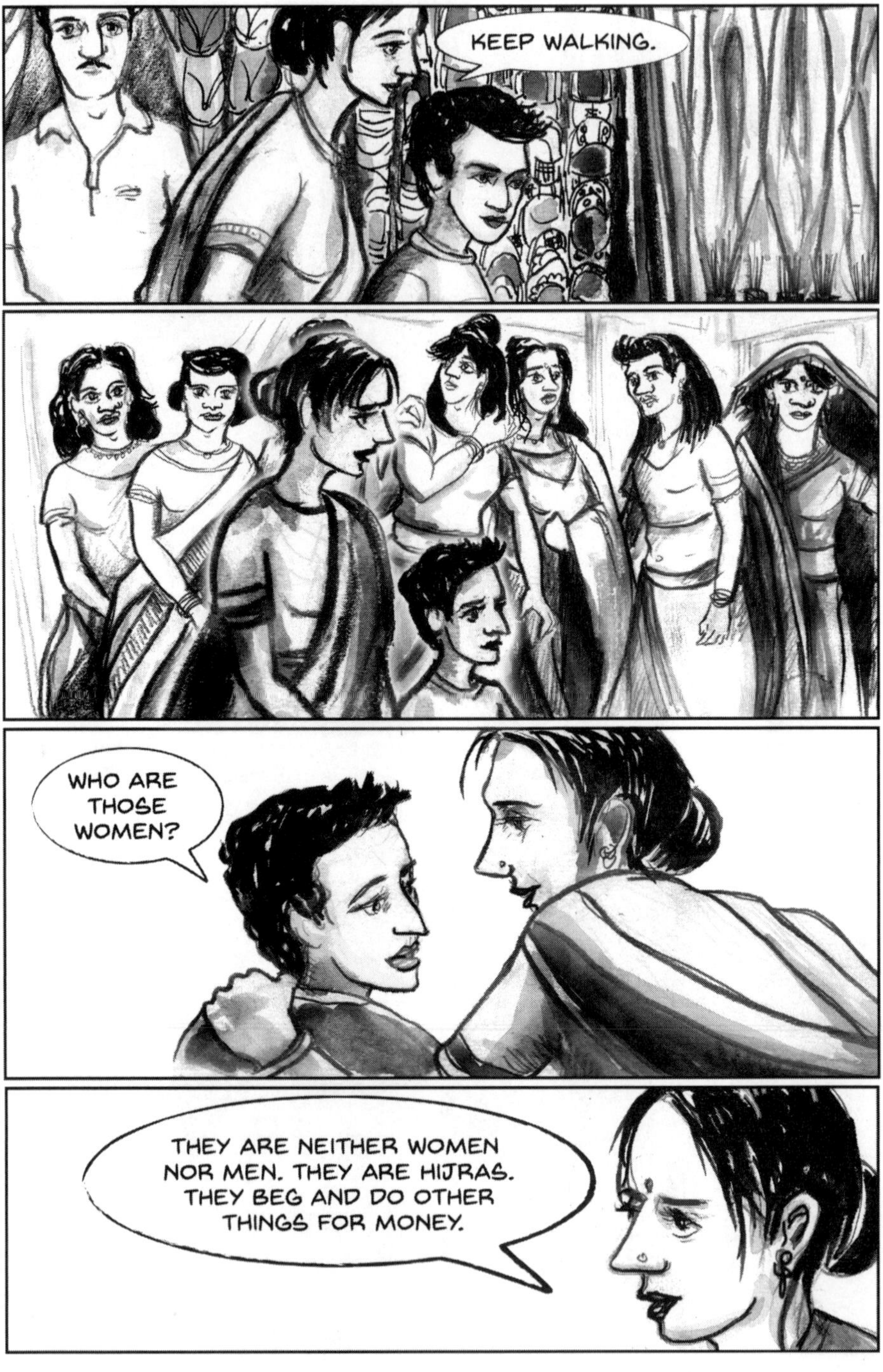
KEEP WALKING.
WHO ARE THOSE WOMEN?
THEY ARE NEITHER WOMEN NOR MEN. THEY ARE HIJRAS. THEY BEG AND DO OTHER THINGS FOR MONEY.

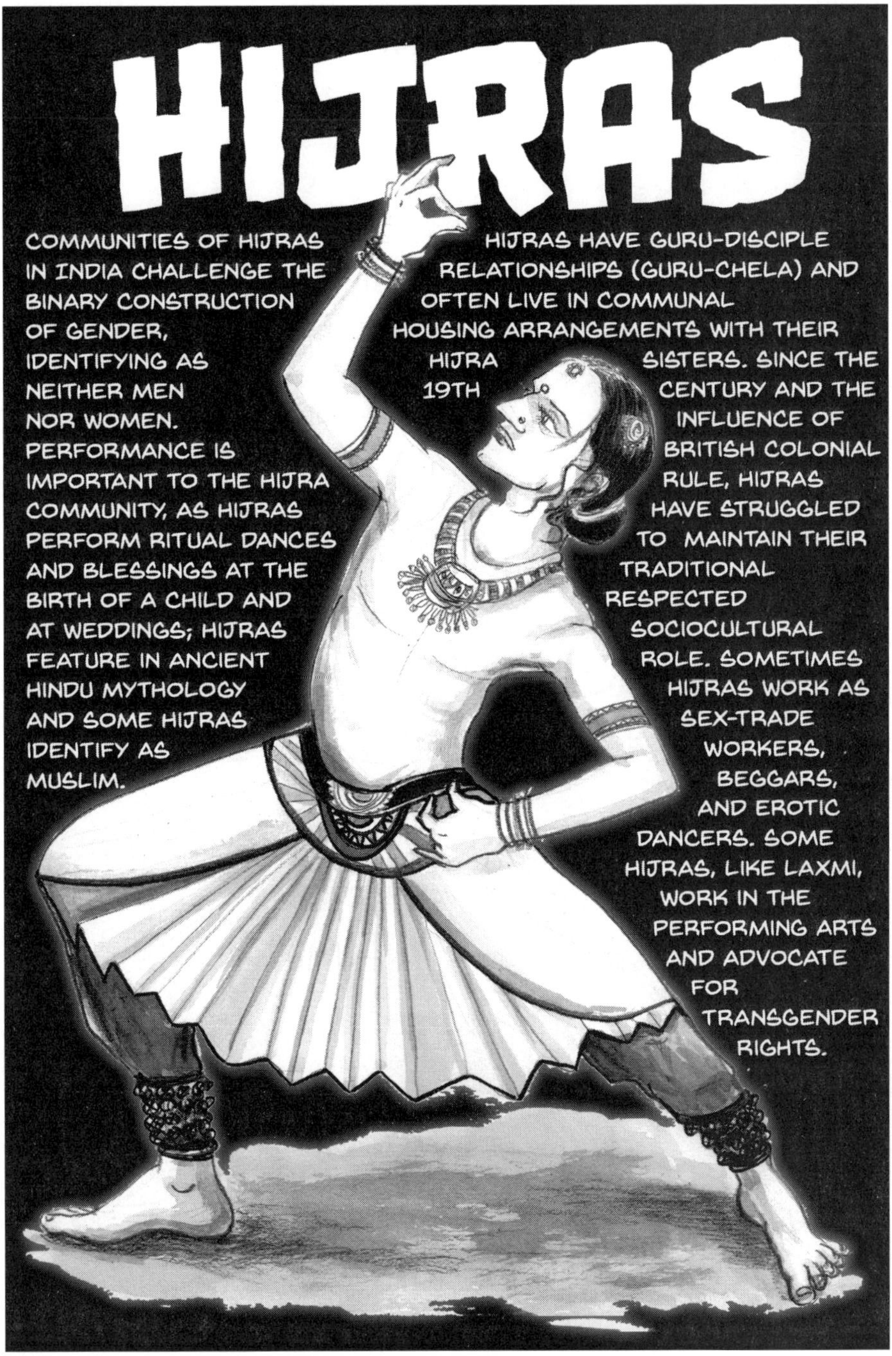
HIJRAS
COMMUNITIES OF HIJRAS IN INDIA CHALLENGE THE BINARY CONSTRUCTION OF GENDER, IDENTIFYING AS NEITHER MEN NOR WOMEN. PERFORMANCE IS IMPORTANT TO THE HIJRA COMMUNITY, AS HIJRAS PERFORM RITUAL DANCES AND BLESSINGS AT THE BIRTH OF A CHILD AND AT WEDDINGS; HIJRAS FEATURE IN ANCIENT HINDU MYTHOLOGY AND SOME HIJRAS IDENTIFY AS MUSLIM.
HIJRAS HAVE GURU-DISCIPLE RELATIONSHIPS (GURU-CHELA) AND OFTEN LIVE IN COMMUNAL HOUSING ARRANGEMENTS WITH THEIR HIJRA SISTERS. SINCE THE 19TH CENTURY AND THE INFLUENCE OF BRITISH COLONIAL RULE, HIJRAS HAVE STRUGGLED TO MAINTAIN THEIR TRADITIONAL RESPECTED SOCIOCULTURAL ROLE. SOMETIMES HIJRAS WORK AS SEX-TRADE WORKERS, BEGGARS, AND EROTIC DANCERS. SOME HIJRAS, LIKE LAXMI, WORK IN THE PERFORMING ARTS AND ADVOCATE FOR TRANSGENDER RIGHTS.

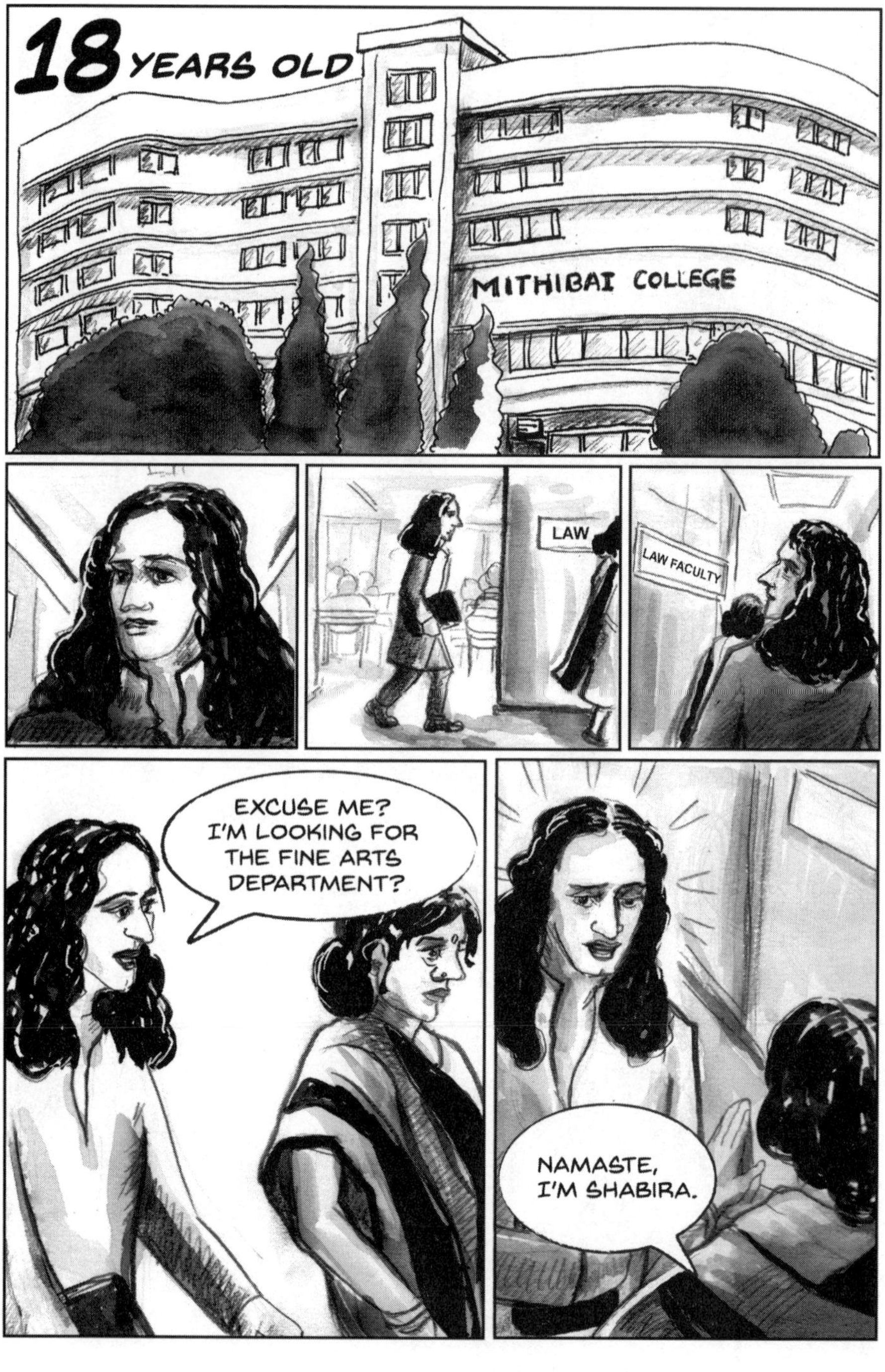
18 YEARS OLD
MITHIBAI COLLEGE
LAW
LAW FACULTY
EXCUSE ME? I'M LOOKING FOR THE FINE ARTS DEPARTMENT?
NAMASTE, I'M SHABIRA.

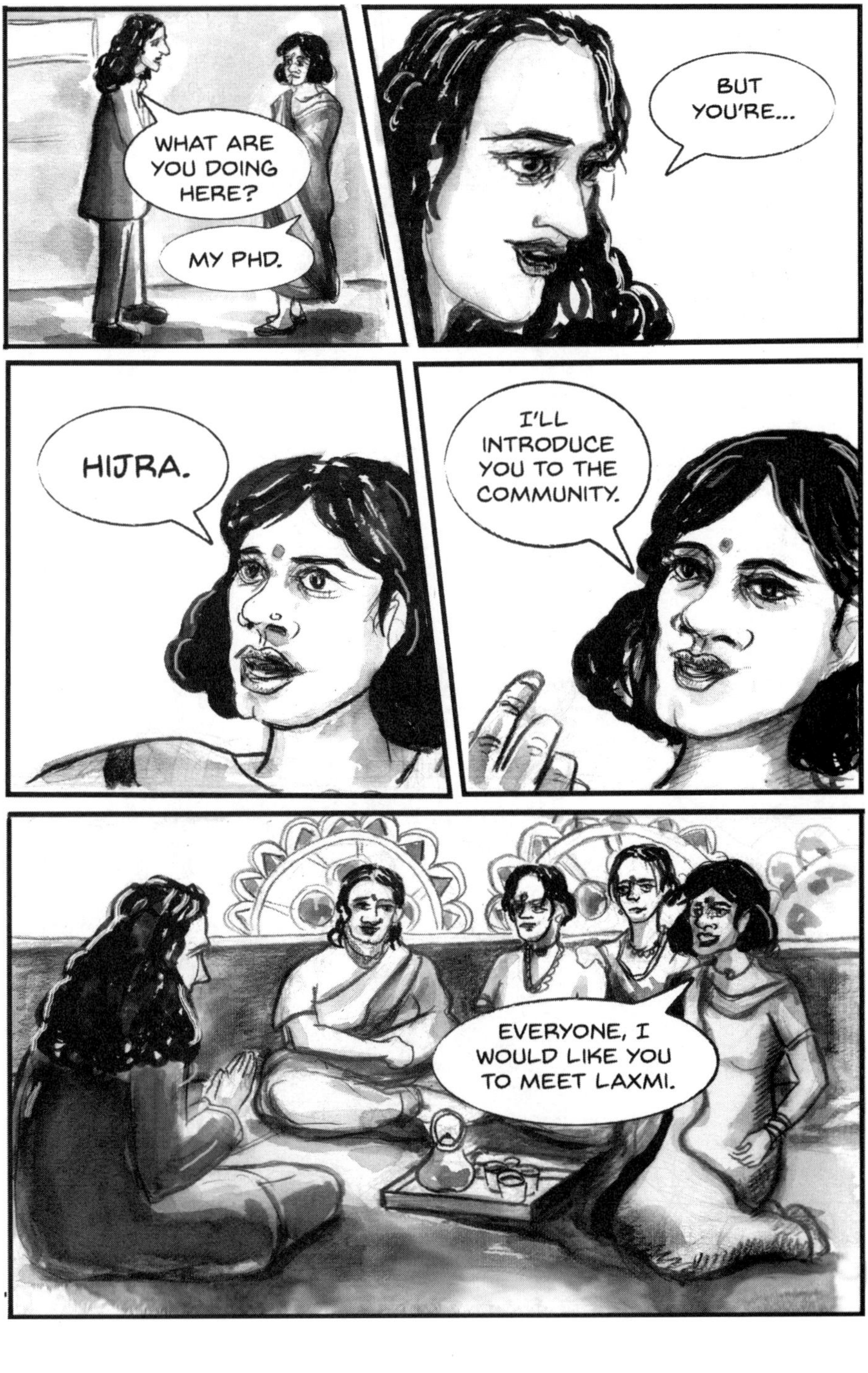
WHAT ARE YOU DOING HERE?
MY PHD.
BUT YOU'RE...
HIJRA.
I'LL INTRODUCE YOU TO THE COMMUNITY.
EVERYONE, I WOULD LIKE YOU TO MEET LAXMI.

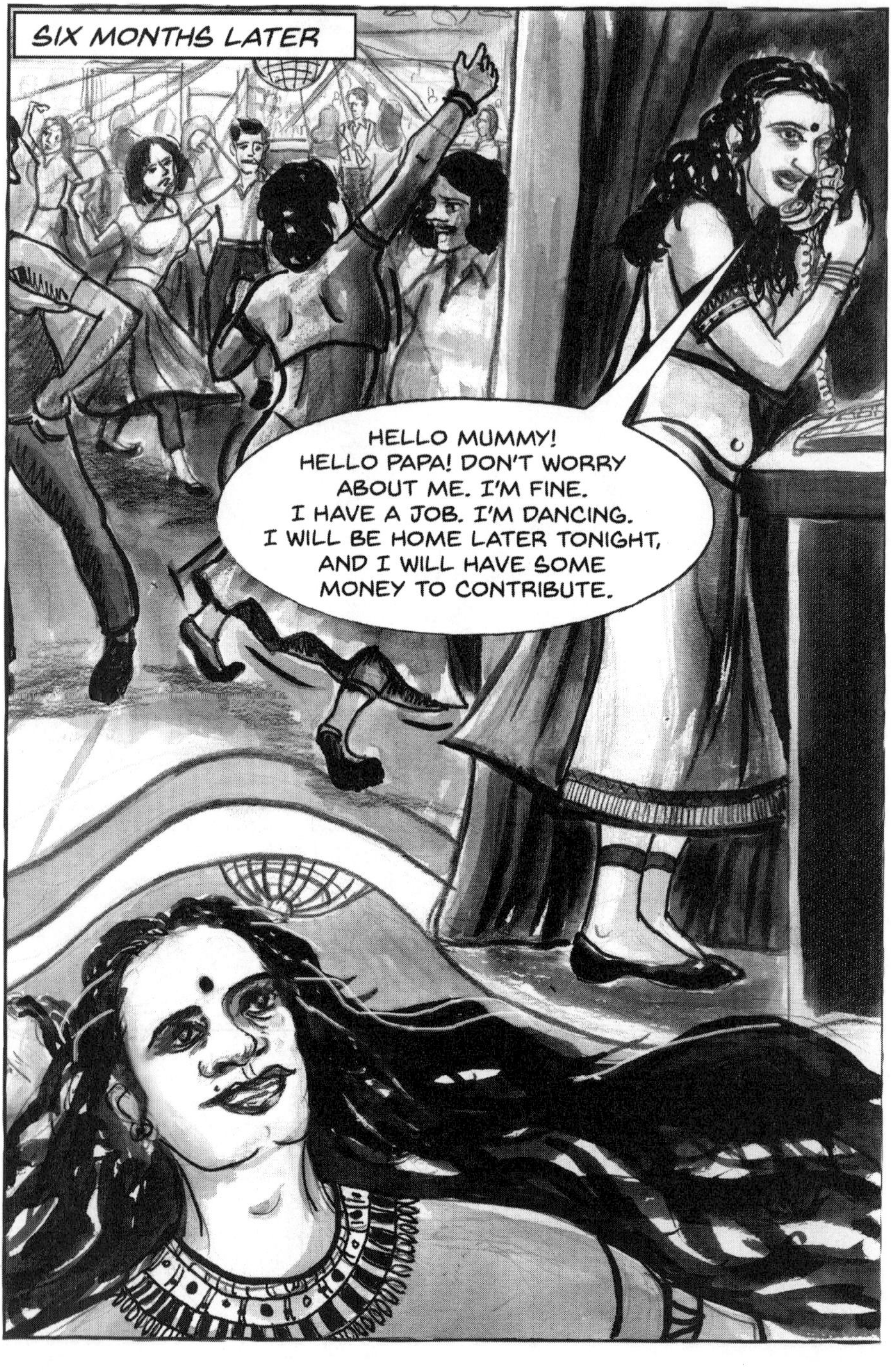
SIX MONTHS LATER
HELLO MUMMY! HELLO PAPA! DON'T WORRY ABOUT ME. I'M FINE. I HAVE A JOB. I'M DANCING. I WILL BE HOME LATER TONIGHT, AND I WILL HAVE SOME MONEY TO CONTRIBUTE.

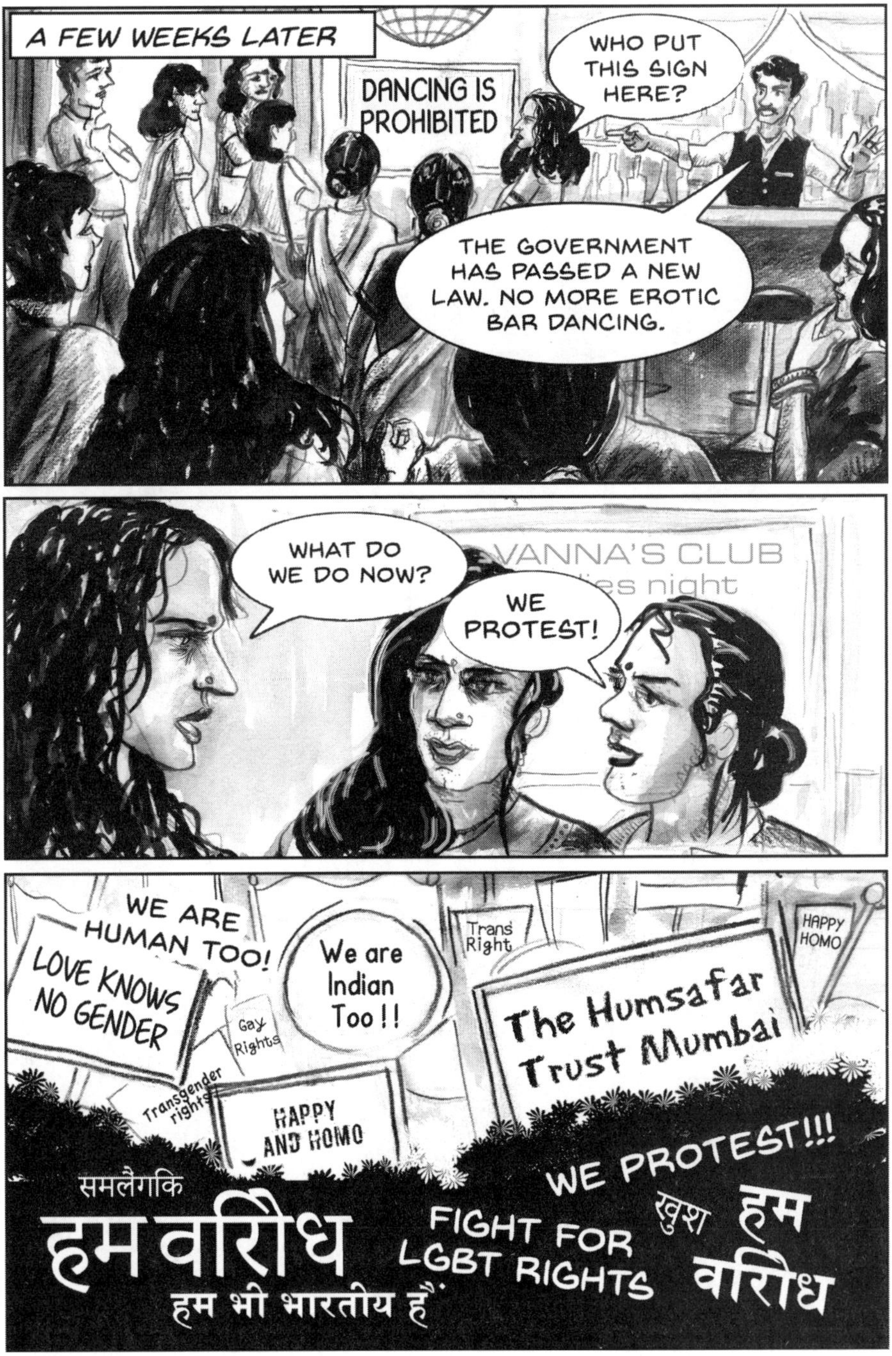
A FEW WEEKS LATER
DANCING IS PROHIBITED
WHO PUT THIS SIGN HERE?
THE GOVERNMENT HAS PASSED A NEW LAW. NO MORE EROTIC BAR DANCING.
VANNA'S CLUB
WHAT DO WE DO NOW?
WE PROTEST!
WE ARE HUMAN TOO!
LOVE KNOWS NO GENDER
We are Indian Too!!
Trans Right
HAPPY HOMO
Gay Rights
The Humsafar Trust Mumbai
Transgender rights
HAPPY AND HOMO
WE PROTEST!!!
समलैगकि
हम वरिोध
हम भी भारतीय हैं
FIGHT FOR LGBT RIGHTS
खुश हम
वरिोध

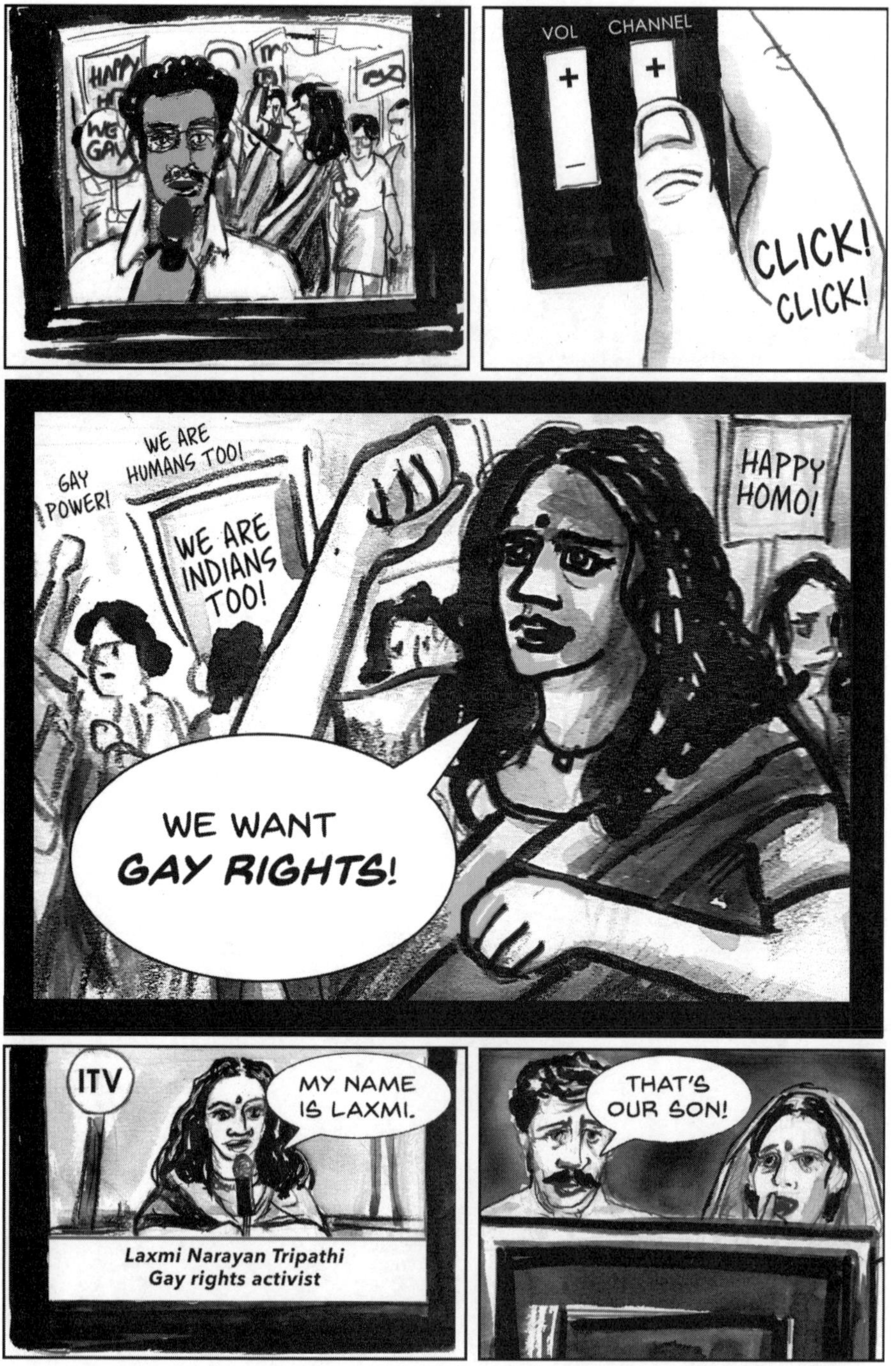
VOL
CHANNEL
CLICK!
CLICK!
WE ARE HUMANS TOO!
GAY POWER!
WE ARE INDIANS TOO!
HAPPY HOMO!
WE WANT GAY RIGHTS!
ITV
MY NAME IS LAXMI.
Laxmi Narayan Tripathi
Gay rights activist
THAT'S OUR SON!

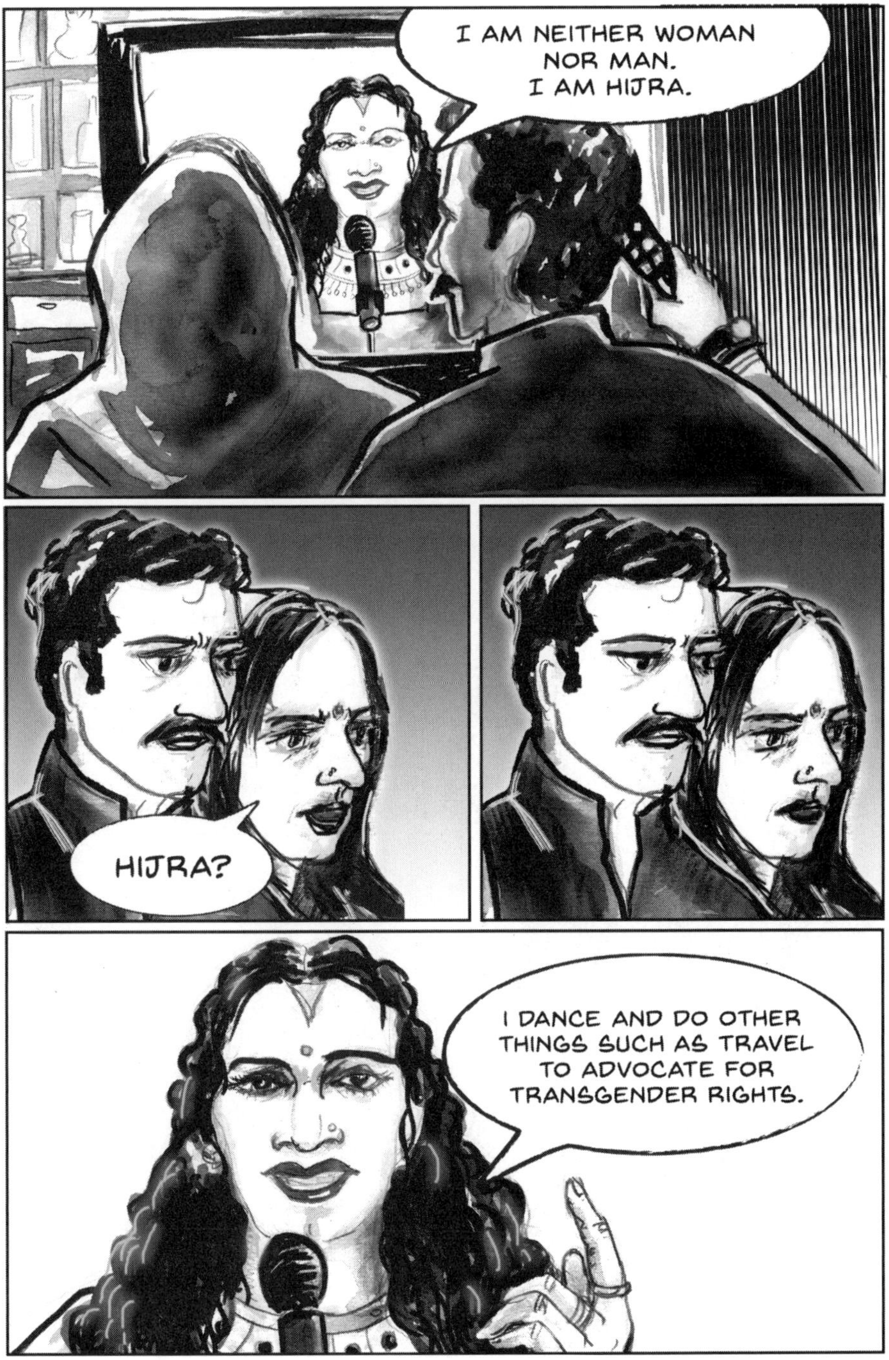
I AM NEITHER WOMAN NOR MAN. I AM HIJRA.
HIJRA?
I DANCE AND DO OTHER THINGS SUCH AS TRAVEL TO ADVOCATE FOR TRANSGENDER RIGHTS.

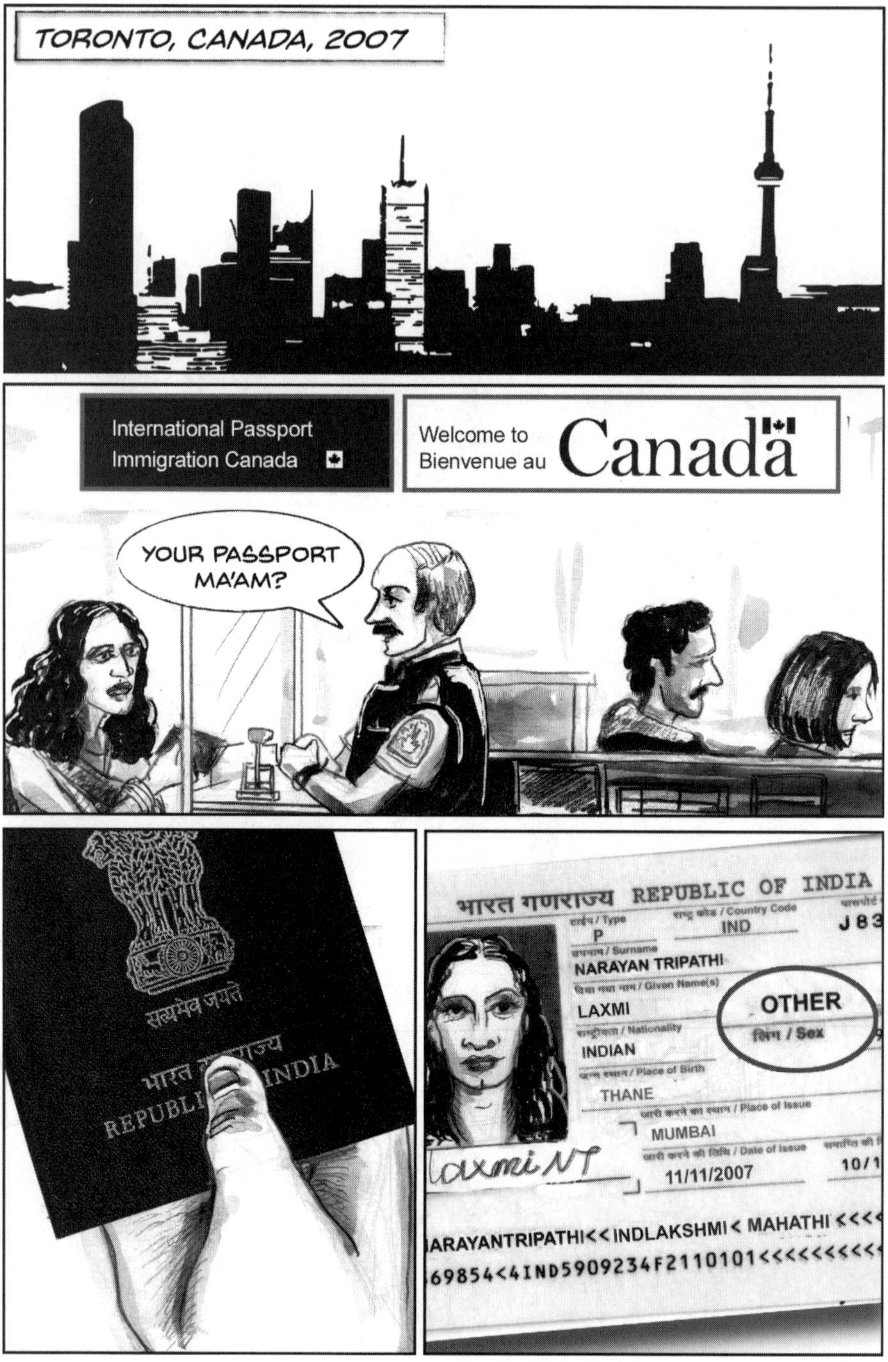

TORONTO, CANADA, 2007
International Passport
Immigration Canada
Welcome to
Bienvenue au
Canada
YOUR PASSPORT MA'AM?
सत्यमेव जयते
भारत गणराज्य REPUBLIC OF INDIA
Type
P
Country Code
IND
Surname
NARAYAN TRIPATHI
Given Name(s)
LAXMI
OTHER
Sex
Nationality
INDIAN
Place of Birth
THANE
Place of Issue
MUMBAI
Date of Issue
11/11/2007
Laxmi NT
ARAYANTRIPATHI<<INDLAKSHMI< MAHATHI <<<
69854<4IND5909234F2110101<<<<<<<<<

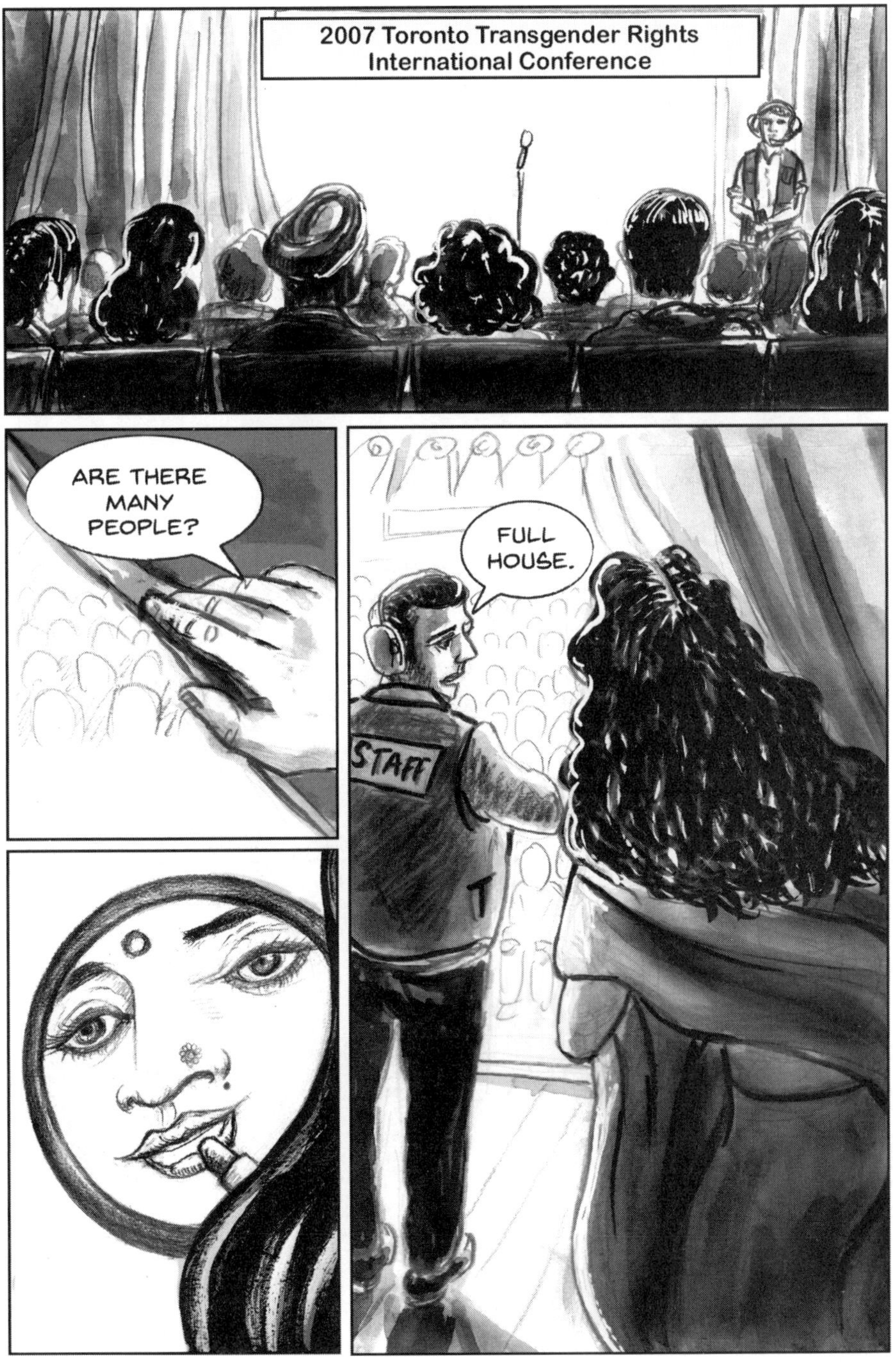
2007 Toronto Transgender Rights International Conference
ARE THERE MANY PEOPLE?
FULL HOUSE.
STAFF

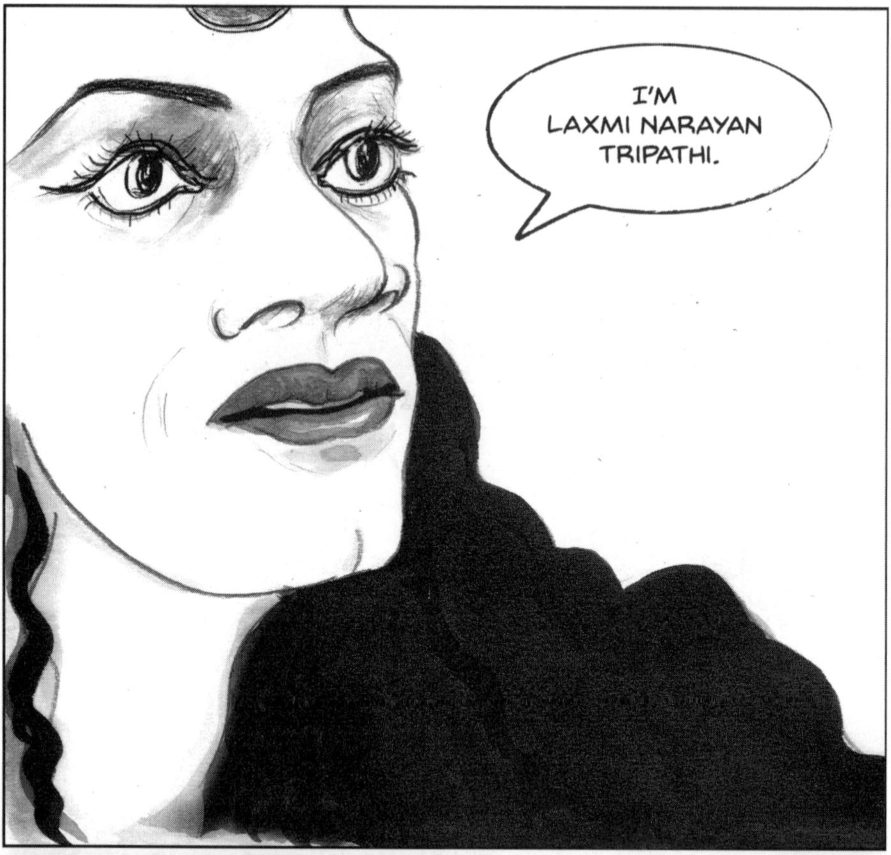
I'M LAXMI NARAYAN TRIPATHI.

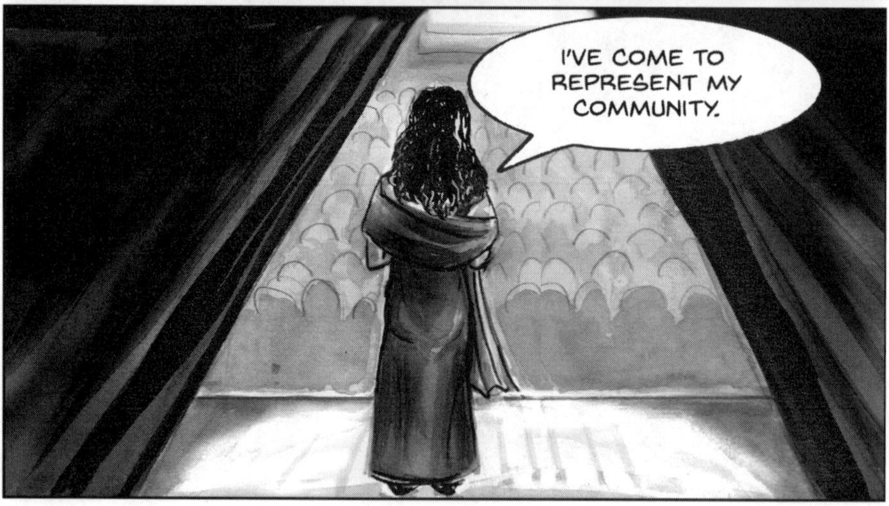
I'VE COME TO REPRESENT MY COMMUNITY.

Born in Thane, India, in 1979, Laxmi Narayan Tripathi is known worldwide as a transgender activist. She is also a film actor and a classically trained Bharatanatyam dancer. Tripathi went to college in Mumbai for an arts degree and a post-graduate degree in classical dance. In her youth, Laxmi Narayan Tripathi joined the hijra community in India, one of the world's oldest transgender communities. While working as a dancer and living as a hijra, Tripathi became an activist for transgender rights, and speaks openly about becoming and being a transgender hijra woman.

Tripathi identifies as belonging to the hijra community of transgender women in India. This means that, while Tripathi's preferred pronouns are she/her, she belongs to a community of women who occupy a gender category that does not easily translate to Western, Eurocentric gender binaries.

The history of hijra communities in India is pre-colonial, and while colonial and post-colonial India led to oppressive conditions for hijra communities, hijra cultural vitality continues to influence twenty-first-century gender rights in India, Southeast Asia, and the world. In Canada, gender expression is a guaranteed protected right since 2017, and people may choose a non-binary, male, or female gender identity; however, this does not quite equate to hijra identity, which acknowledges transgender hijra women as a unique third gender. Trans women in India are not all hijra. We hope that learning about Tripathi encourages you to study the ways in which culture informs gender and sex identity.

Tripathi advocates for sexual orientation and gender expression freedom, seeing them as interrelated. In 2007, Indian gay rights activist and celebrity Kavi, along with an HIV/AIDS awareness organization, started to appeal Section 377 of the Indian Penal Act, the act that criminalized gay sex. Laxmi Narayan Tripathi joined his team. During a press conference Laxmi appeared in full make-up and women's clothing. It was through this TV appearance that her parents learned about her association with the hijra community.

They were surprised but ultimately supportive and they continue to love and support their daughter.

In 2007, Tripathi left India for the first time and traveled to Toronto, Canada, to meet with the Asia-Pacific sex workers network. Her passport stated that she was a transgender female, an identification she had lobbied for. In 2008, Laxmi Narayan Tripathi was the first transgender woman to represent an Asia-Pacific nation at the United Nations. She spoke about transgender rights and experiences. She also spoke in favor of LGBTQIIA and women's rights at the United Nations in 2014.

In April 2014 the Indian Supreme Court recognized transgender rights and recognized a third gender. All government documents in India now include the option for a third gender, by law transgender health needs must be provided for in health clinics, and transgender persons may adopt children. However, it was only in 2018 that same-sex sex was decriminalized; gender expression rights were years ahead of sexual orientation rights. Tripathi continues her work as an international LGBTQIIA activist, and has published two books about her experiences belonging to the hijra community and as an activist.

Discussion Questions

1 How did Laxmi Narayan Tripathi find allies to support her transition from male to female? Who were these allies?
2 What kinds of activism did Tripathi engage in, and what skills did these acts demand of her?
3 How did clothing and dance play a role in Laxmi's gender expression in the context of becoming a member of the hijra community?

Research Questions and Activities

1 Research the history of the hijra community in India. Find out how the role and status of the community have changed over the past century.
2 Find out if your governments – federal, state, or provincial – legislate or protect sexual orientation and gender expression. Compare the

rights in your jurisdiction to those of a nearby state, province, or country.

3 Are there cultural spaces that are safe, thriving, and celebrated for transgender culture in your home state or province? Find out more about these cultural spaces and consider how they are like, or unlike, the music, dance, and cultural spaces of hijra communities in India.

Further Reading and Viewing

Agoramoorthy, Govindasamy, and Minna Hsu. "Living on the Societal Edge: India's Transgender Realities." *Journal of Religion and Health* 54.4 (2015): 1451–59.

Coyote, Ivan E., and Rae Spoon. *Gender Failure*. Vancouver: Arsenal Pulp Press, 2014.

My Prairie Home. Dir. Chelsea McMullan. Perf. Rae Spoon. National Film Board of Canada, 2013.

Tripathi, Laxmi Narayan. *Me Laxmi, Me Hijra*. Oxford: Oxford University Press, 2015.

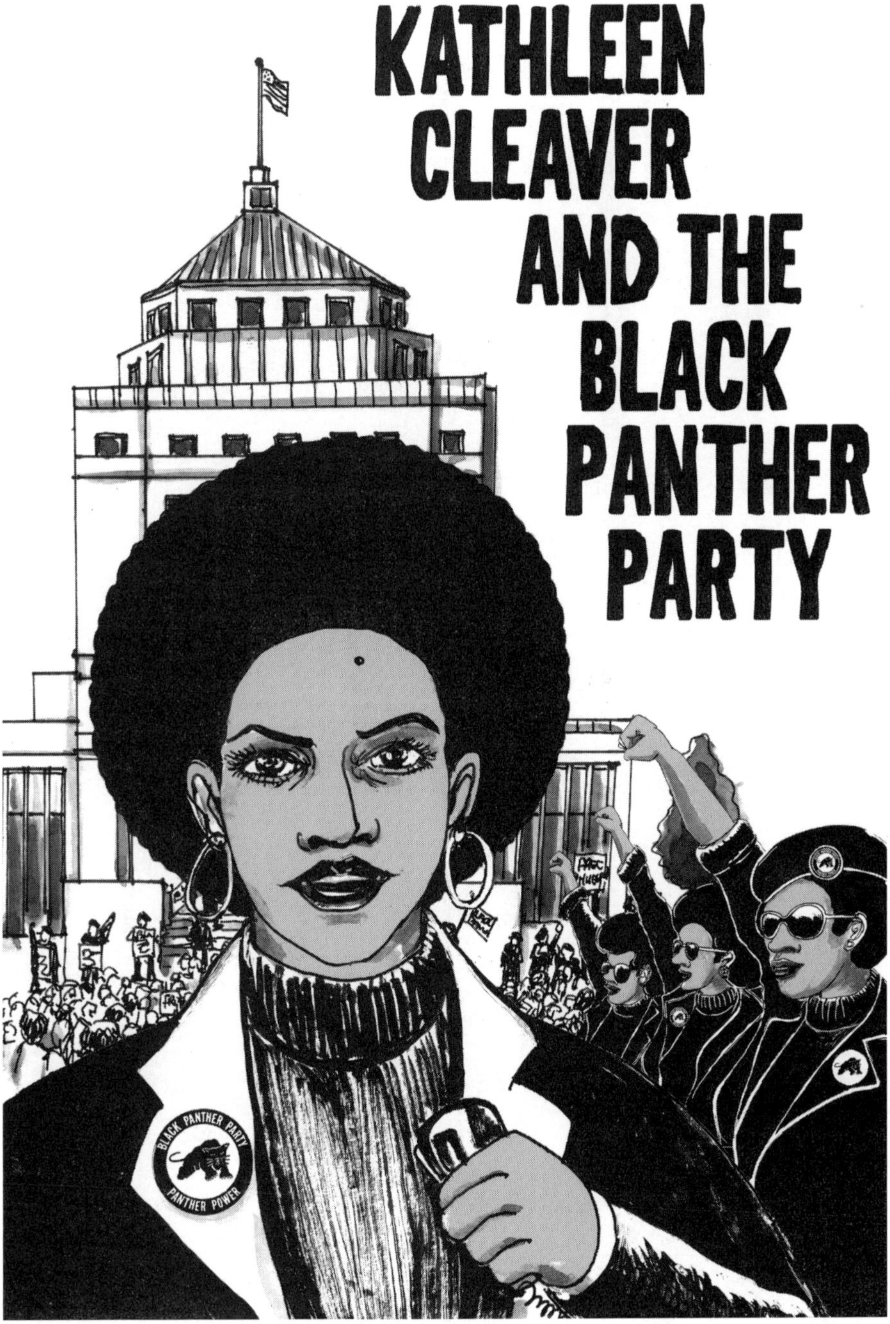
KATHLEEN
CLEAVER
AND THE
BLACK
PANTHER
PARTY
BLACK PANTHER PARTY
PANTHER POWER

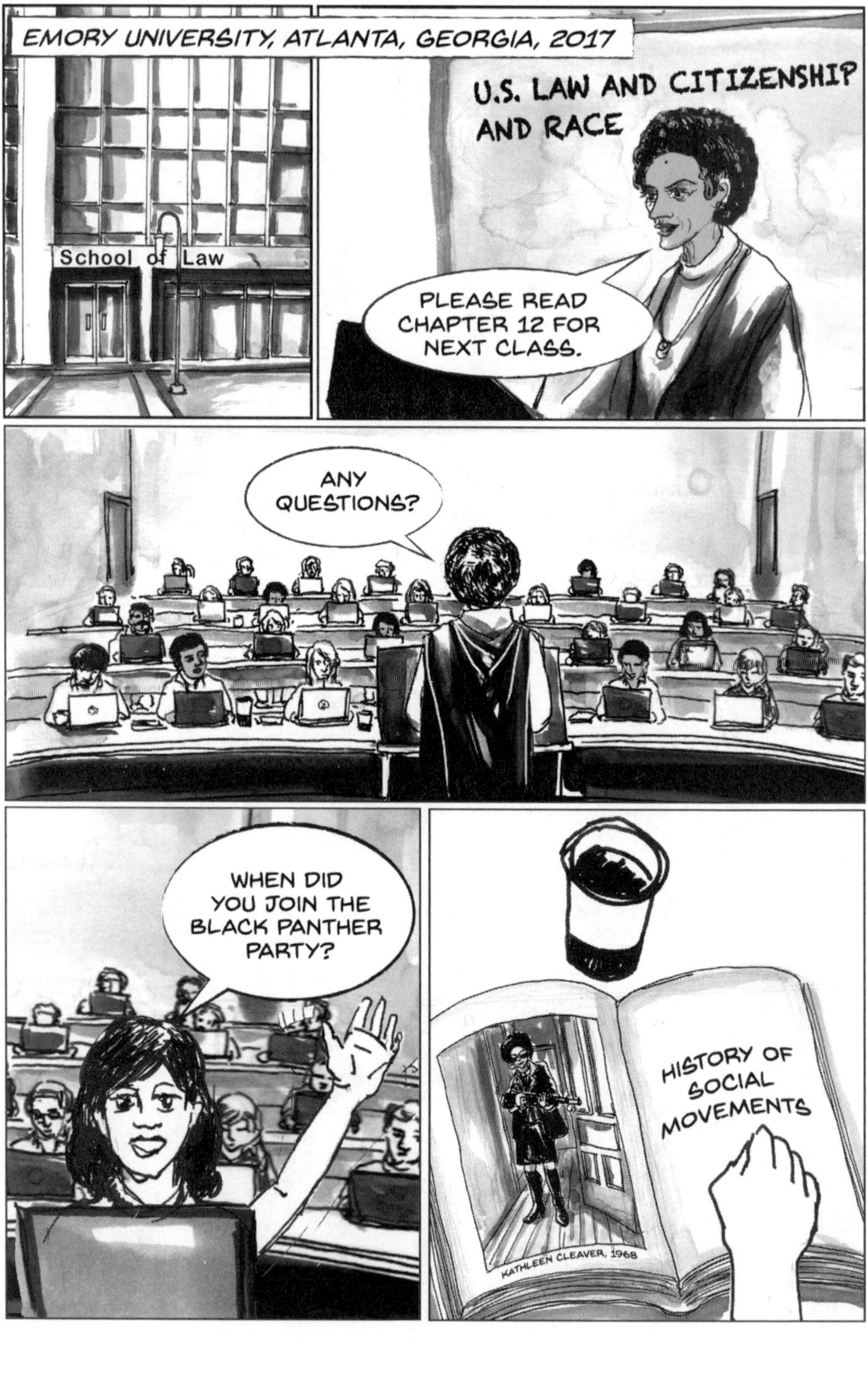
EMORY UNIVERSITY, ATLANTA, GEORGIA, 2017
School of Law
U.S. LAW AND CITIZENSHIP AND RACE
PLEASE READ CHAPTER 12 FOR NEXT CLASS.
ANY QUESTIONS?
WHEN DID YOU JOIN THE BLACK PANTHER PARTY?
HISTORY OF SOCIAL MOVEMENTS
KATHLEEN CLEAVER, 1968

In 1966, Huey P. Newtown, along with Bobby Seale, founded the Black Panther Party in Oakland, California. Unlike other black rights movements in the United States at the time, the BPP was an armed self-defense movement. Police began to target BPP members with random stops and searches. On October 28, 1967, Officer John Frey had a list of BPP cars taped to his dashboard. When Frey saw Newton's VW, he pulled him over. In the ensuing confrontation, Newton was shot in the abdomen and Frey was shot dead. Newton was charged with voluntary manslaughter and sentenced to prison.

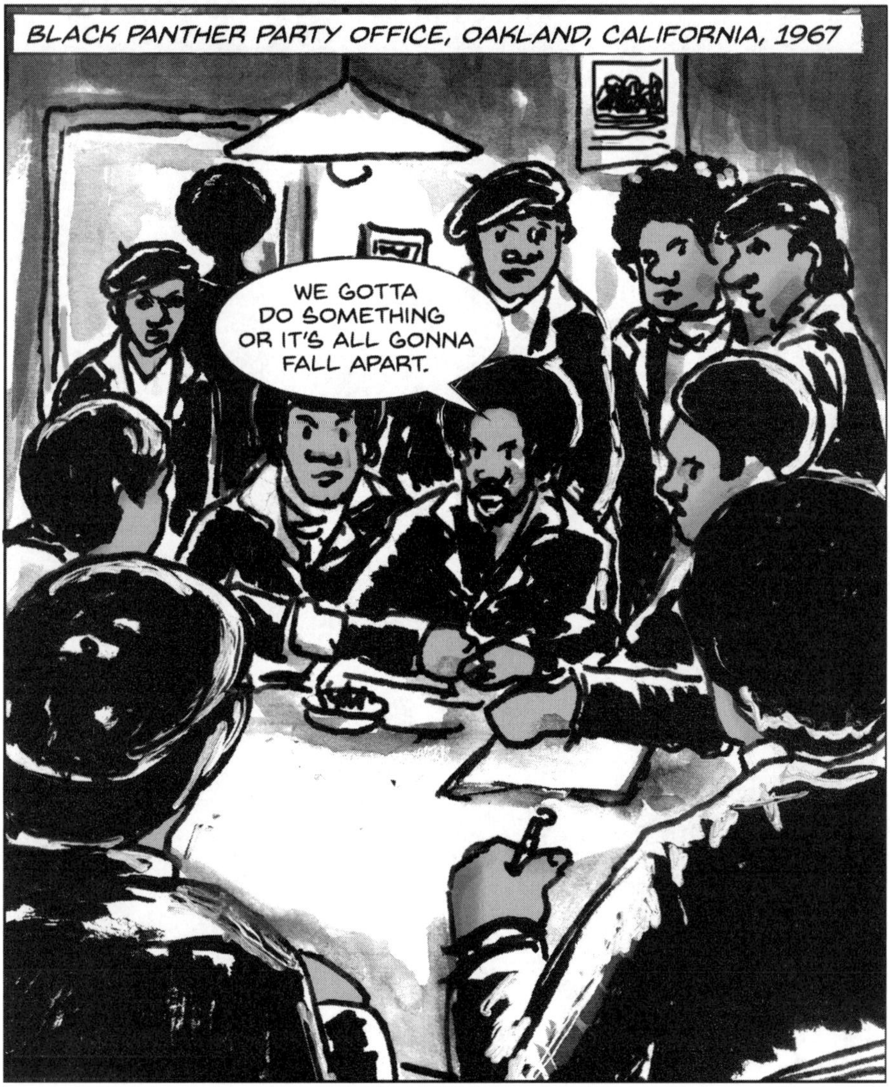
BLACK PANTHER PARTY OFFICE, OAKLAND, CALIFORNIA, 1967
WE GOTTA DO SOMETHING OR IT'S ALL GONNA FALL APART.

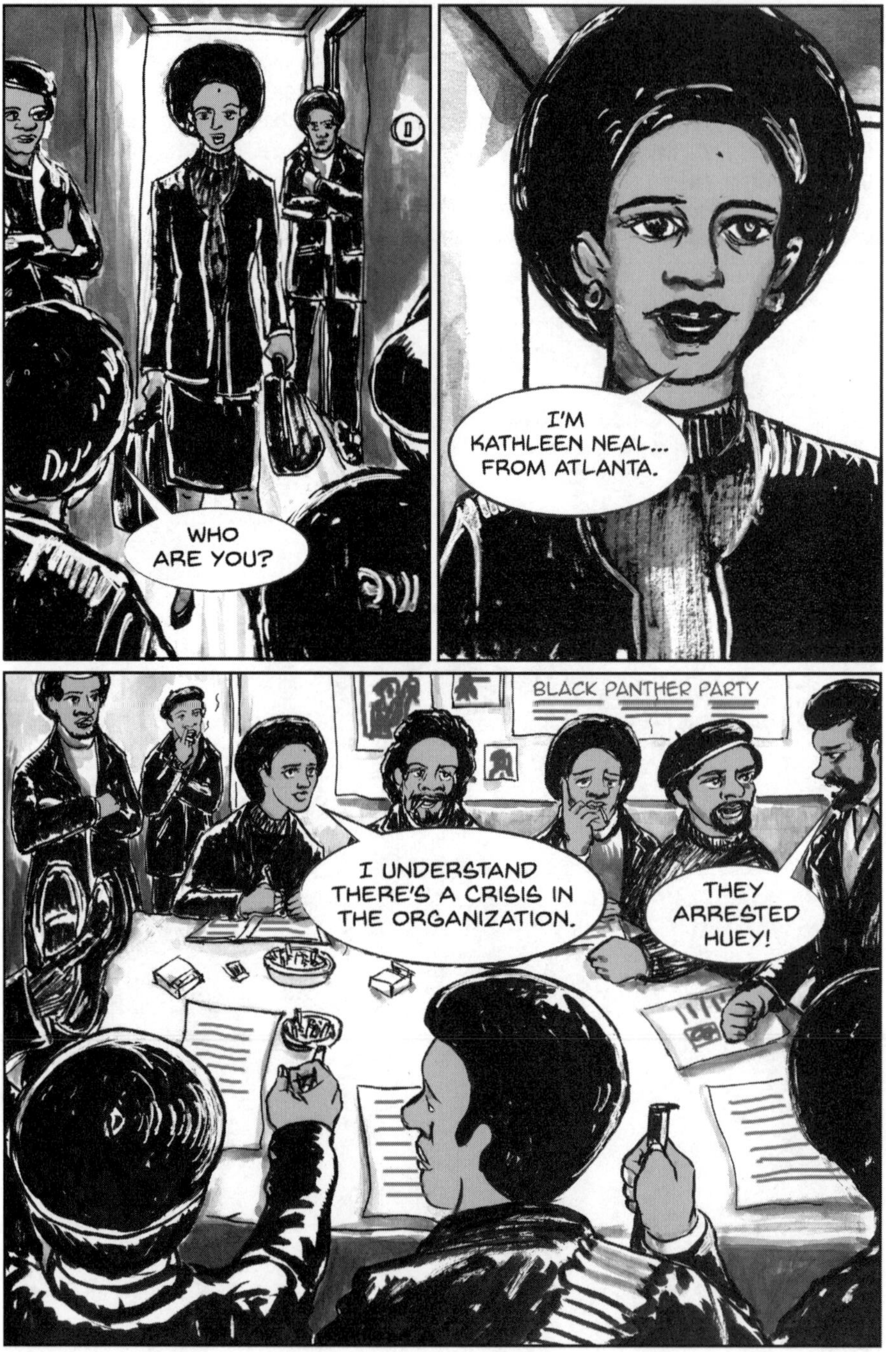
WHO ARE YOU?
I'M KATHLEEN NEAL... FROM ATLANTA.
BLACK PANTHER PARTY
I UNDERSTAND THERE'S A CRISIS IN THE ORGANIZATION.
THEY ARRESTED HUEY!

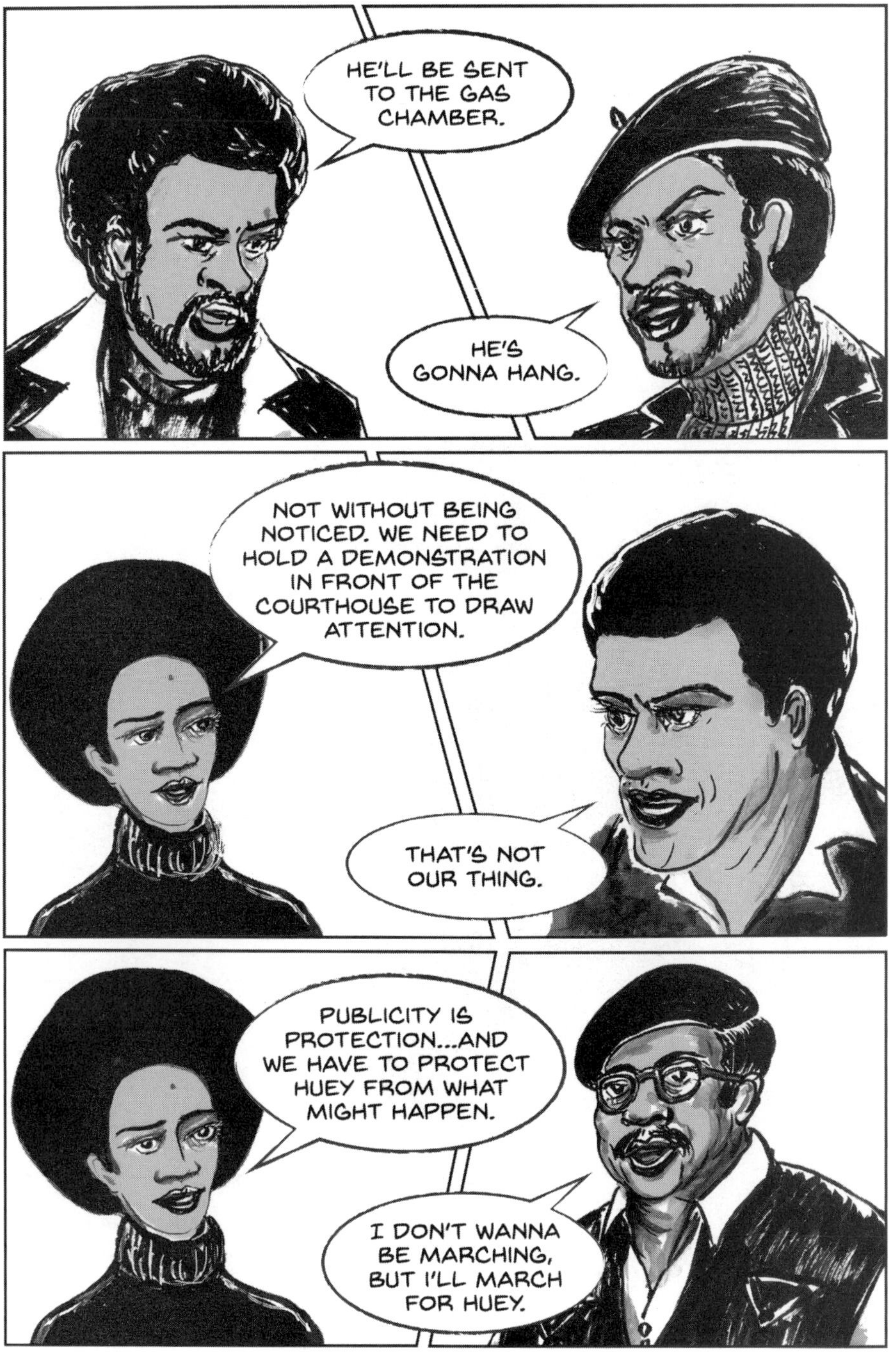
HE'LL BE SENT TO THE GAS CHAMBER.
HE'S GONNA HANG.
NOT WITHOUT BEING NOTICED. WE NEED TO HOLD A DEMONSTRATION IN FRONT OF THE COURTHOUSE TO DRAW ATTENTION.
THAT'S NOT OUR THING.
PUBLICITY IS PROTECTION...AND WE HAVE TO PROTECT HUEY FROM WHAT MIGHT HAPPEN.
I DON'T WANNA BE MARCHING, BUT I'LL MARCH FOR HUEY.

TACK! TACK!

Press Release:
Free Huey Rally, Alameda Court House
August 25, 1967

TACK! TICK! TACK! TACK!

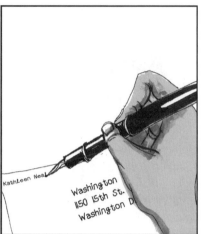

KathLeen Neal

Washington
1150 15th St.
Washington D

KathLeen Neal
Communications Secretary,
Black Panther Party

Washington Post
1150 15th St. NW
Washington D.C. 20005

New York Times,
123 Washington Square,
P.O.Box 2423, New York City,
New York, 236457

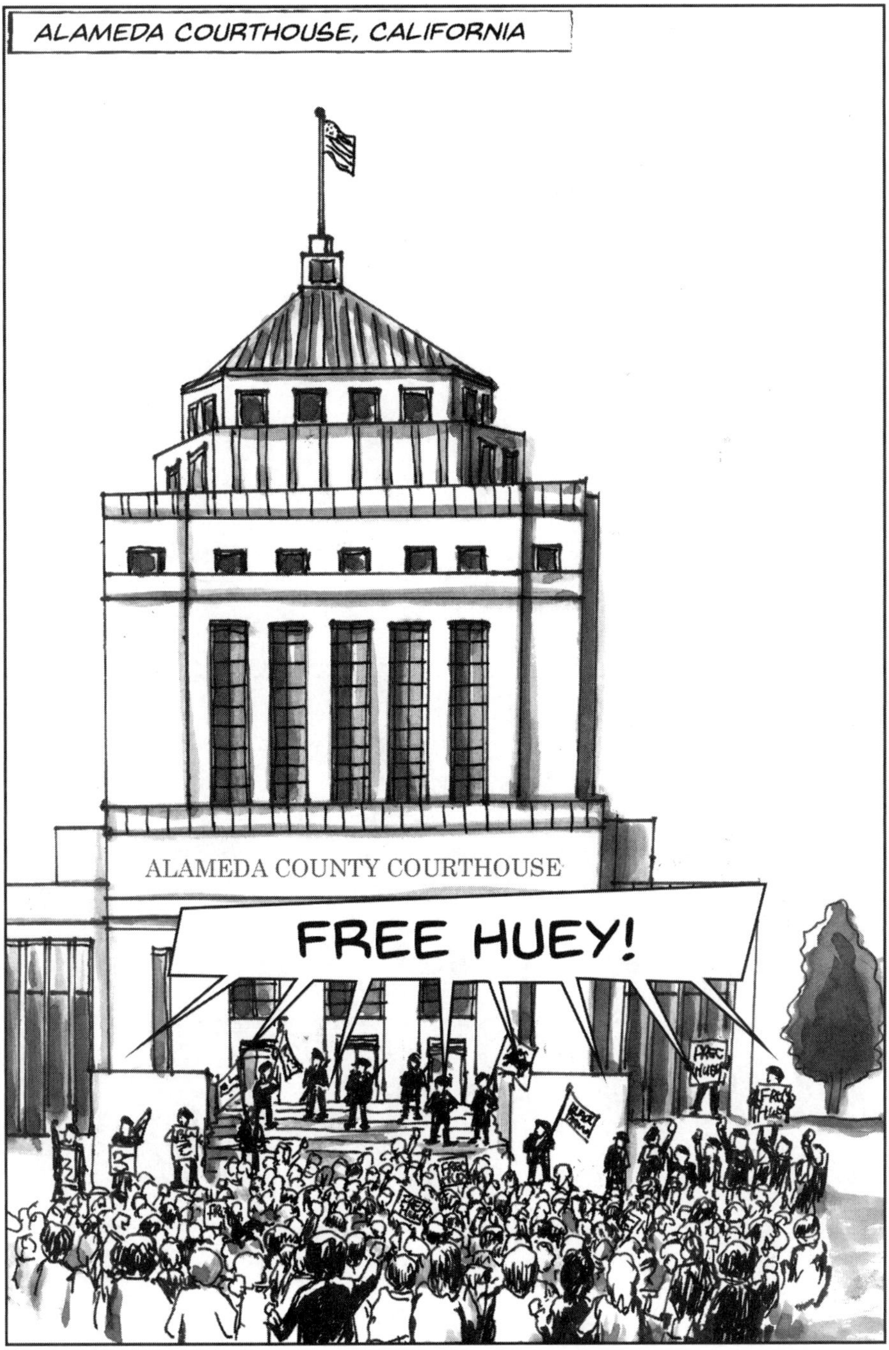
ALAMEDA COURTHOUSE, CALIFORNIA
ALAMEDA COUNTY COURTHOUSE
FREE HUEY!

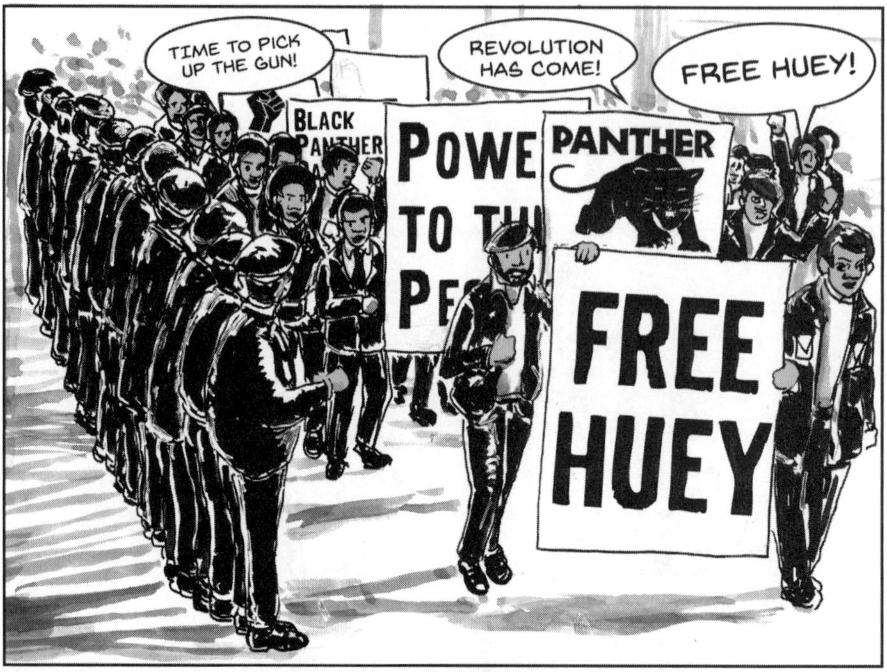
TIME TO PICK UP THE GUN!
REVOLUTION HAS COME!
FREE HUEY!
BLACK
PANTHER
FREE HUEY

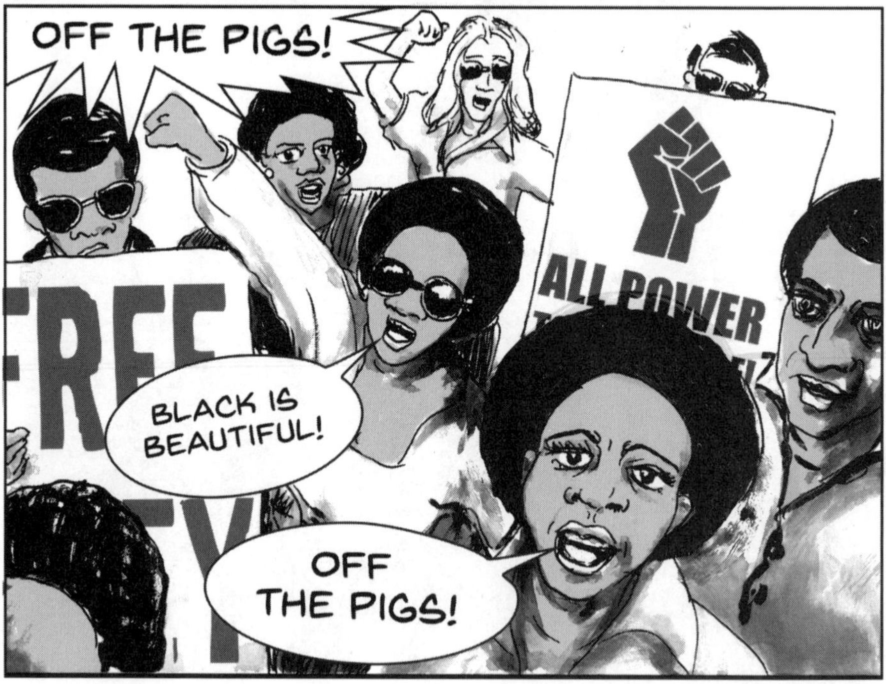
OFF THE PIGS!
ALL POWER
BLACK IS BEAUTIFUL!
OFF THE PIGS!

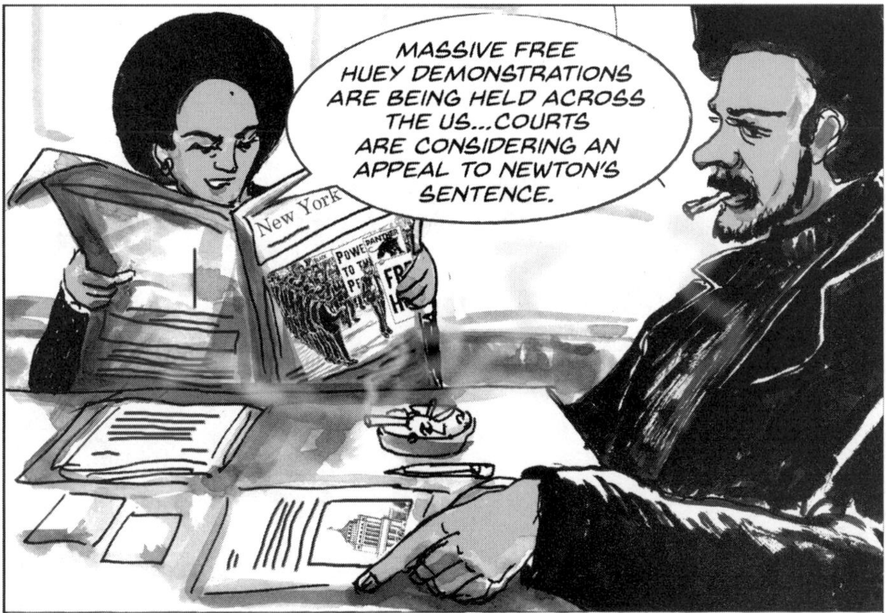
MASSIVE FREE HUEY DEMONSTRATIONS ARE BEING HELD ACROSS THE US...COURTS ARE CONSIDERING AN APPEAL TO NEWTON'S SENTENCE.
New York

Along with being the communications secretary, Kathleen Neal Cleaver (now married to Eldridge Cleaver) was the press coordinator, party spokesperson, and first female member of the Central Committee of the Black Panther Party.

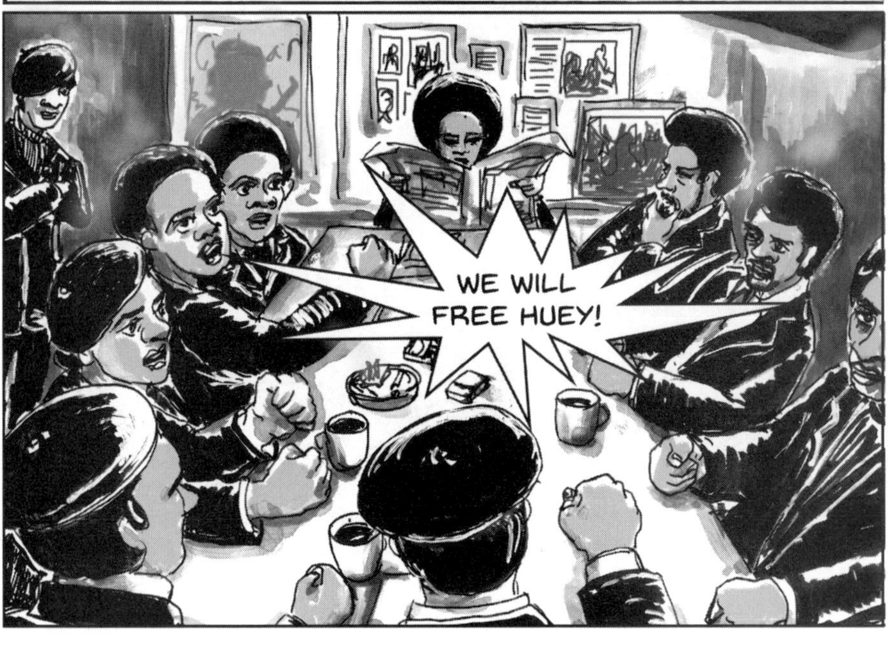
WE WILL FREE HUEY!

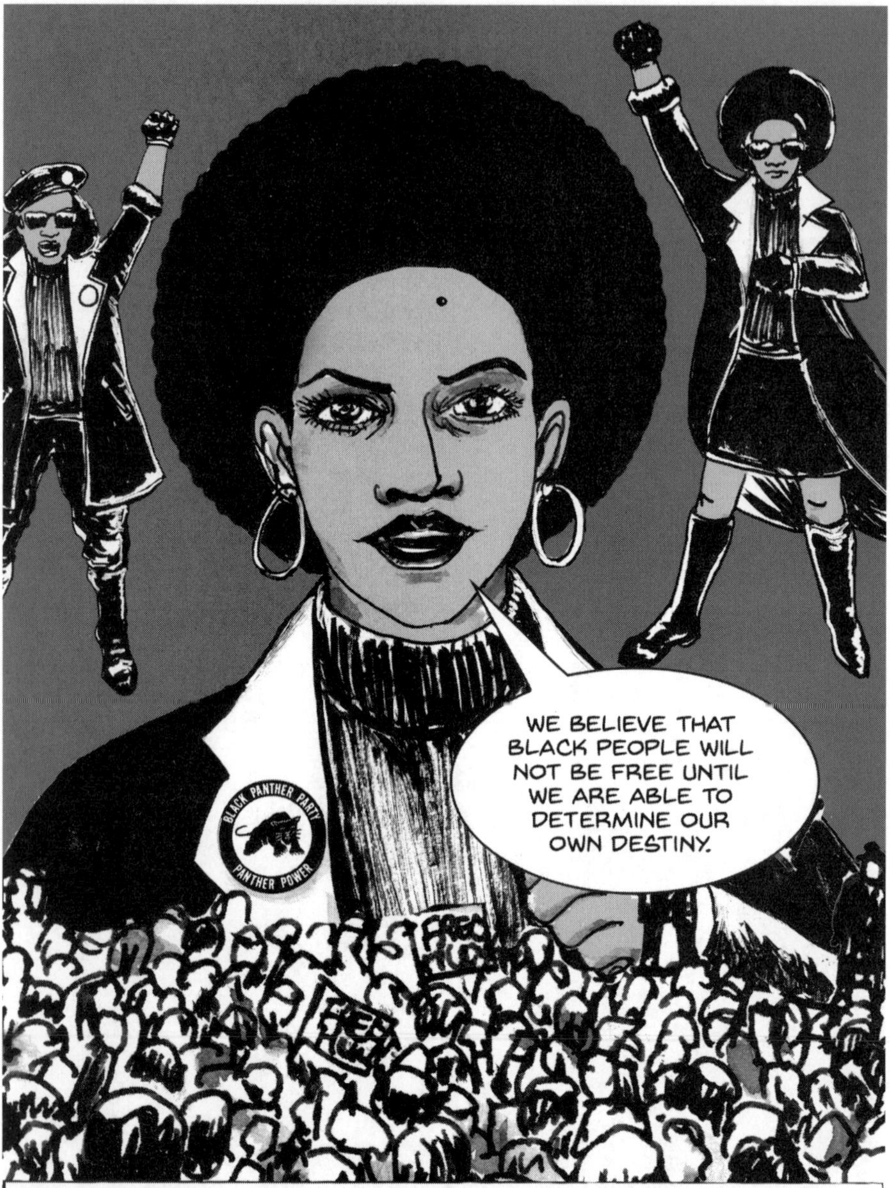
WE BELIEVE THAT BLACK PEOPLE WILL NOT BE FREE UNTIL WE ARE ABLE TO DETERMINE OUR OWN DESTINY.
BLACK PANTHER PARTY PANTHER POWER
Black Panther women were influential and powerful members of the black liberation movement. Other female leaders of the BPP: Assata Shakur, Elaine Brown, Angela Davis, Barbara Easley, Charlotte O'Neal, Tarika Matilaba, Judy Hart, Chaka Khan. The women had roles in communications, education, organizing, and finance.

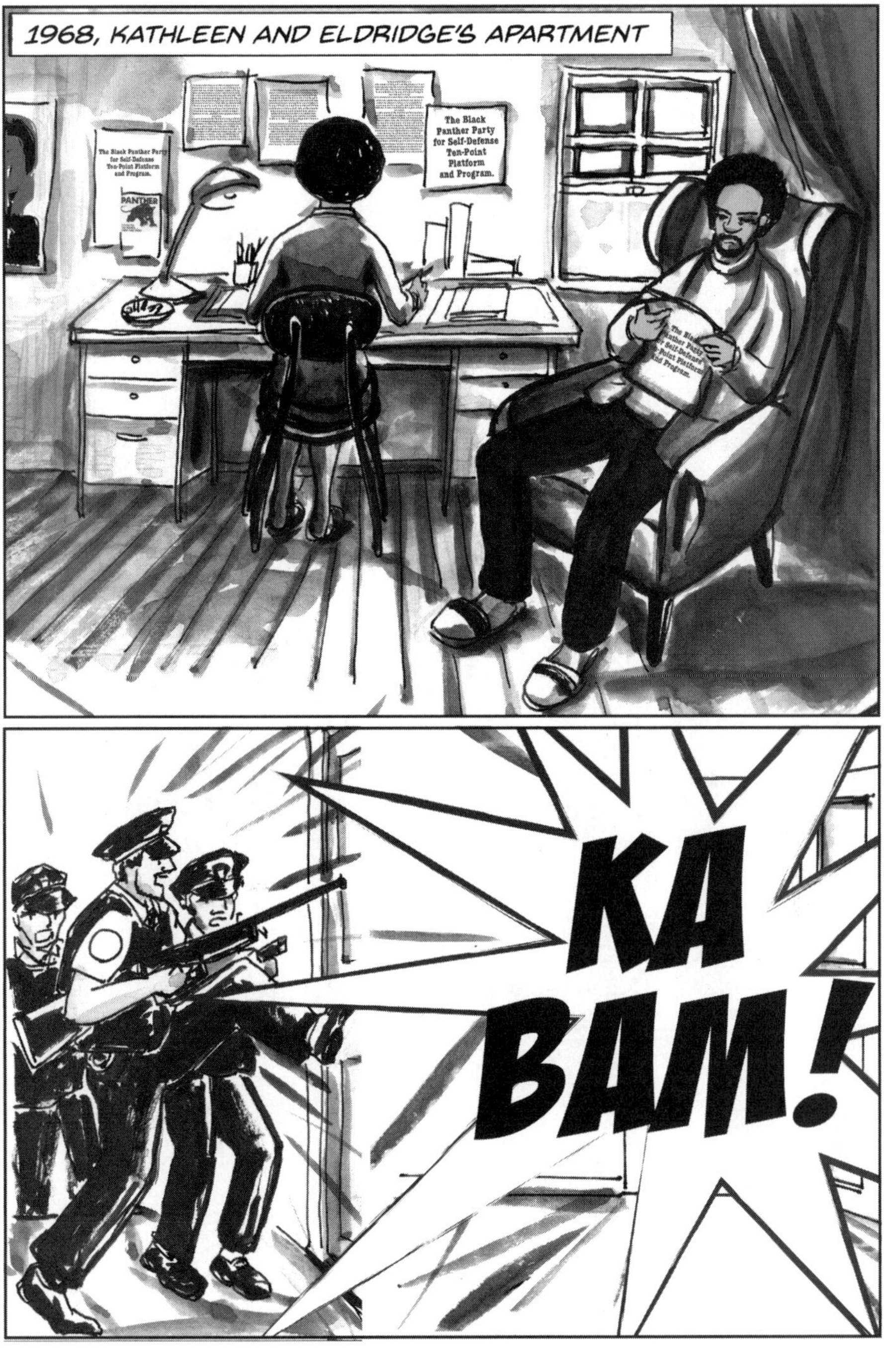
1968, KATHLEEN AND ELDRIDGE'S APARTMENT
The Black Panther Party for Self-Defense Ten-Point Platform and Program.
PANTHER
The Black Panther Party for Self-Defense Ten-Point Platform and Program.
KA BAM!

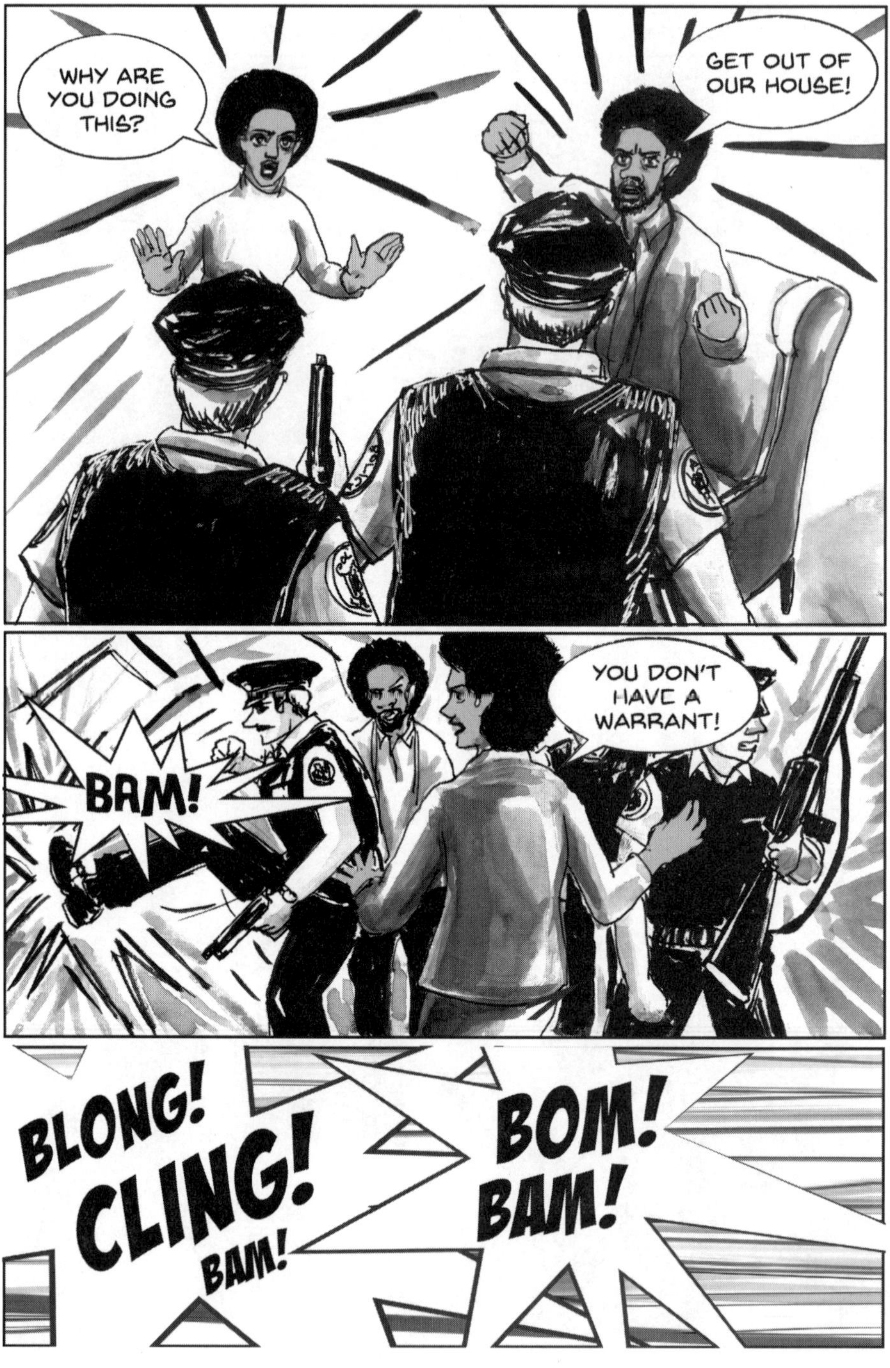
WHY ARE YOU DOING THIS?
GET OUT OF OUR HOUSE!
BAM!
YOU DON'T HAVE A WARRANT!
BLONG!
CLING!
BAM!
BOM!
BAM!

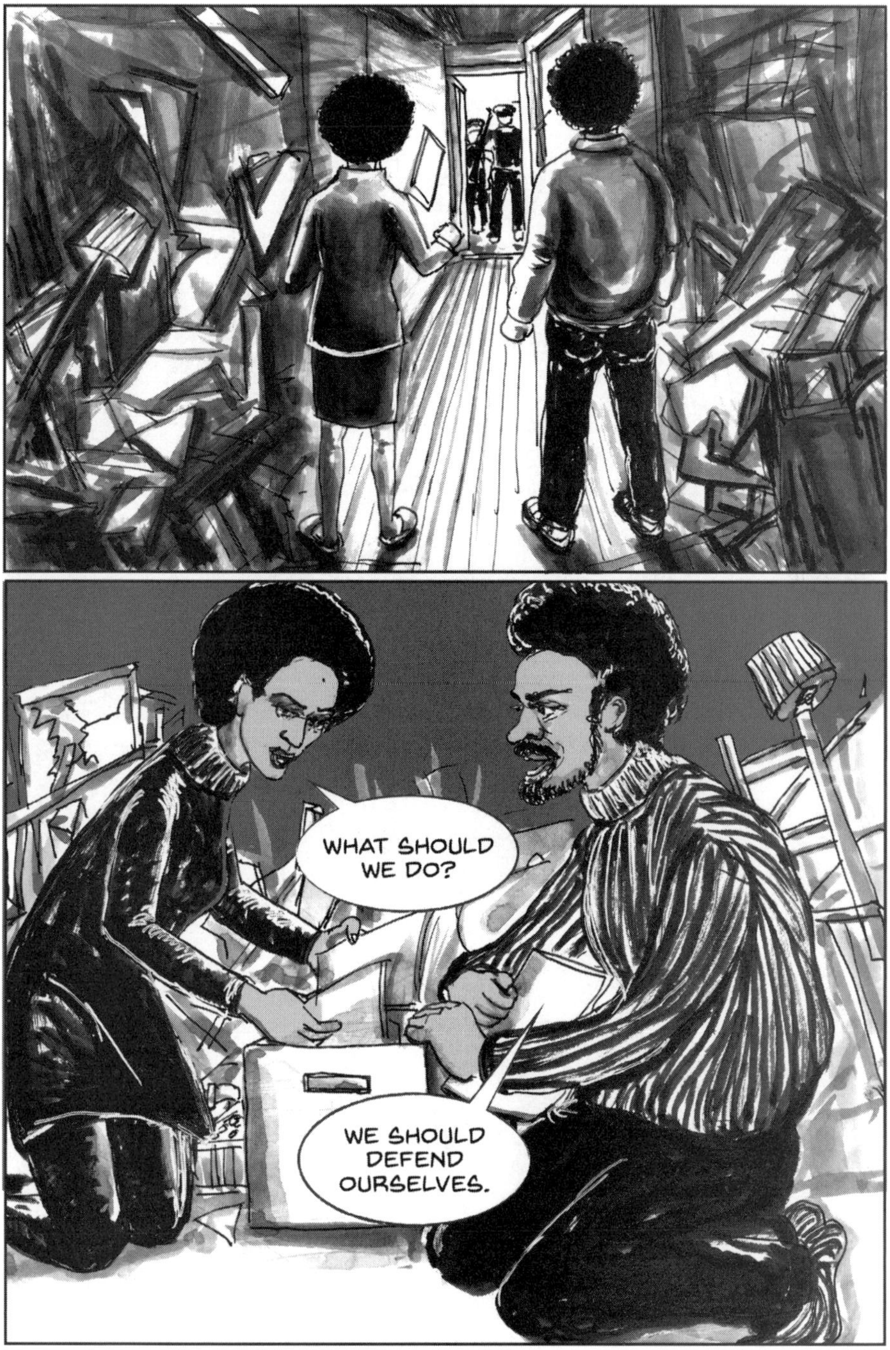
WHAT SHOULD WE DO?
WE SHOULD DEFEND OURSELVES.

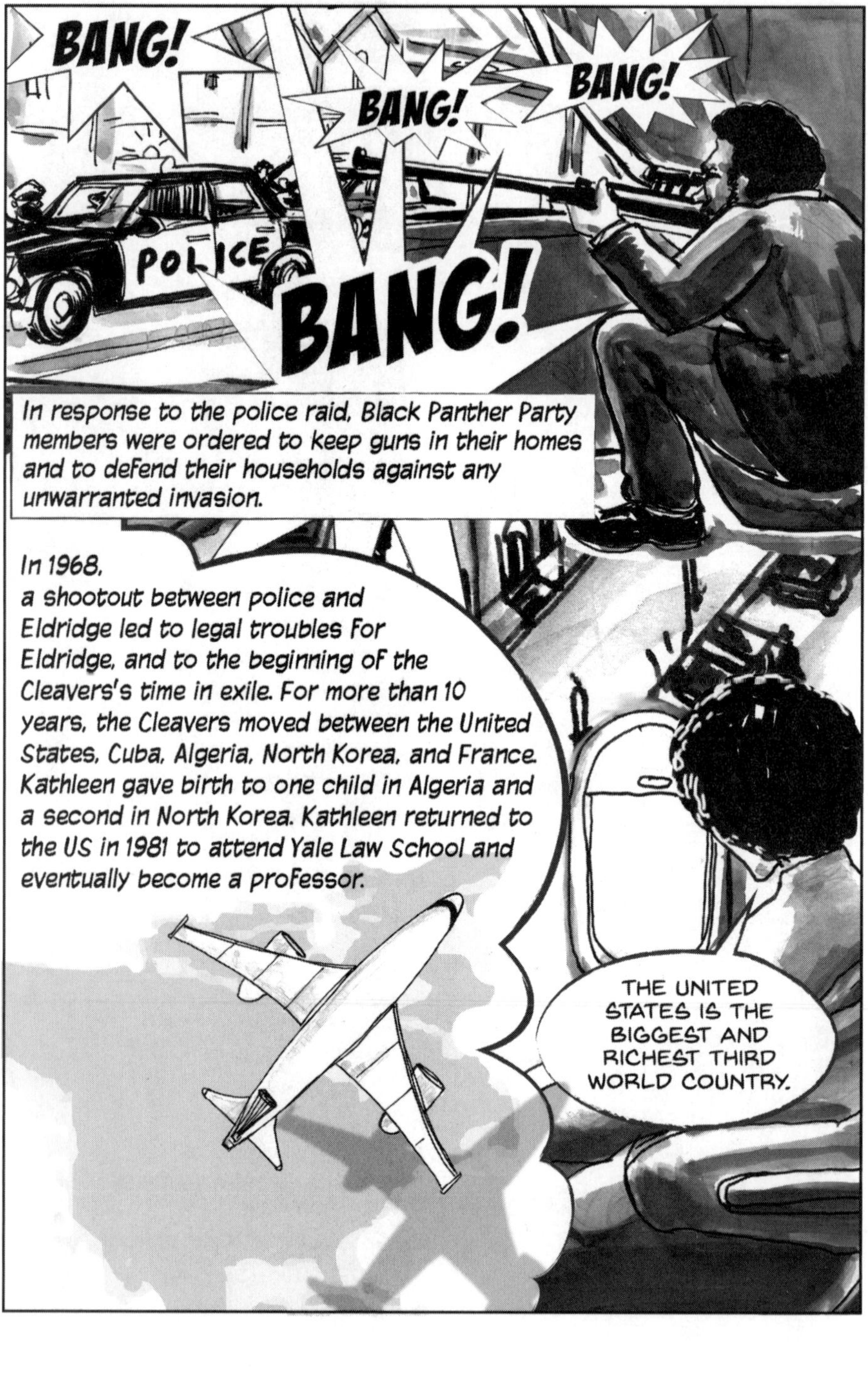
BANG!
BANG!
BANG!
POLICE
BANG!
In response to the police raid, Black Panther Party members were ordered to keep guns in their homes and to defend their households against any unwarranted invasion.
In 1968, a shootout between police and Eldridge led to legal troubles for Eldridge, and to the beginning of the Cleavers's time in exile. For more than 10 years, the Cleavers moved between the United States, Cuba, Algeria, North Korea, and France. Kathleen gave birth to one child in Algeria and a second in North Korea. Kathleen returned to the US in 1981 to attend Yale Law School and eventually become a professor.
THE UNITED STATES IS THE BIGGEST AND RICHEST THIRD WORLD COUNTRY.

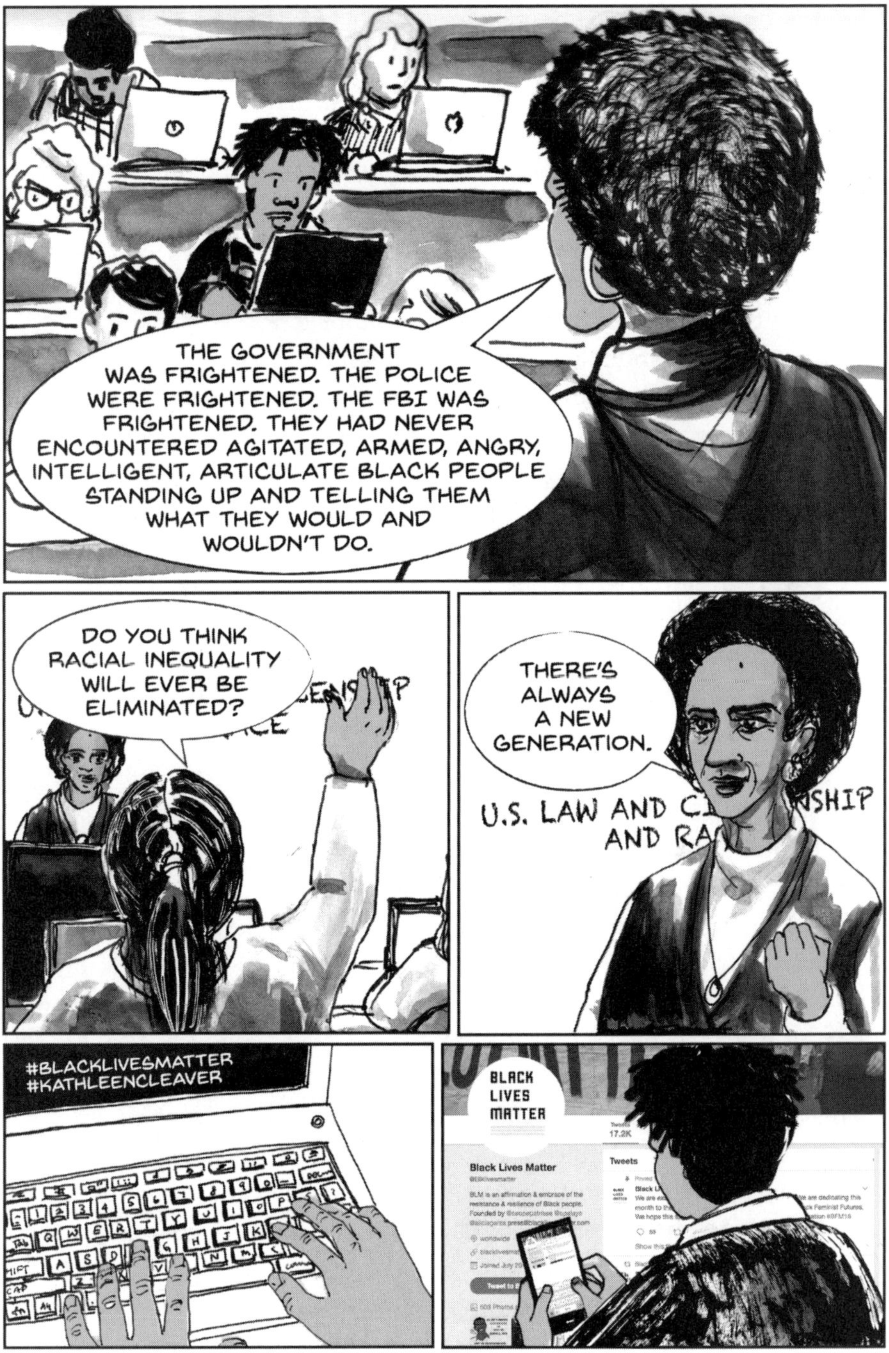
THE GOVERNMENT WAS FRIGHTENED. THE POLICE WERE FRIGHTENED. THE FBI WAS FRIGHTENED. THEY HAD NEVER ENCOUNTERED AGITATED, ARMED, ANGRY, INTELLIGENT, ARTICULATE BLACK PEOPLE STANDING UP AND TELLING THEM WHAT THEY WOULD AND WOULDN'T DO.
DO YOU THINK RACIAL INEQUALITY WILL EVER BE ELIMINATED?
THERE'S ALWAYS A NEW GENERATION.
U.S. LAW AND
#BLACKLIVESMATTER
#KATHLEENCLEAVER
BLACK LIVES MATTER
Black Lives Matter
Tweets
17.2K

Kathleen Cleaver (née Neal) grew up in Tuskegee, Alabama, in a climate of racism and racial segregation. Neal's father was a sociology professor and her mother had a master's degree in mathematics. When Neal was a girl, her family lived for some time in India and the Philippines. In India, Neal was inspired witnessing a nation that had thrown off its white colonists. She was inspired by this resistance, and she saw the fundamental injustice of racialized oppression. Neal returned to the United States, and by 1963, she was a college student involved in the US civil rights movement. In 1966, Neal began working for the Student Nonviolent Coordinating Committee (SNCC) New York office. While at a black student conference in March 1967 in Nashville, Tennessee, Neal met Eldridge Cleaver, an outspoken black activist. By December 1967, Neal had quit the SNCC, moved to San Francisco to join the Black Panther Party (BPP), and married Eldridge Cleaver.

Kathleen Cleaver took up the BPP campaign to free Huey P. Newton. Newton, one of the BPP founders, was in prison under voluntary manslaughter charges, and Cleaver believed Newton was innocent. With her education, intelligence, and organizational skills, Cleaver successfully organized demonstrations, wrote leaflets, held press conferences, attended court hearings, and spoke at rallies. Soon Cleaver sat on the BPP's Central Committee as communications secretary, the first woman to hold a position on the committee.

The original structure of the Black Panther Party was created by and for armed men organized to defend black communities from police violence. Women in the BPP influenced party structure and made it a broader movement that grew to provide free breakfast programs, schools for urban children, and medical services; however, women of the BPP also took part in defense of their communities. But while BPP women worked for liberation and resisted state violence, they often faced sexism within their own organizing communities. Cleaver faced not only racist oppression but also misogyny from people within and outside the civil rights movement. For women of the party, this took the form of verbal and sometimes physical abuse.

As the BPP's influence and membership grew, so did police attention to the activities of party members. In 1968 armed officers raided the Cleaver home without a warrant, violently ransacking the apartment and ultimately finding nothing suspicious. In response, Huey P. Newton ordered all Black Panther members to keep guns in their homes and to defend their households against invasion. This order was illustrated by a photo of an unsmiling Kathleen Cleaver in a leather trench coat, holding a rifle at the door of her apartment, with the caption "Shoot your Shot!"

Soon after, a shootout between police and Eldridge led to legal troubles for Eldridge, and to the beginning of the Cleavers' time in exile. For more than ten years, they moved between the United States, Cuba, Algeria, North Korea, and France. Kathleen gave birth to one child in Algeria and a second in North Korea. In the early 1970s, the Black Panther Party disbanded. In 1981, Kathleen Cleaver returned to the United States permanently and resumed her university studies, eventually studying law at Yale University. Kathleen Cleaver is now an accomplished lawyer and an Ivy League law professor.

Discussion Questions

1 What different kinds of organizing work and action did Kathleen Cleaver take part in or contribute to?
2 What experiences did Kathleen Cleaver have that prepared her for her work with the Black Panther Party?
3 Why did the Black Panther Party encourage party members to keep weapons in their homes?

Research Questions and Activities

1 Feminist writers asha bandele and Patrisse Khan-Cullors write about the ongoing state violence against black men and women in the United States, and from their anti-racist organizing came the #BlackLivesMatter movement. Compare and analyze the rates of

police violence, police killing, and incarceration of black men and women in the United States in the 1960s and 1970s, when the BPP was active, and in the 2010s.

2 Research the term *afrofuturism*. Watch the 2018 film *Black Panther* and compare the roles of women and men in Wakanda to the roles of men and women in the BPP.

3 Read the 1977 Combahee River Collective Statement, written by a black feminist collective. The four-point statement calls for the inclusion of black feminism in black rights organizing and in feminist organizing. Compare the feminist politics of the Combahee River Collective to the politics of the #BlackLivesMatter movement.

Further Reading and Viewing

The Black Panthers: Vanguard of the Revolution. Dir. Stanley Nelson Jr. Firelight Films, 2016.

Cleaver, Kathleen, and Julia Herve. "Black Scholar Interviews: Kathleen Cleaver." *The Black Scholar* 4 (1971): 54–59.

Khan-Cullors, Patrisse, and asha bandele. *When They Call You a Terrorist.* New York: St. Martin's Press, 2017.

Taylor, Keeanga-Yamahtta, ed. *How We Get Free. Black Feminism and the Combahee River Collective.* Chicago: Haymarket Books, 2017.

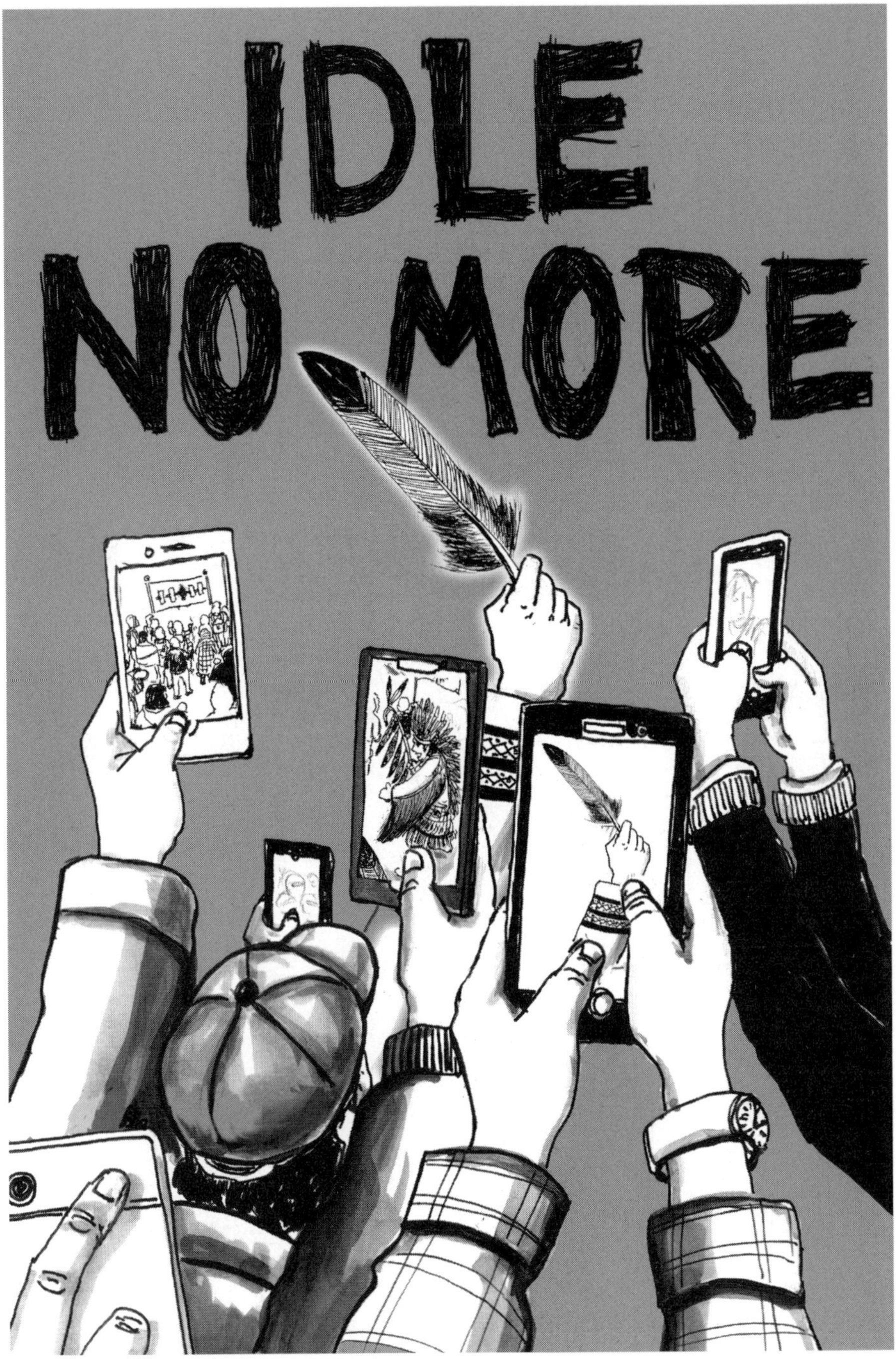
IDLE
NO MORE

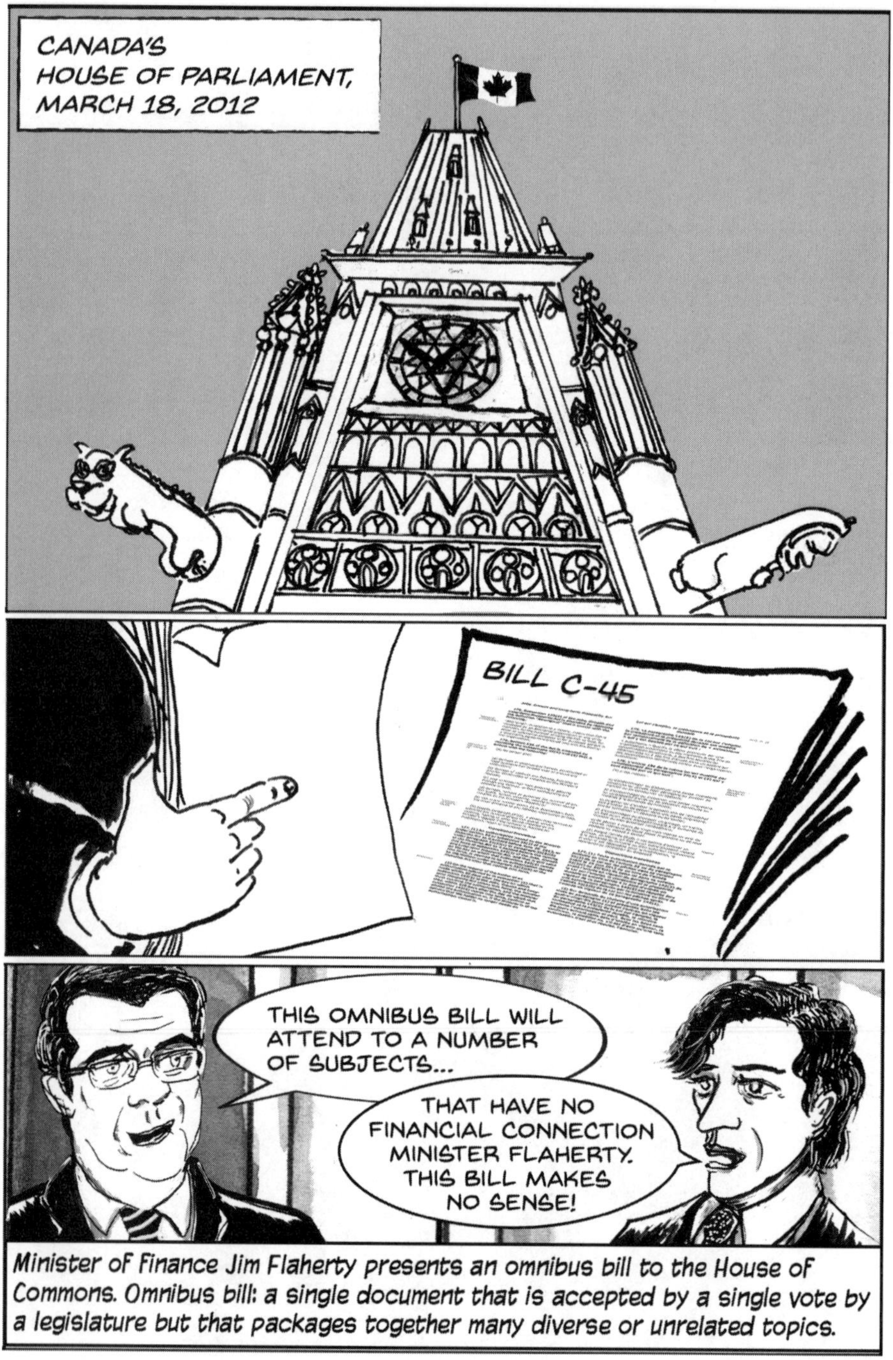
CANADA'S HOUSE OF PARLIAMENT, MARCH 18, 2012
BILL C-45
THIS OMNIBUS BILL WILL ATTEND TO A NUMBER OF SUBJECTS...
THAT HAVE NO FINANCIAL CONNECTION MINISTER FLAHERTY. THIS BILL MAKES NO SENSE!
Minister of Finance Jim Flaherty presents an omnibus bill to the House of Commons. Omnibus bill: a single document that is accepted by a single vote by a legislature but that packages together many diverse or unrelated topics.

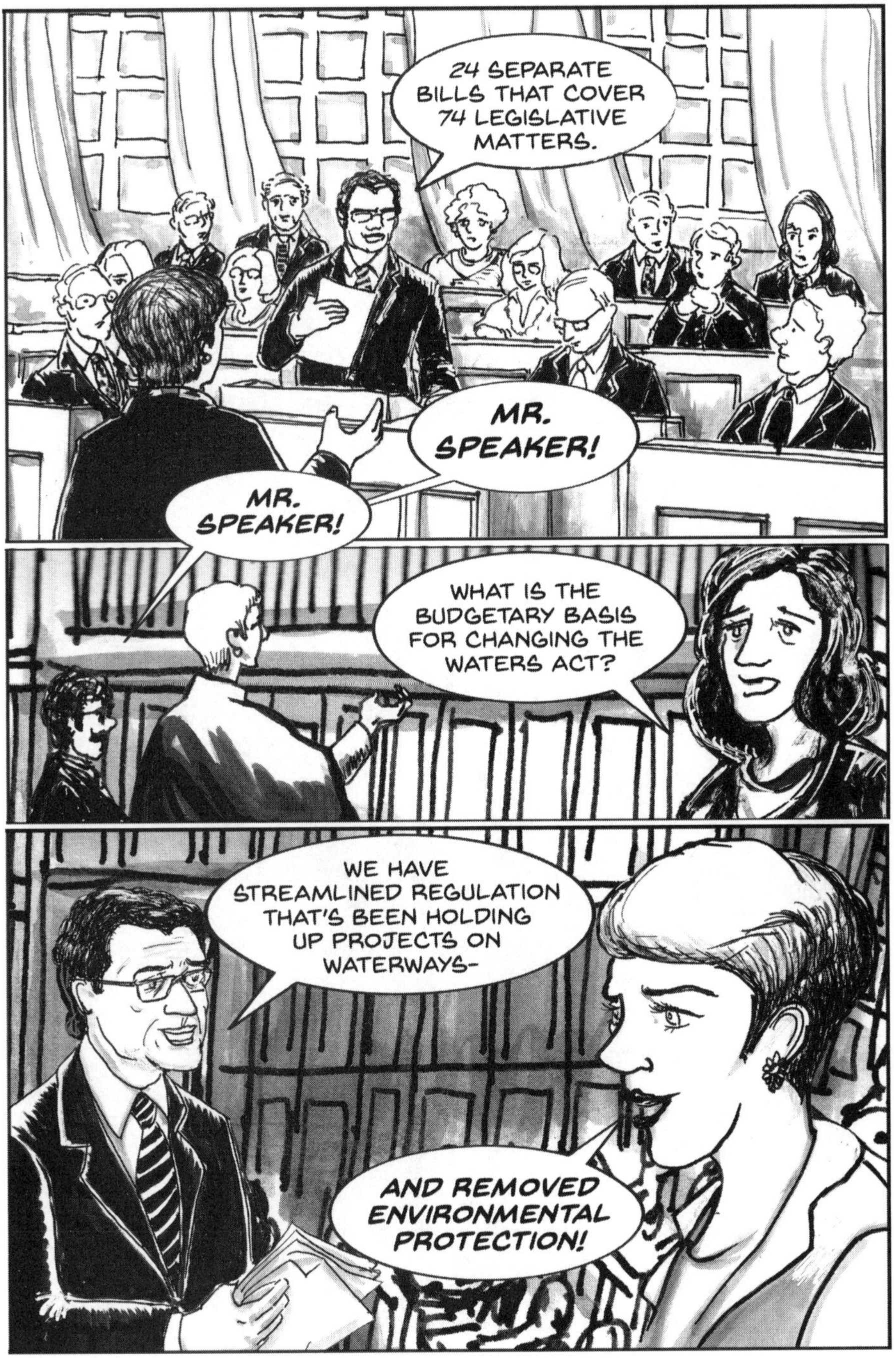
24 SEPARATE BILLS THAT COVER 74 LEGISLATIVE MATTERS.
MR. SPEAKER!
MR. SPEAKER!
WHAT IS THE BUDGETARY BASIS FOR CHANGING THE WATERS ACT?
WE HAVE STREAMLINED REGULATION THAT'S BEEN HOLDING UP PROJECTS ON WATERWAYS-
AND REMOVED ENVIRONMENTAL PROTECTION!

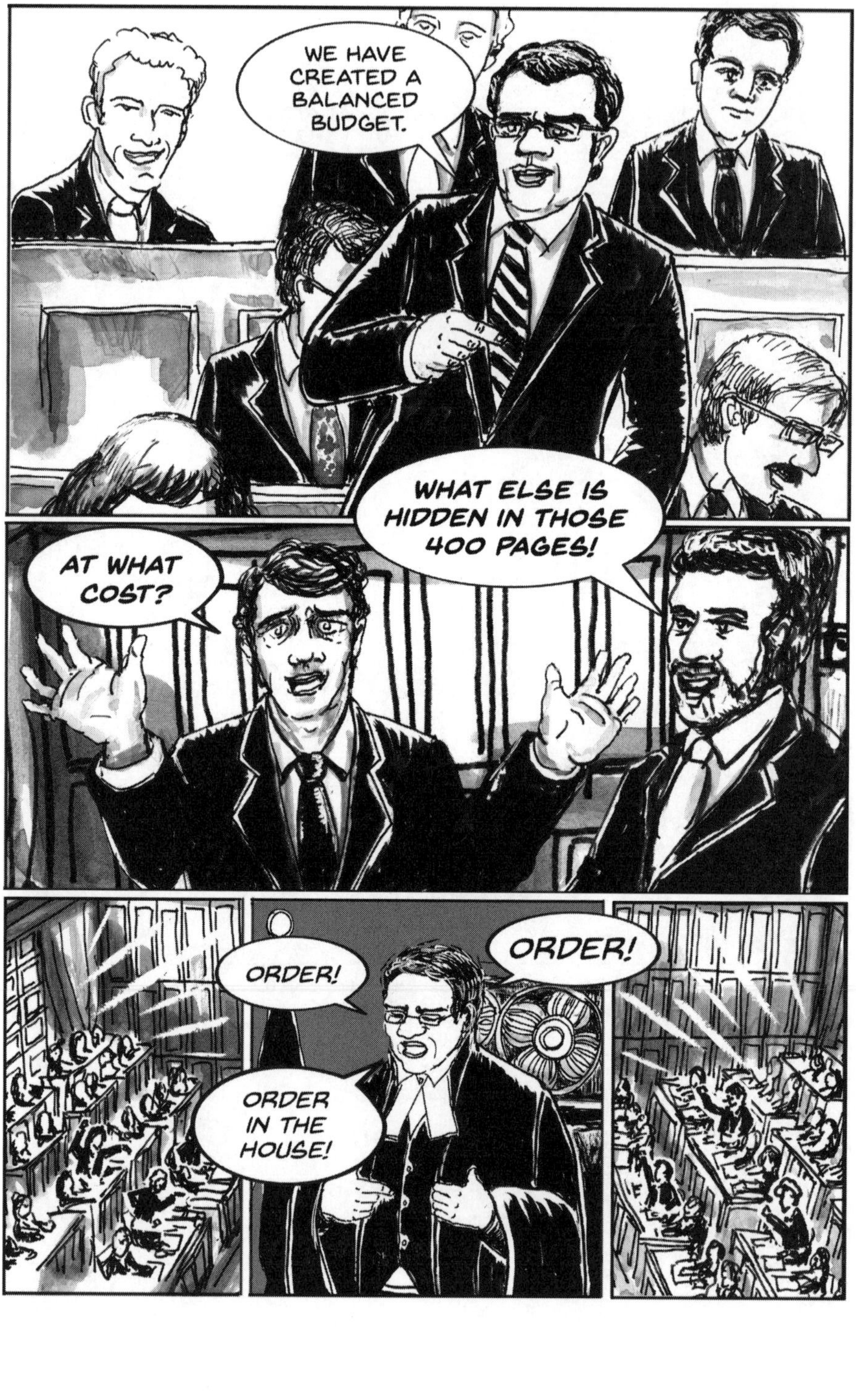
WE HAVE CREATED A BALANCED BUDGET.
AT WHAT COST?
WHAT ELSE IS HIDDEN IN THOSE 400 PAGES!
ORDER!
ORDER!
ORDER IN THE HOUSE!

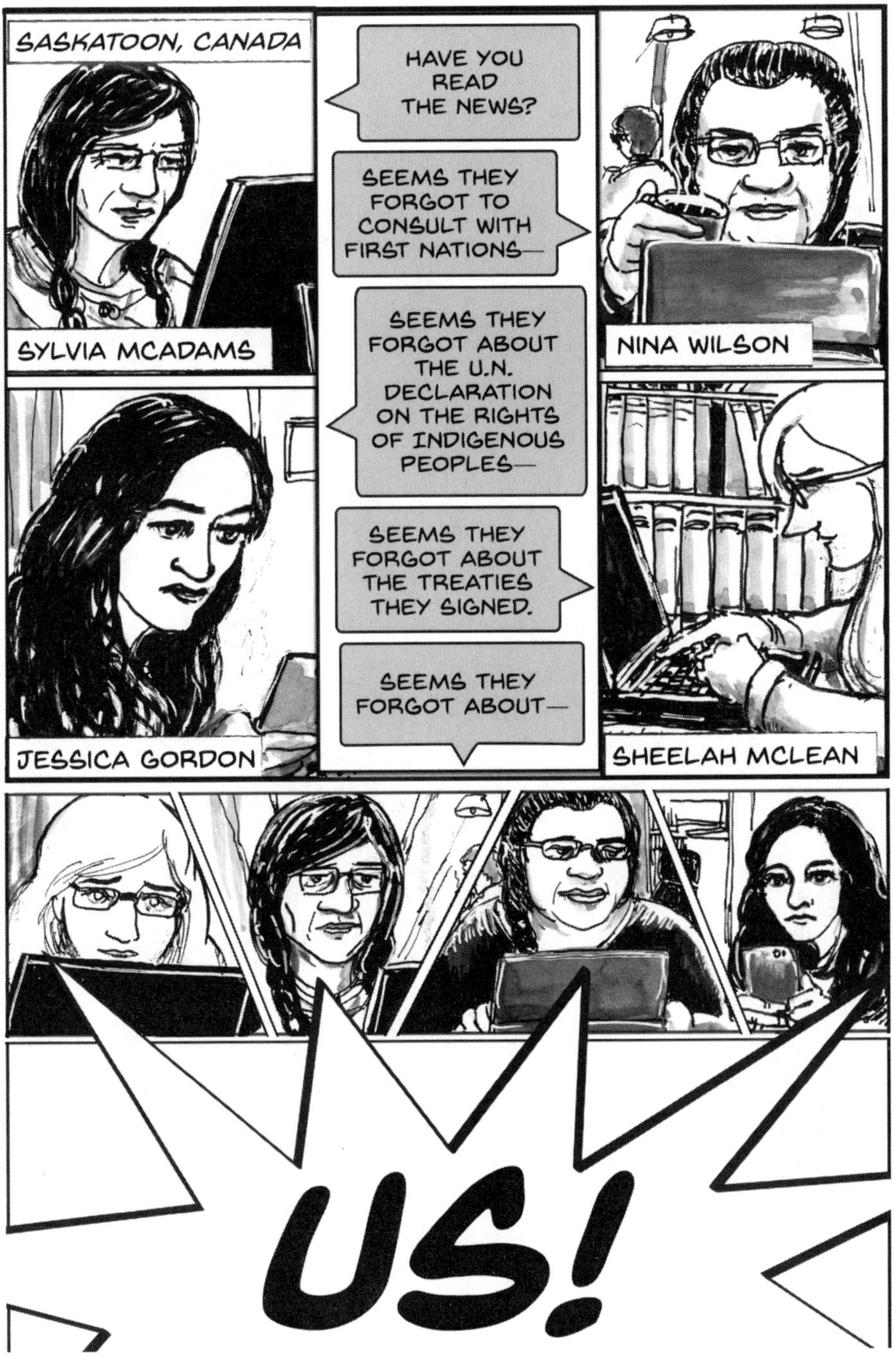
SASKATOON, CANADA
HAVE YOU READ THE NEWS?
SEEMS THEY FORGOT TO CONSULT WITH FIRST NATIONS—
SYLVIA MCADAMS
NINA WILSON
SEEMS THEY FORGOT ABOUT THE U.N. DECLARATION ON THE RIGHTS OF INDIGENOUS PEOPLES—
SEEMS THEY FORGOT ABOUT THE TREATIES THEY SIGNED.
SEEMS THEY FORGOT ABOUT—
JESSICA GORDON
SHEELAH MCLEAN
US!

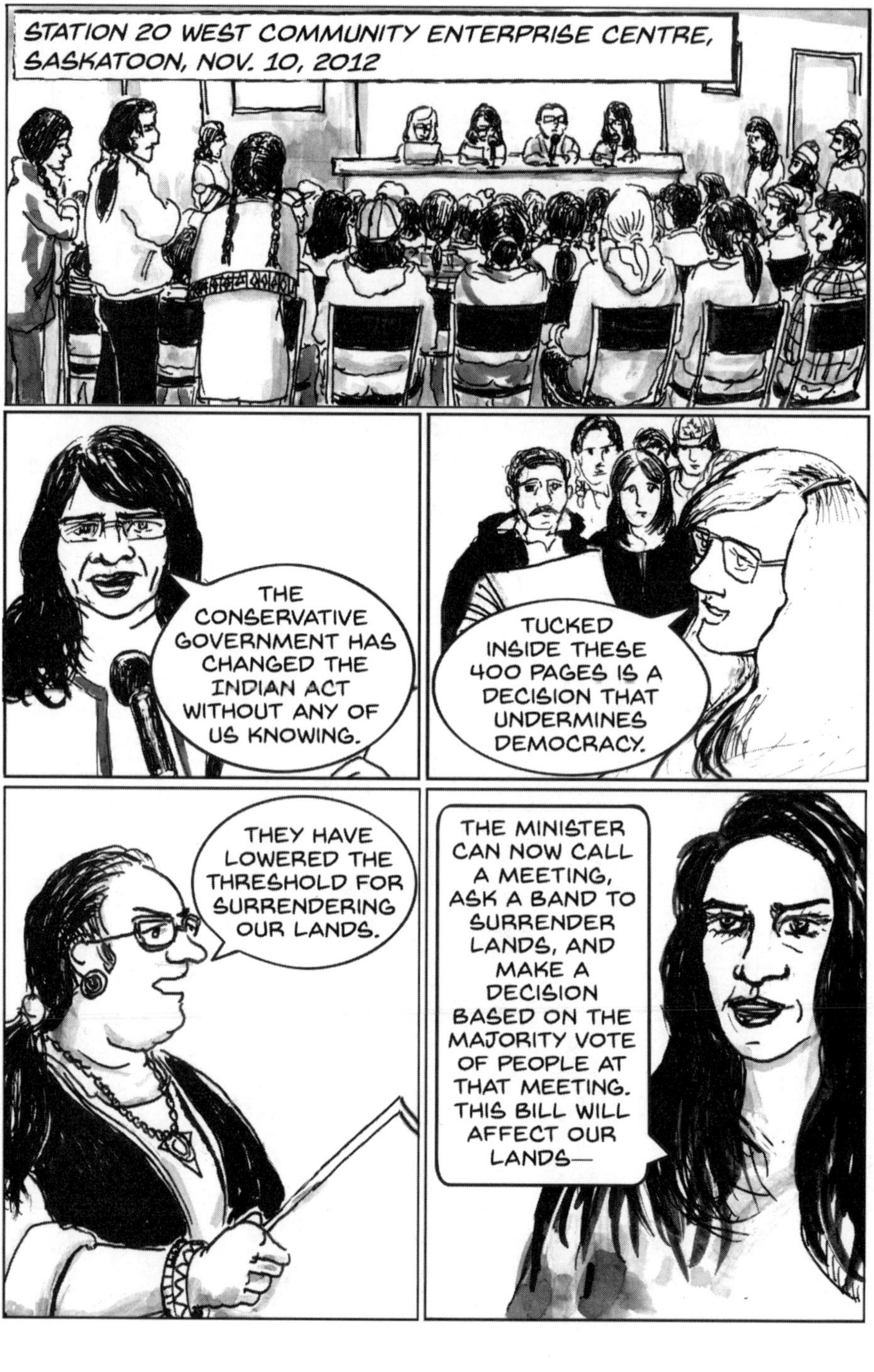
STATION 20 WEST COMMUNITY ENTERPRISE CENTRE, SASKATOON, NOV. 10, 2012
THE CONSERVATIVE GOVERNMENT HAS CHANGED THE INDIAN ACT WITHOUT ANY OF US KNOWING.
TUCKED INSIDE THESE 400 PAGES IS A DECISION THAT UNDERMINES DEMOCRACY.
THEY HAVE LOWERED THE THRESHOLD FOR SURRENDERING OUR LANDS.
THE MINISTER CAN NOW CALL A MEETING, ASK A BAND TO SURRENDER LANDS, AND MAKE A DECISION BASED ON THE MAJORITY VOTE OF PEOPLE AT THAT MEETING. THIS BILL WILL AFFECT OUR LANDS—

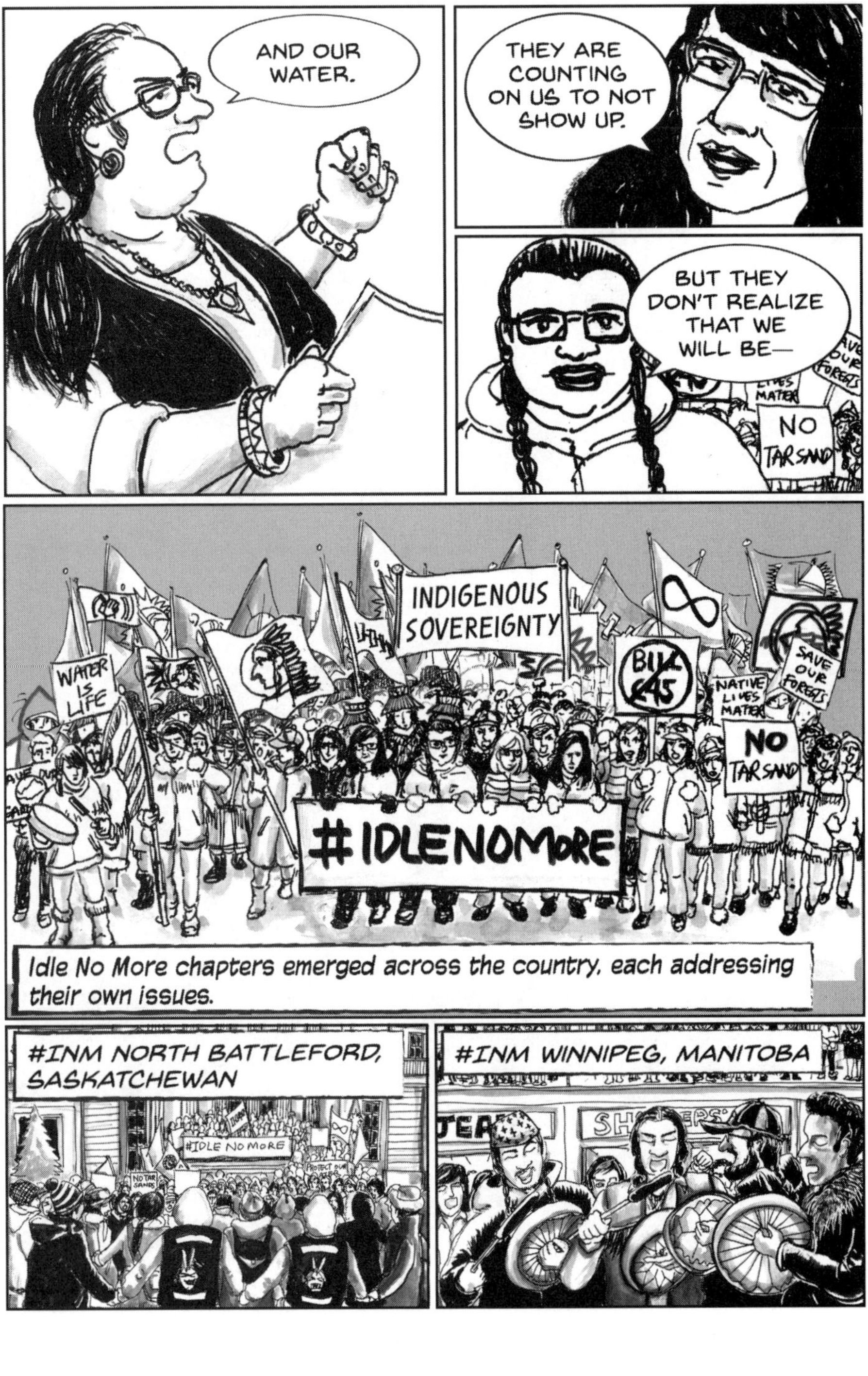
AND OUR WATER.
THEY ARE COUNTING ON US TO NOT SHOW UP.
BUT THEY DON'T REALIZE THAT WE WILL BE—
NO TARSAND
INDIGENOUS SOVEREIGNTY
WATER IS LIFE
NATIVE LIVES MATTER
SAVE OUR FORESTS
NO TARSAND
#IDLENOMORE
Idle No More chapters emerged across the country, each addressing their own issues.
#INM NORTH BATTLEFORD, SASKATCHEWAN
#IDLE NO MORE
#INM WINNIPEG, MANITOBA

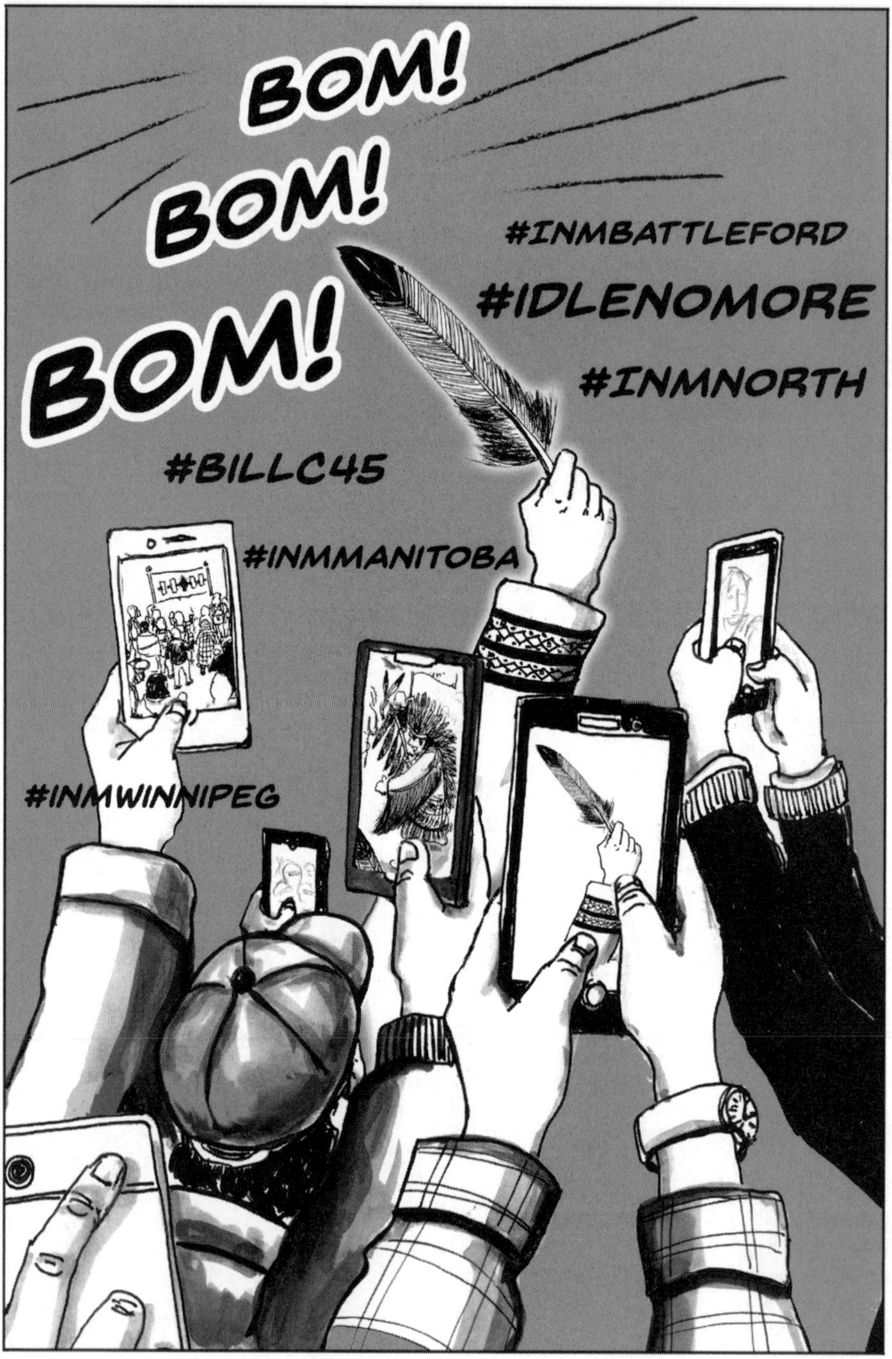
BOM!
BOM!
BOM!
#INMBATTLEFORD
#IDLENOMORE
#INMNORTH
#BILLC45
#INMMANITOBA
#INMWINNIPEG

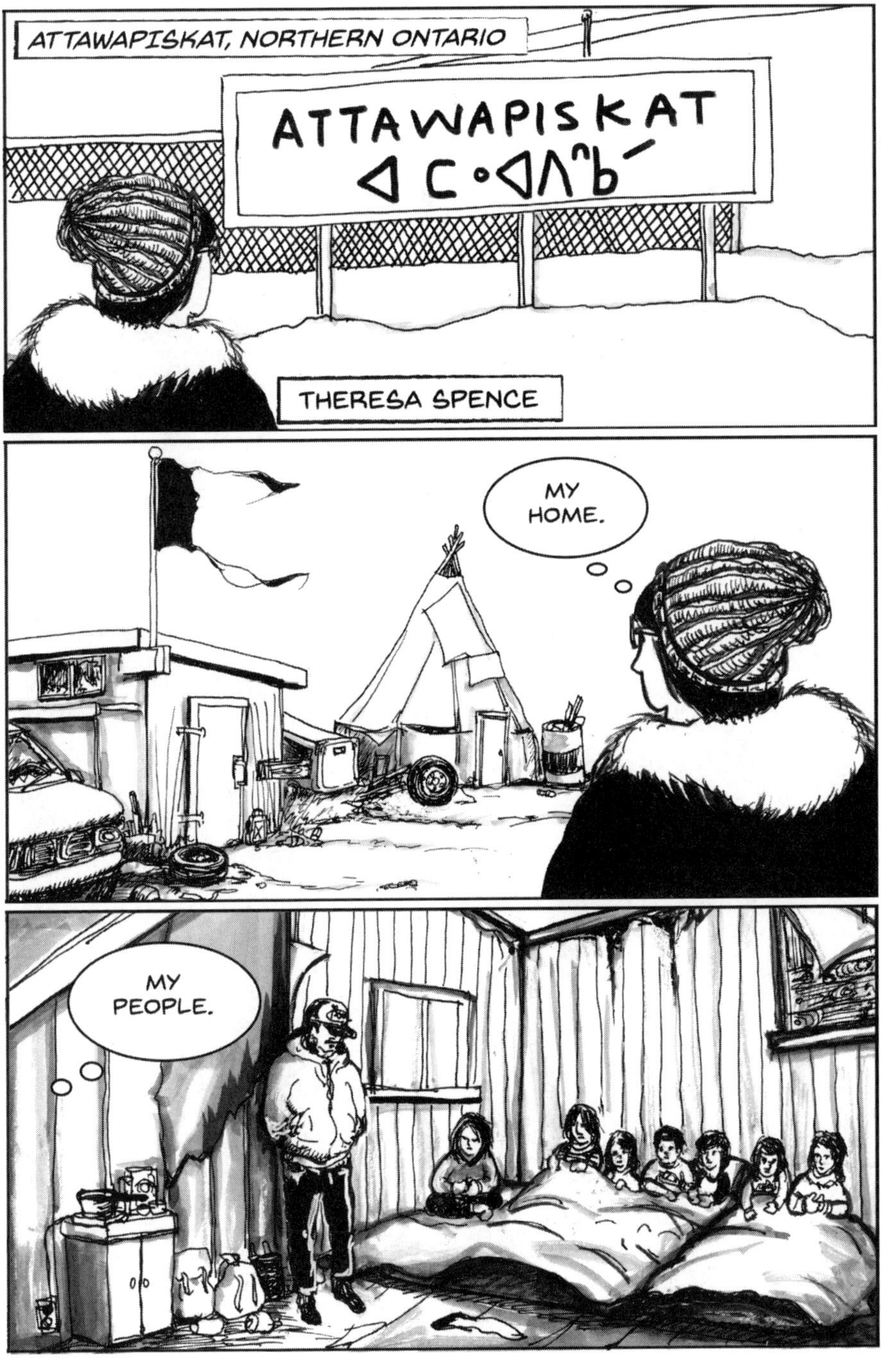
ATTAWAPISKAT, NORTHERN ONTARIO
ATTAWAPISKAT
THERESA SPENCE
MY HOME.
MY PEOPLE.

OUR CRISIS.
DING! DING!
#INMATTAWAPISKAT
In the settler state of Canada, Indigenous
women are still fighting for equal rights

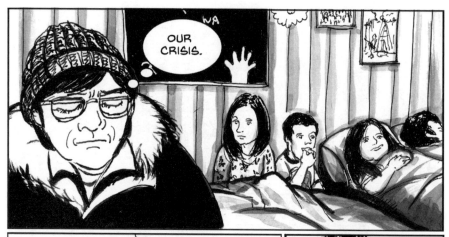

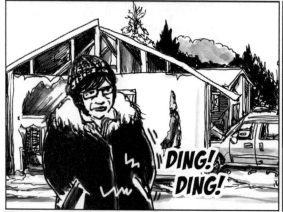

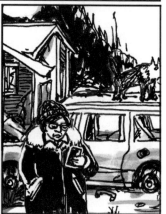

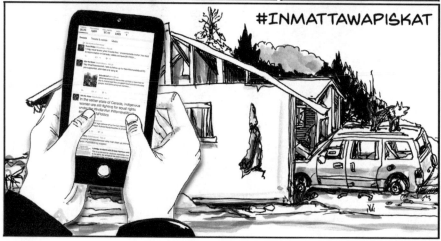

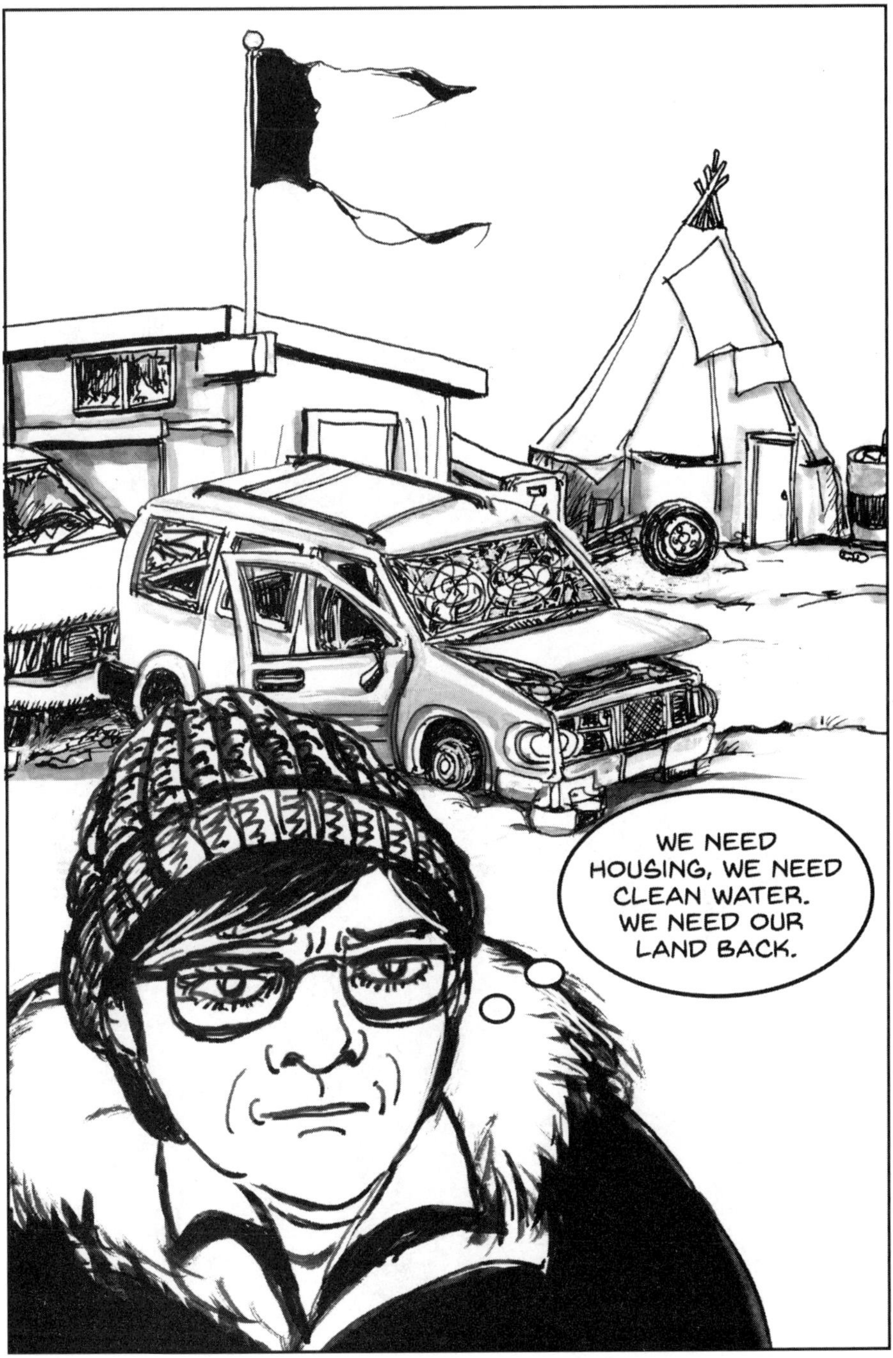
WE NEED HOUSING, WE NEED CLEAN WATER. WE NEED OUR LAND BACK.

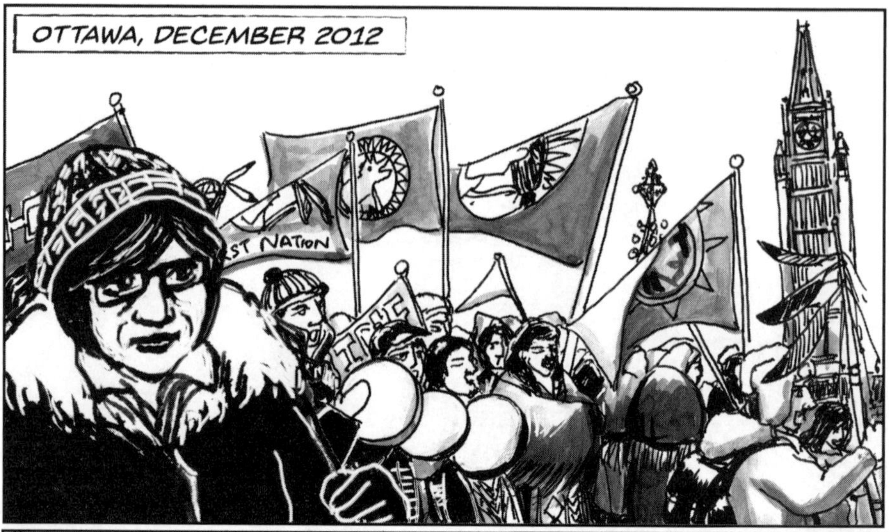
OTTAWA, DECEMBER 2012

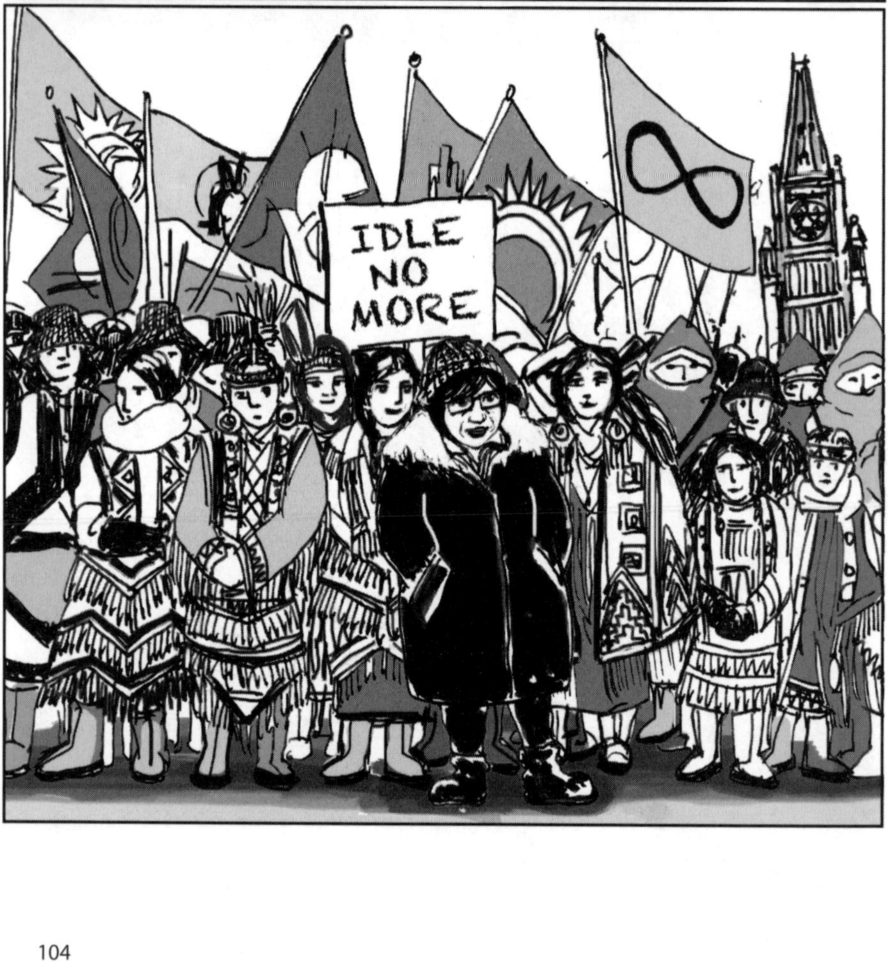
IDLE NO MORE

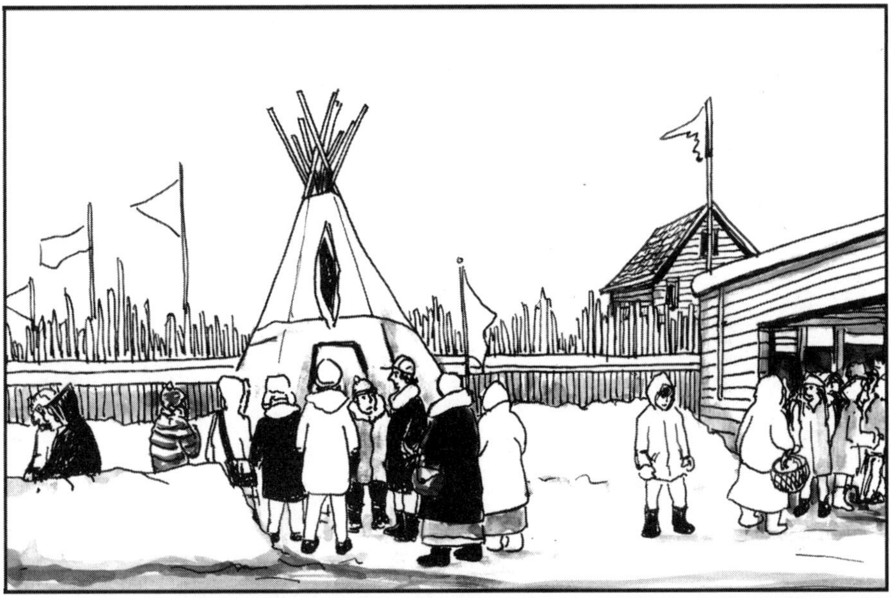

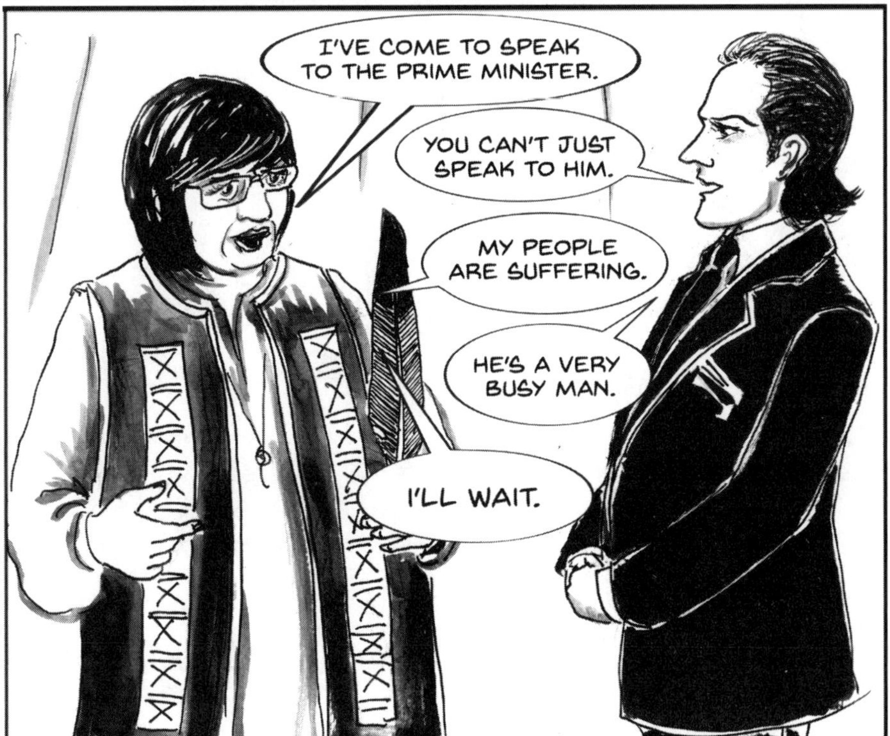

I'VE COME TO SPEAK TO THE PRIME MINISTER.
YOU CAN'T JUST SPEAK TO HIM.
MY PEOPLE ARE SUFFERING.
HE'S A VERY BUSY MAN.
I'LL WAIT.

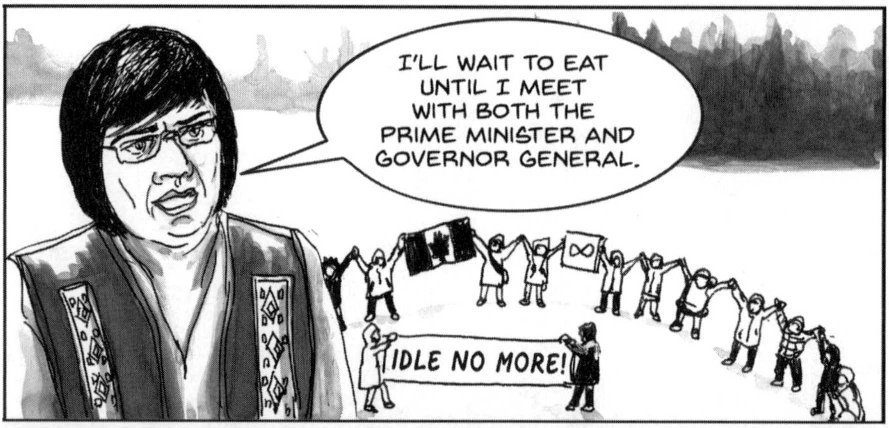
I'LL WAIT TO EAT UNTIL I MEET WITH BOTH THE PRIME MINISTER AND GOVERNOR GENERAL.
IDLE NO MORE!

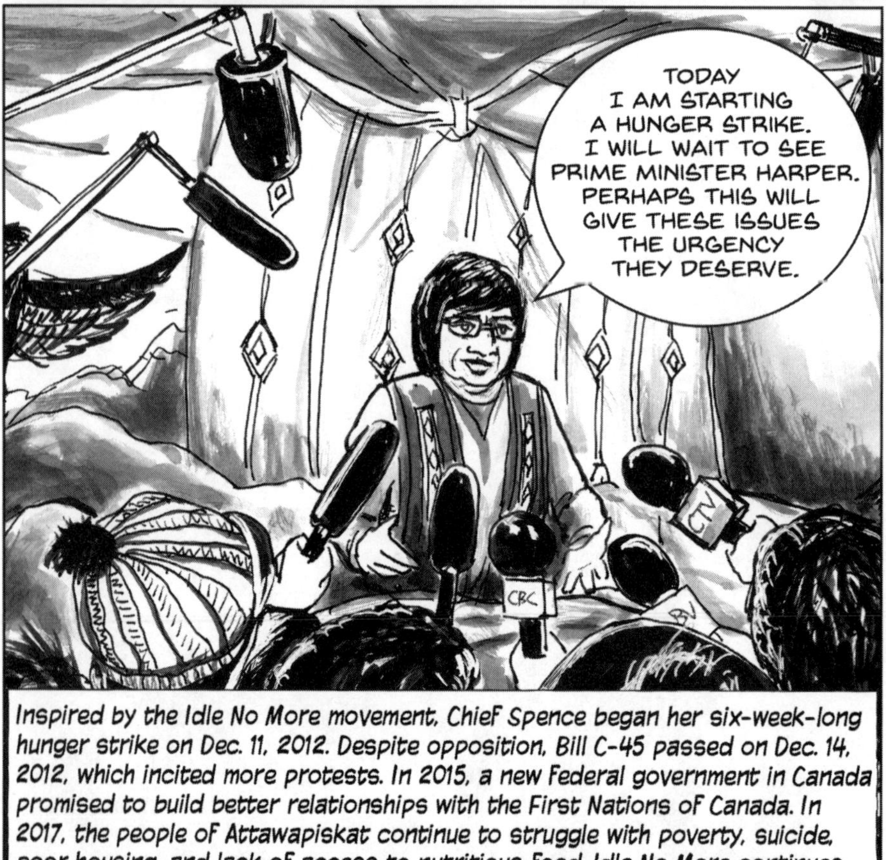
TODAY I AM STARTING A HUNGER STRIKE. I WILL WAIT TO SEE PRIME MINISTER HARPER. PERHAPS THIS WILL GIVE THESE ISSUES THE URGENCY THEY DESERVE.
CTV
CBC
Inspired by the Idle No More movement, Chief Spence began her six-week-long hunger strike on Dec. 11, 2012. Despite opposition, Bill C-45 passed on Dec. 14, 2012, which incited more protests. In 2015, a new Federal government in Canada promised to build better relationships with the First Nations of Canada. In 2017, the people of Attawapiskat continue to struggle with poverty, suicide, poor housing, and lack of access to nutritious Food. Idle No More continues as a global political advocacy movement For Indigenous rights.

In October 2012, the Canadian federal government brought forward Bill C-45, a bill that would remove Indigenous people's rights and weaken protection of the land and waters in Indigenous territories. First Nations groups objected, saying they weren't consulted, and in November 2012, Sylvia McAdams, Nina Wilson, Jessica Gordon, and Sheelah McLean decided they'd had enough of government oppression of Indigenous people. They held a conference in Saskatoon that they called "Idle No More" and they outlined their opposition to measures in Bill C-45. Foremost they opposed changes that would allow "for easier opening of treaty lands and territory."

#IdleNoMore became a viral hashtag, gathering momentum in its use for rallying conferences, protests, and teach-ins across Canada. Thousands of supporters gathered in cities across Canada on December 10, 2012, protesting widespread poverty in Indigenous communities and the loss of treaty lands and territory, and demanding the federal government meet with leaders of the now national Idle No More movement.

Across Canada, organized through social media and #IdleNoMore emails, Indigenous people and allies gathered in flash mobs at shopping malls (warm indoor places during cold winter months) for massive round dances. Accompanied by Indigenous hand-drums, the dancers declared the intentions of the Idle No More movement, and demanded that the federal government stop its patronizing, racist governance of Indigenous people in Canada.

In December 2012, Attawapiskat Chief Theresa Spence announced that she would fast until the prime minister and the governor general met with her to listen to her demands for justice for her people. Attawapiskat has long been a community facing grinding poverty, racism, lack of access to education and food, high suicide rates, and geographic isolation, exacerbated by political indifference. Chief Theresa Spence fasted for forty-three days, yet the prime minister refused to meet with her.

Bill C-45 passed in late December 2012. Angered at patronizing and unfair treatment by the Canadian government, Indigenous people across Canada blocked trains and highways and held large rallies and protests. After the bill had passed, the prime minister, but not the governor general, offered to meet with Chief Spence. Chief Spence refused the offer; she insisted on meeting with the governor general, the executive representative of the monarch, who is the titular head of state in Canada.

Canada is a colonial country, and the colonization of the lands, waters, and Indigenous people has been a violent process of land theft and cultural genocide. Indigenous women now lead much of the political organizing for First Nations across the country, and the Idle No More movement still provides educational, organizational, and media support for Indigenous rights activists in Canada and around the world.

Discussion Questions

1 How did the Idle No More movement communicate the message of Indigenous solidarity?
2 How did the women of Idle No More confront and challenge the political establishment in their own country? What happened when Chief Theresa Spence tried to meet with the prime minister?
3 Based on what you know about intersectional feminism from the introduction of this book, what do you think are the intersecting oppressions and privileges that the actions of the women of Idle No More address?

Research Questions and Activities

1 The round dance became a symbol of the Idle No More movement. Research historical and contemporary round dances; how have round dances been, and how do they continue to be, a site of political activism?
2 In response to a national crisis, the Government of Canada has launched the National Inquiry into Murdered and Missing Indigenous Women and Girls (MMIWG). Research the official

inquiry into MMIWG in Canada, and find out what the inquiry has recommended. How do these recommendations compare to the calls of the Idle No More movement?

3 What Indigenous nation lives on the land where you study? What is the current treaty or title agreement between Indigenous people and colonial powers on the land where you study?

4 In the Chiapas region of Mexico, the Zapatistas are an Indigenous collective with strong women's leadership. Find out about the legacy and leadership of Commandanta Ramona, and compare her leadership and resistance with that of Chief Theresa Spence.

Further Reading

Brownlie, Robin Jarvis, and Valerie J. Korinek, eds. *Finding a Way to the Heart: Feminist Writings on Aboriginal and Women's History in Canada.* Winnipeg: University of Manitoba Press, 2012.

Kino-Nda-Niimi Collective. *The Winter We Danced: Voices from the Past, the Future, and the Idle No More Movement.* Winnipeg: ARP Books, 2014.

Maracle, Lee. *I Am Woman: A Native Perspective on Sociology and Feminism.* Vancouver: Press Gang Publishers, 1996.

Simpson, Betasamosake Leanne. *Lighting the Eighth Fire: The Liberation, Resurgence and Protection of Indigenous Nations.* Winnipeg: ARP Books, 2008.

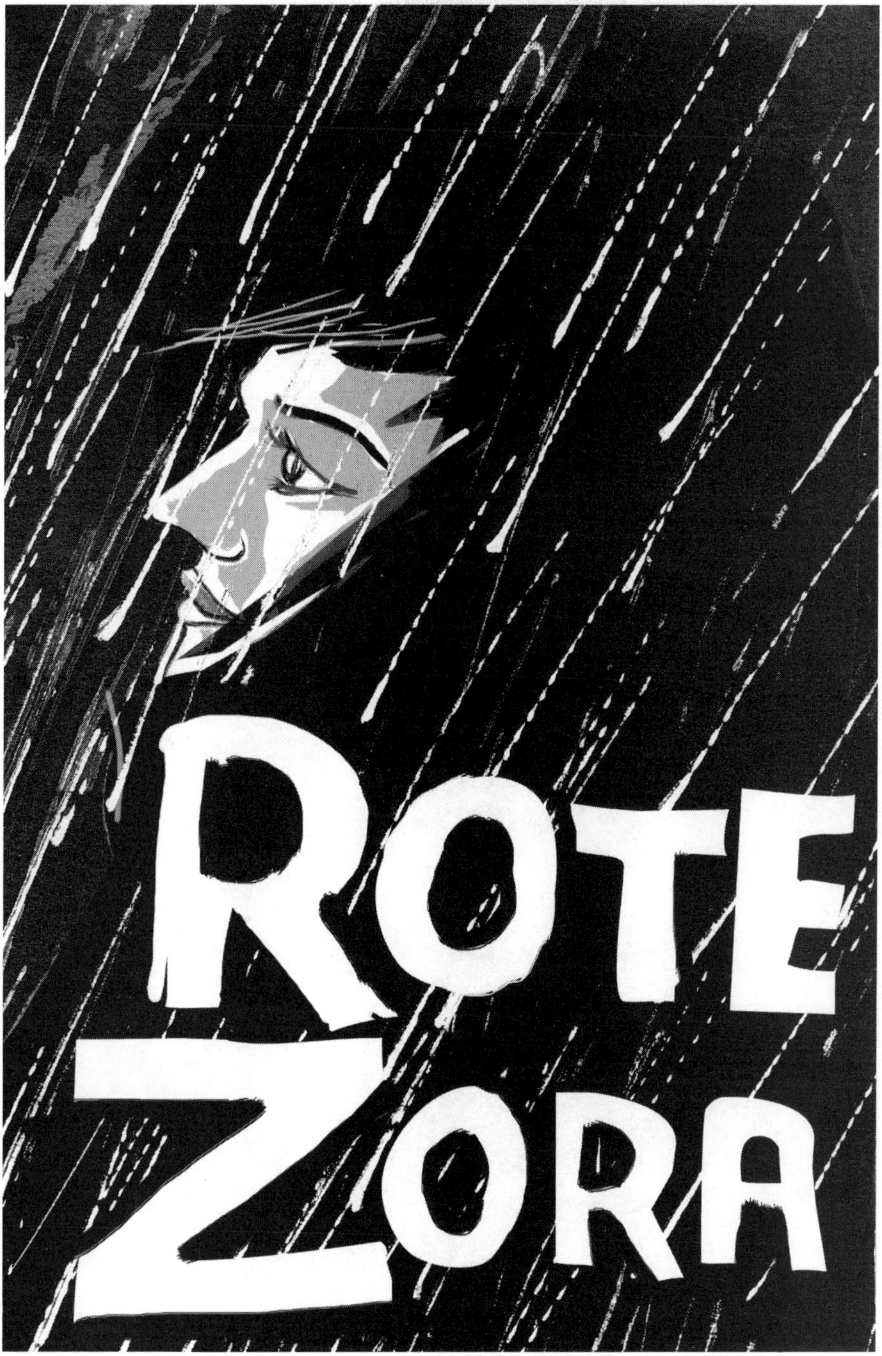
ROTE
ZORA

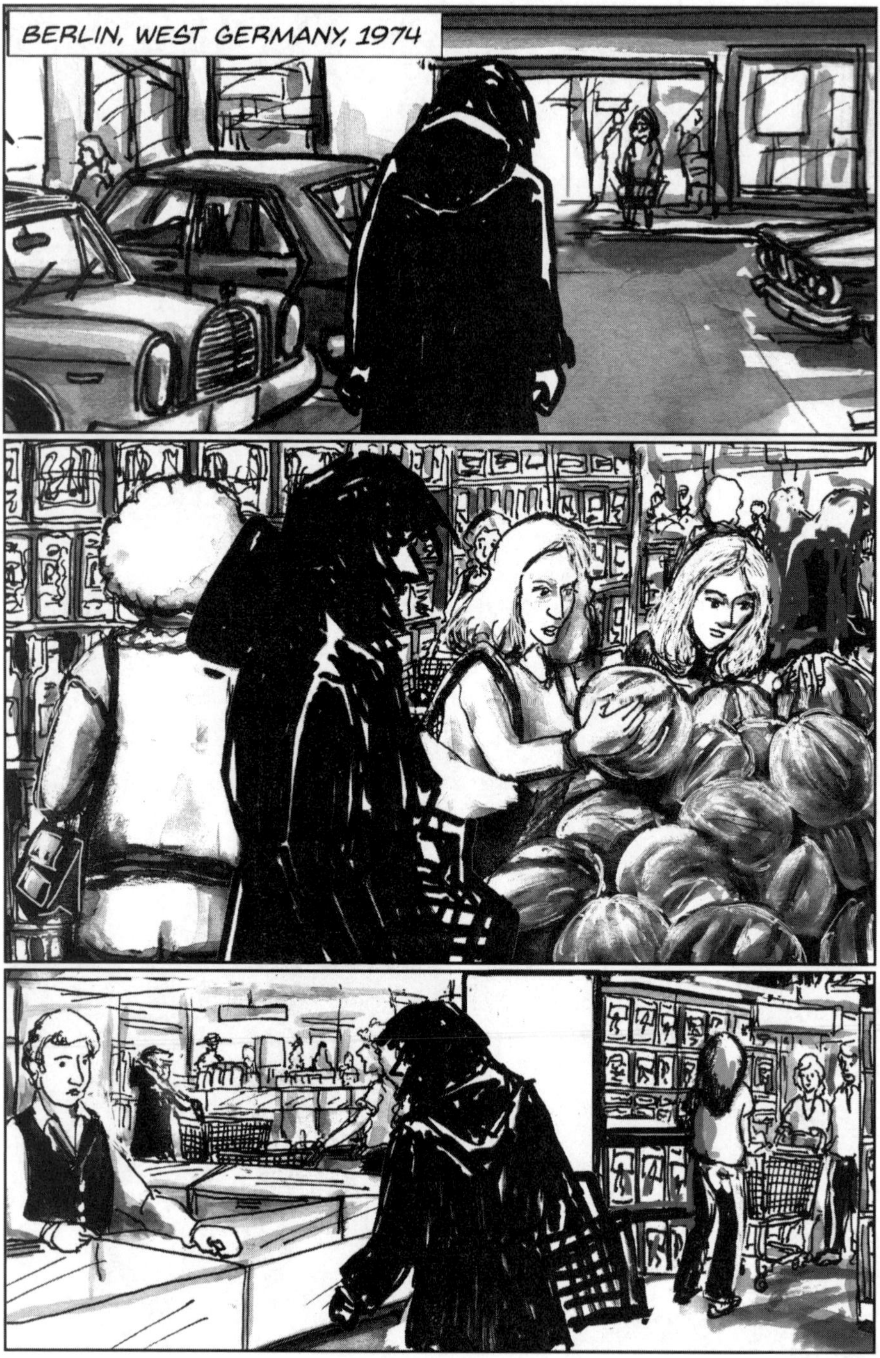
BERLIN, WEST GERMANY, 1974

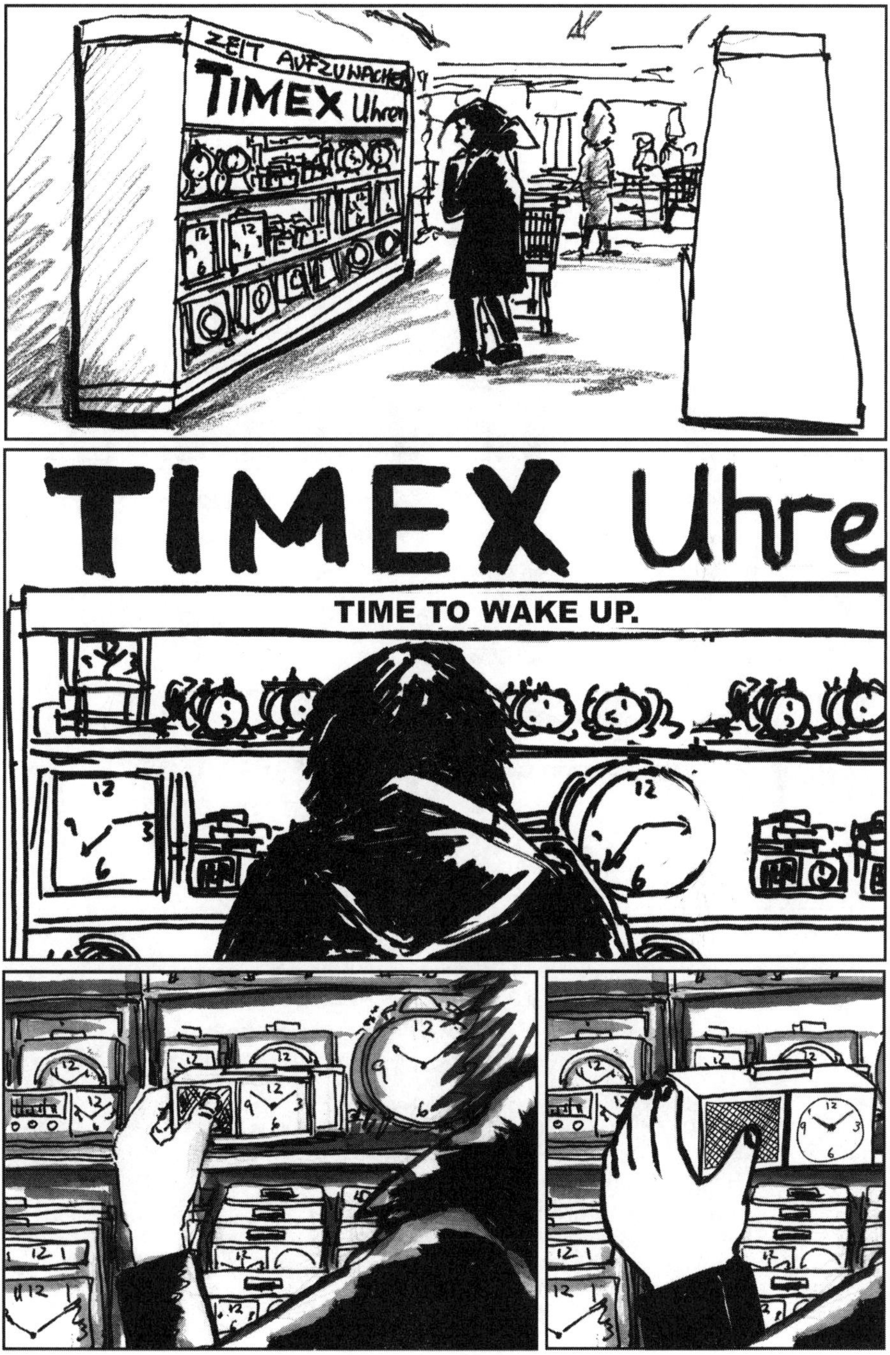
ZEIT AUFZUNACHEN
TIMEX Uhren
TIMEX Uhre
TIME TO WAKE UP.

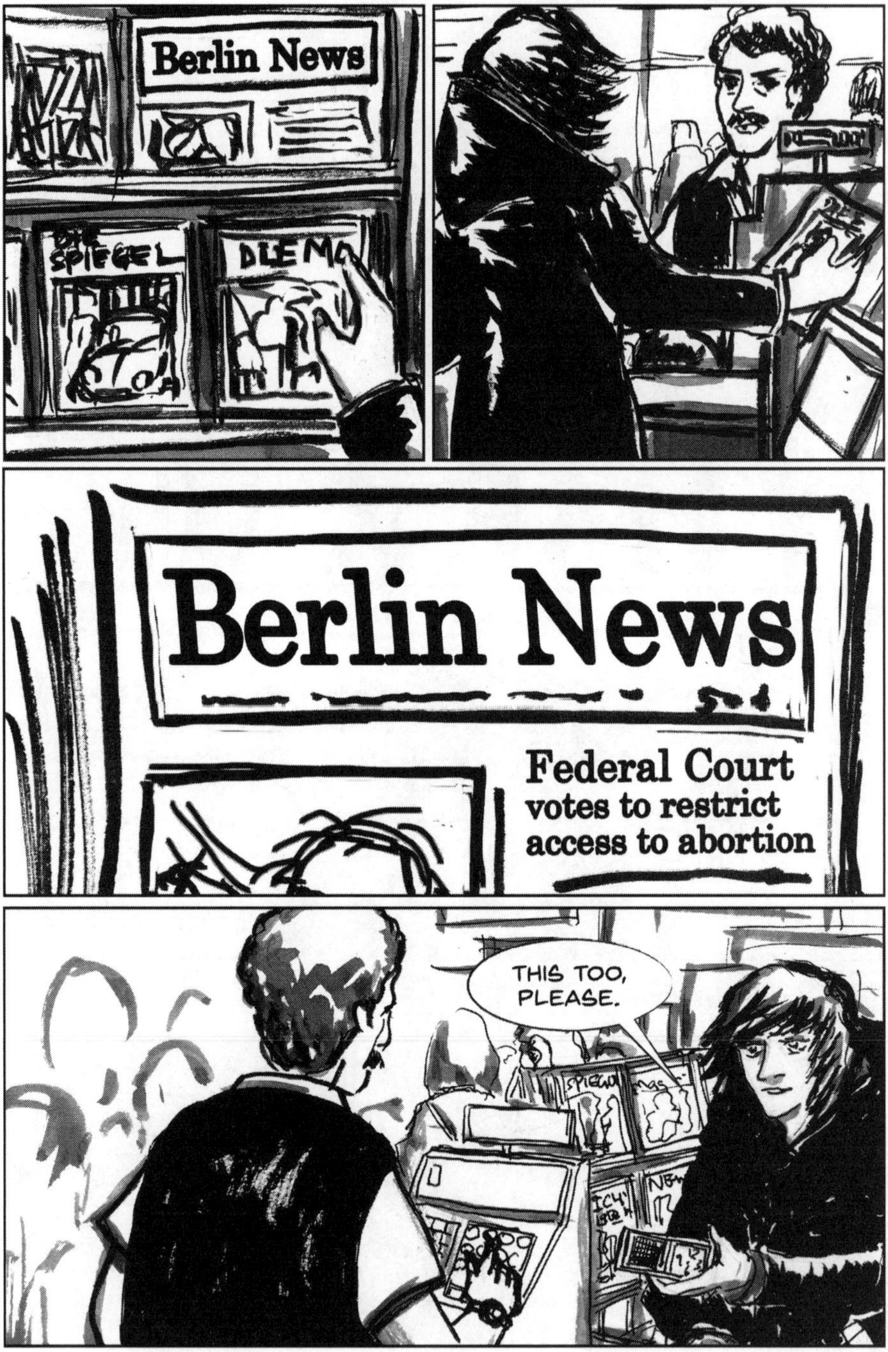
Berlin News
Berlin News
Federal Court votes to restrict access to abortion
THIS TOO, PLEASE.

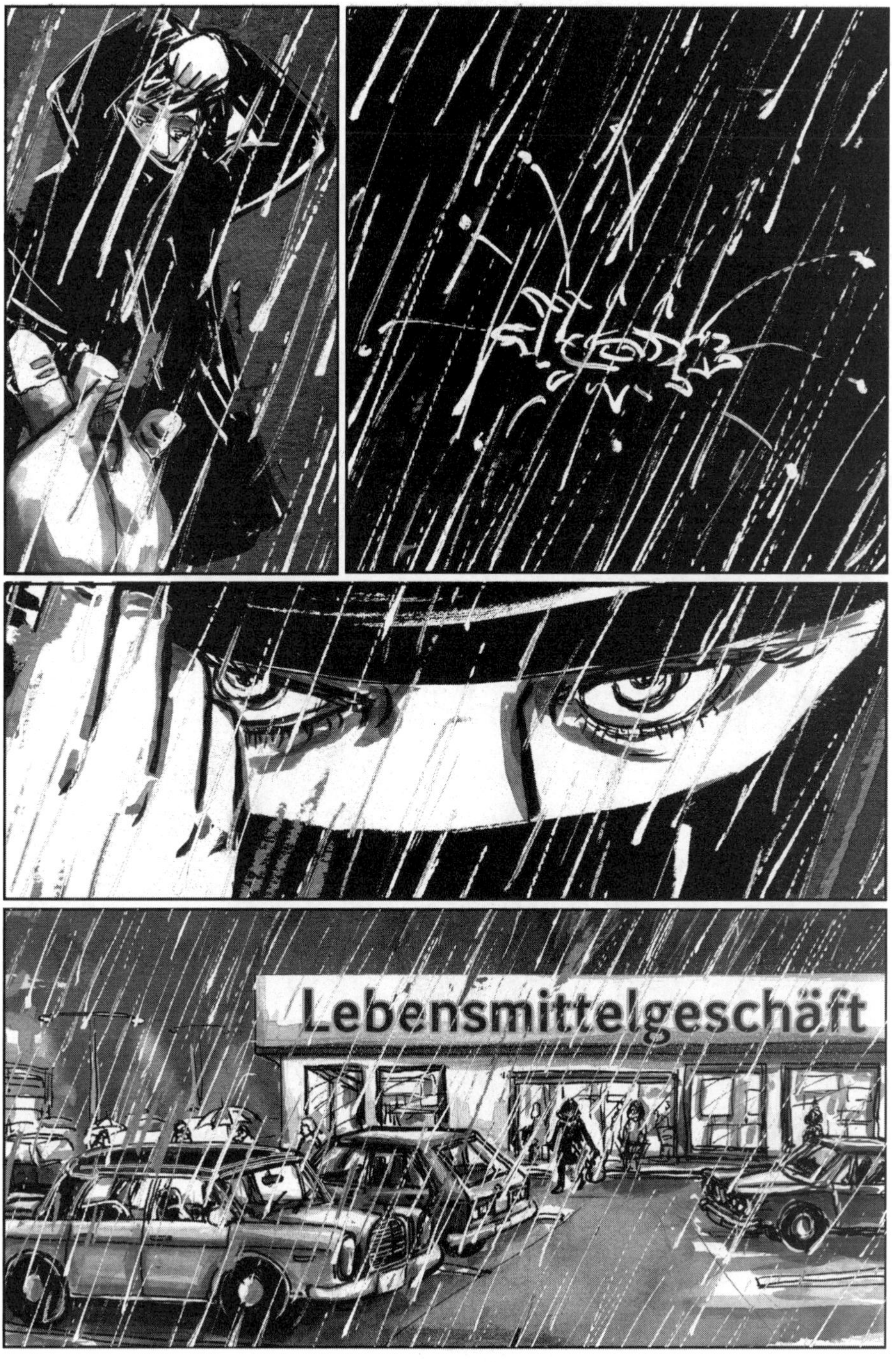
Lebensmittelgeschäft

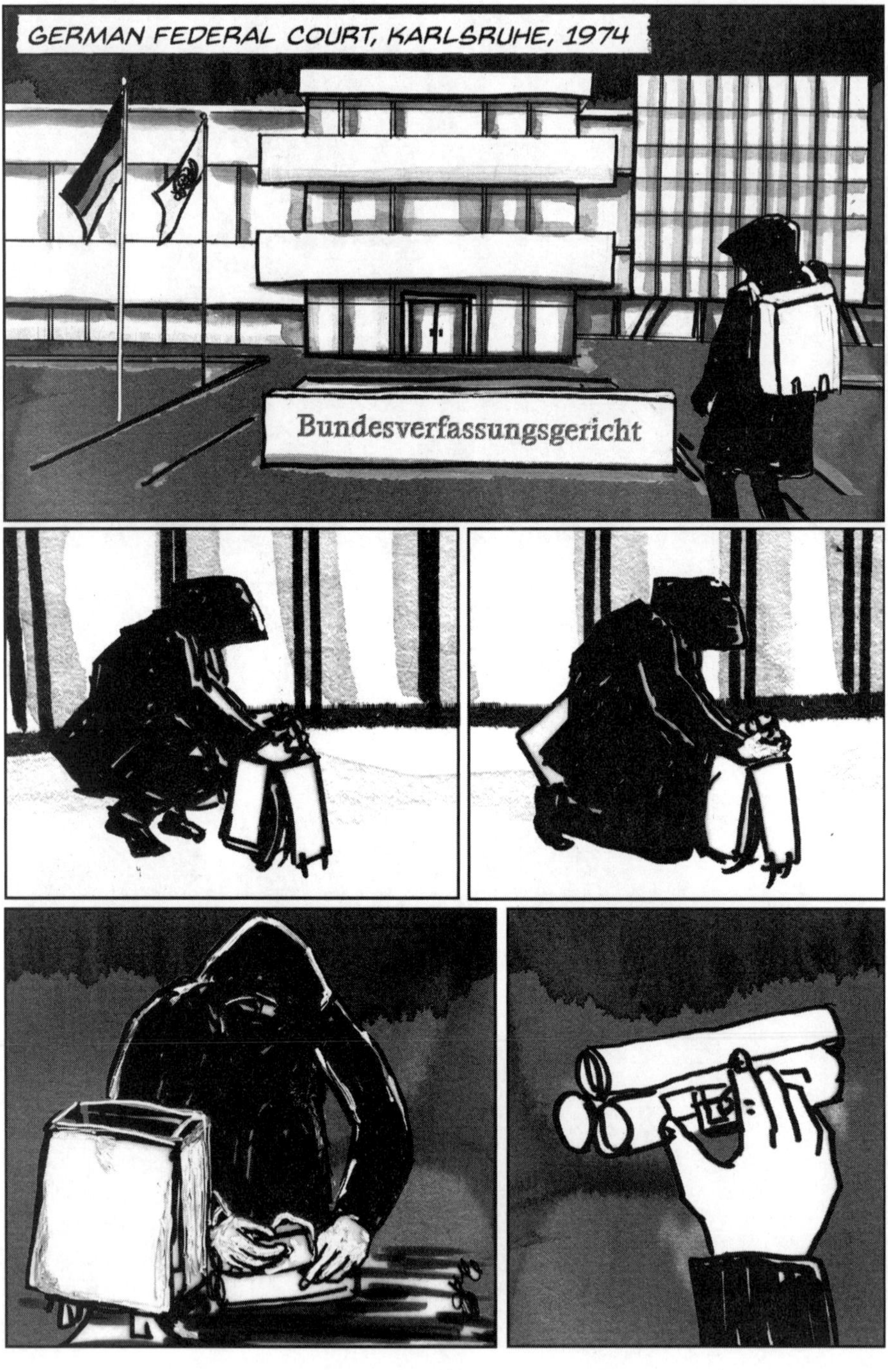
GERMAN FEDERAL COURT, KARLSRUHE, 1974
Bundesverfassungsgericht

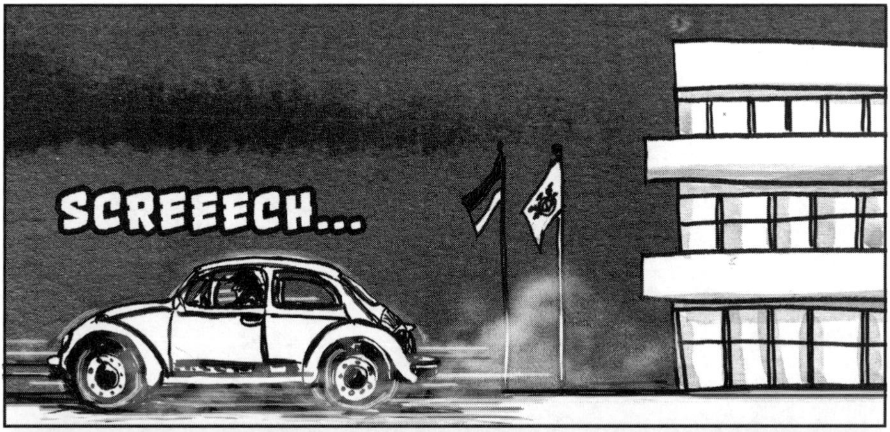
SCREEECH...

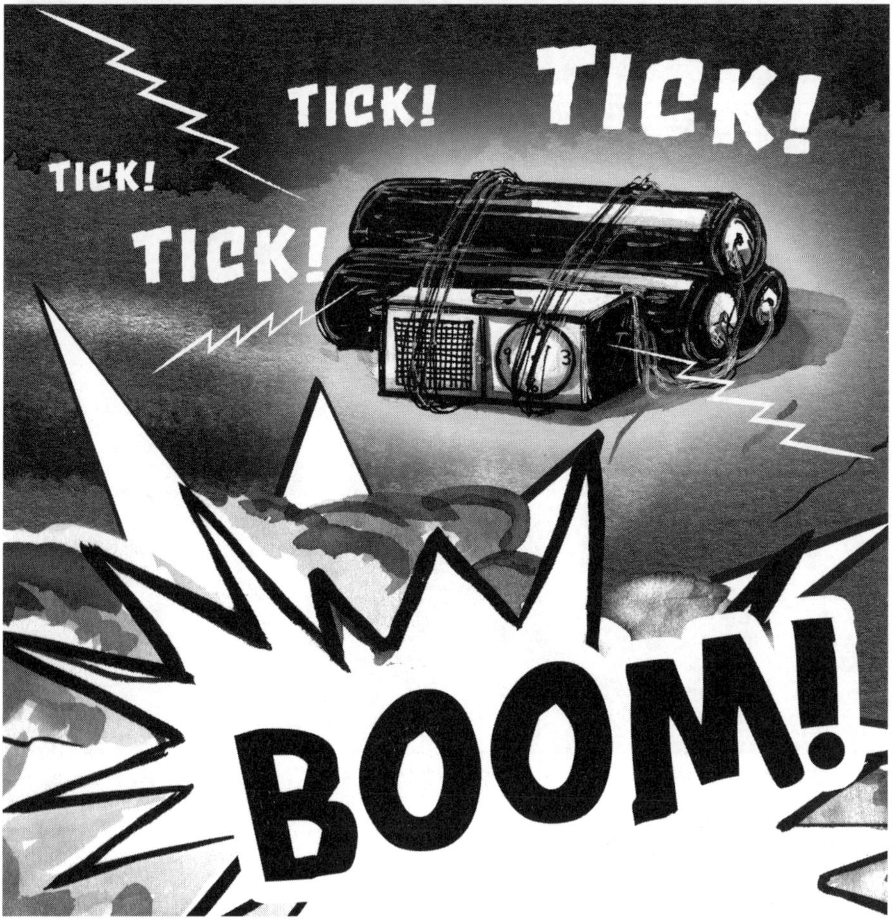
TICK!
TICK!
TICK!
TICK!
BOOM!

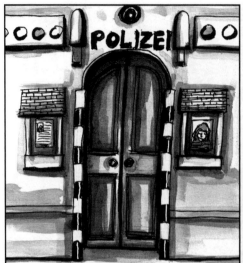

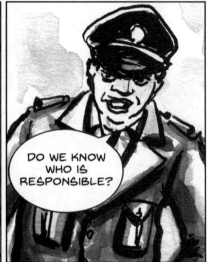

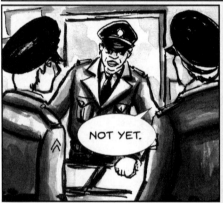

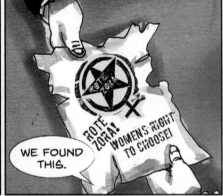

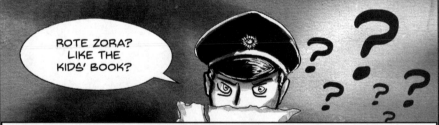

POLIZEI
DO WE KNOW WHO IS RESPONSIBLE?
NOT YET.
WE FOUND THIS.
ROTE ZORA
ROTE ZORA! WOMEN'S RIGHT TO CHOOSE!
ROTE ZORA? LIKE THE KIDS' BOOK?
"Rote Zora and Her Gang" (1941) by Kurt Held is a German children's book about red-headed Zora and her band of fellow orphans. Together they look after each other in a heartless world. In 1974, a group of German underground feminist radicals took the name Rote Zora for their group activist work.

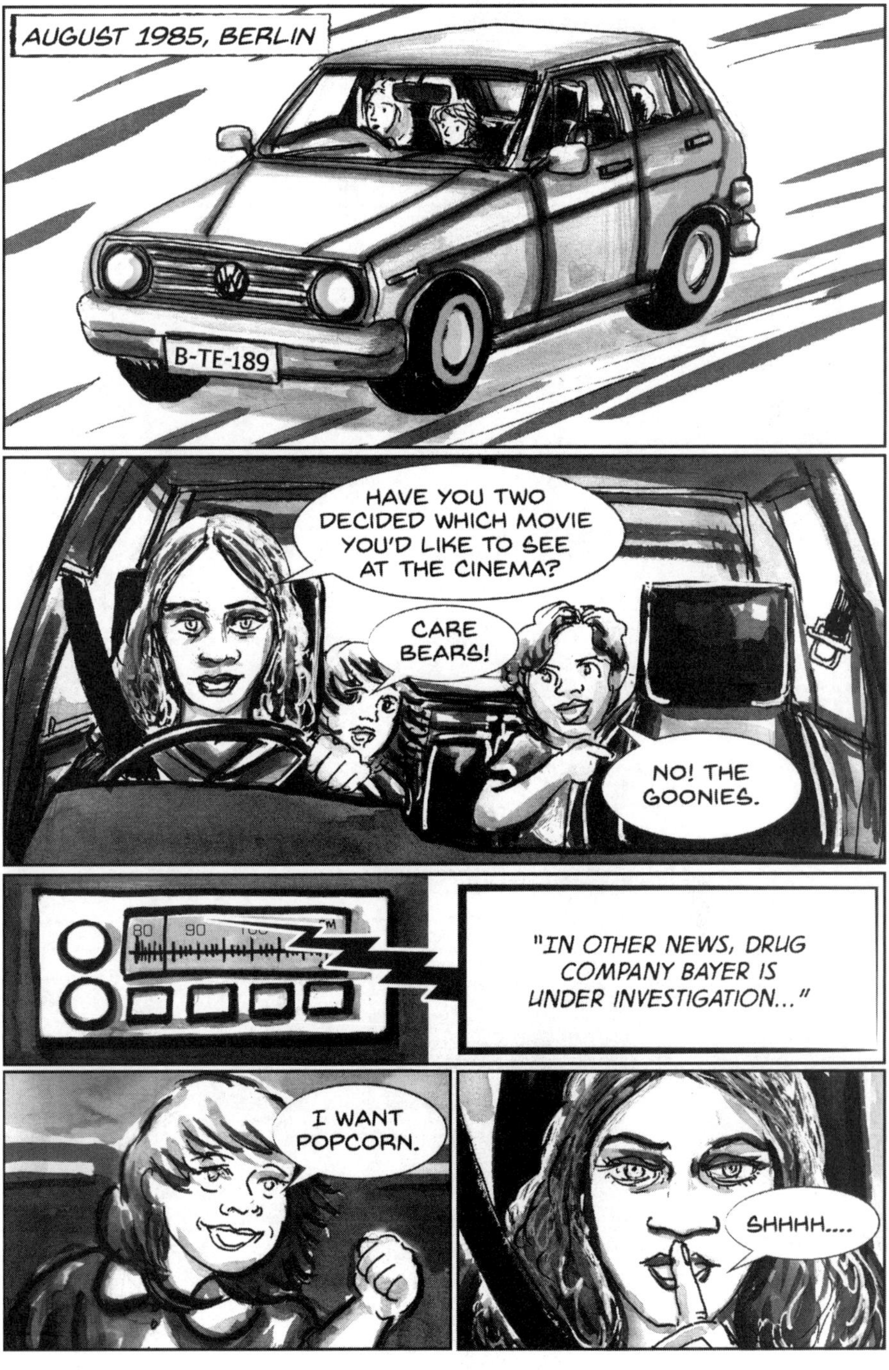
AUGUST 1985, BERLIN
B-TE-189
HAVE YOU TWO DECIDED WHICH MOVIE YOU'D LIKE TO SEE AT THE CINEMA?
CARE BEARS!
NO! THE GOONIES.
"IN OTHER NEWS, DRUG COMPANY BAYER IS UNDER INVESTIGATION..."
I WANT POPCORN.
SHHHH....

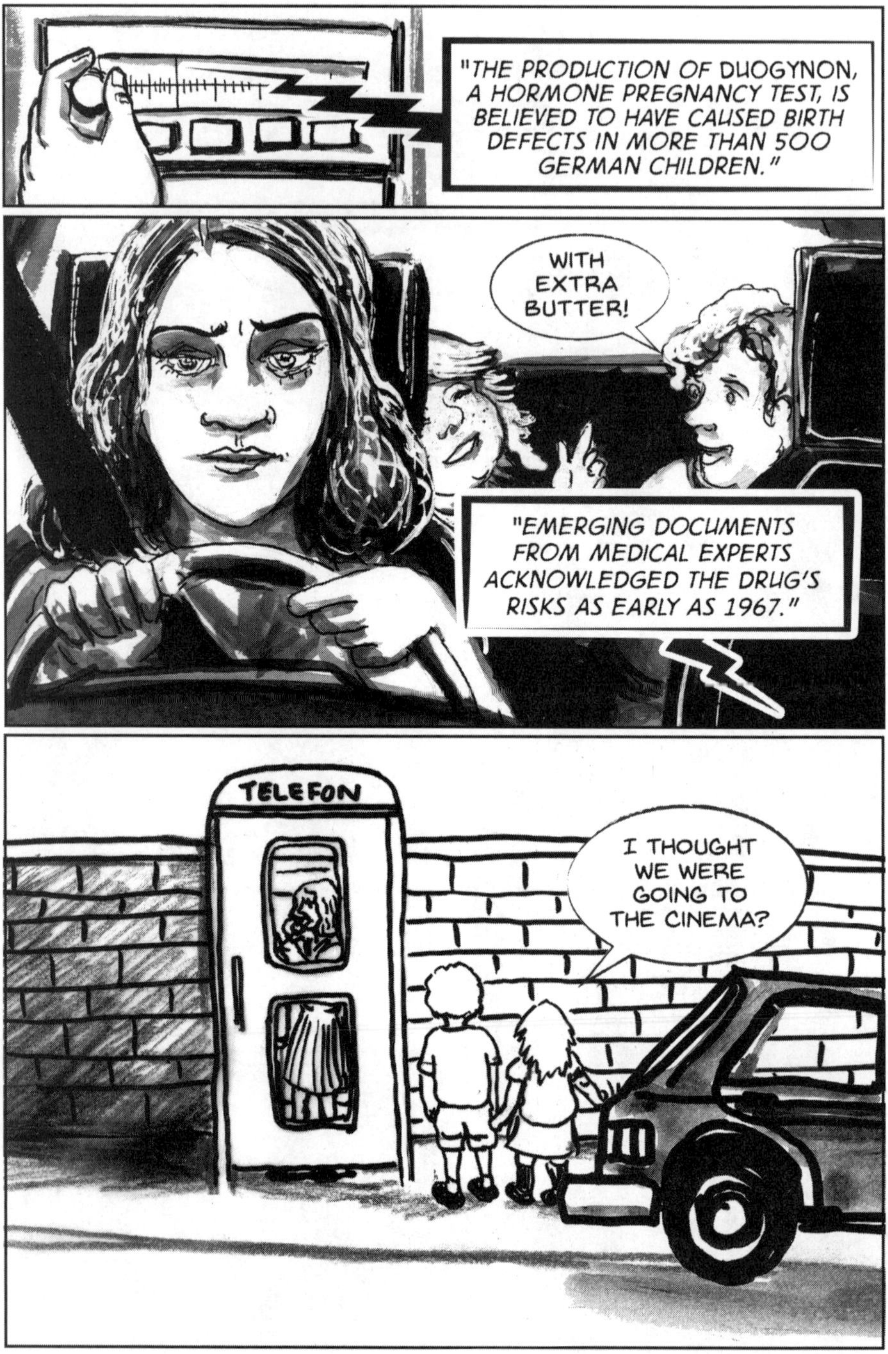
"THE PRODUCTION OF DUOGYNON, A HORMONE PREGNANCY TEST, IS BELIEVED TO HAVE CAUSED BIRTH DEFECTS IN MORE THAN 500 GERMAN CHILDREN."
WITH EXTRA BUTTER!
"EMERGING DOCUMENTS FROM MEDICAL EXPERTS ACKNOWLEDGED THE DRUG'S RISKS AS EARLY AS 1967."
TELEFON
I THOUGHT WE WERE GOING TO THE CINEMA?

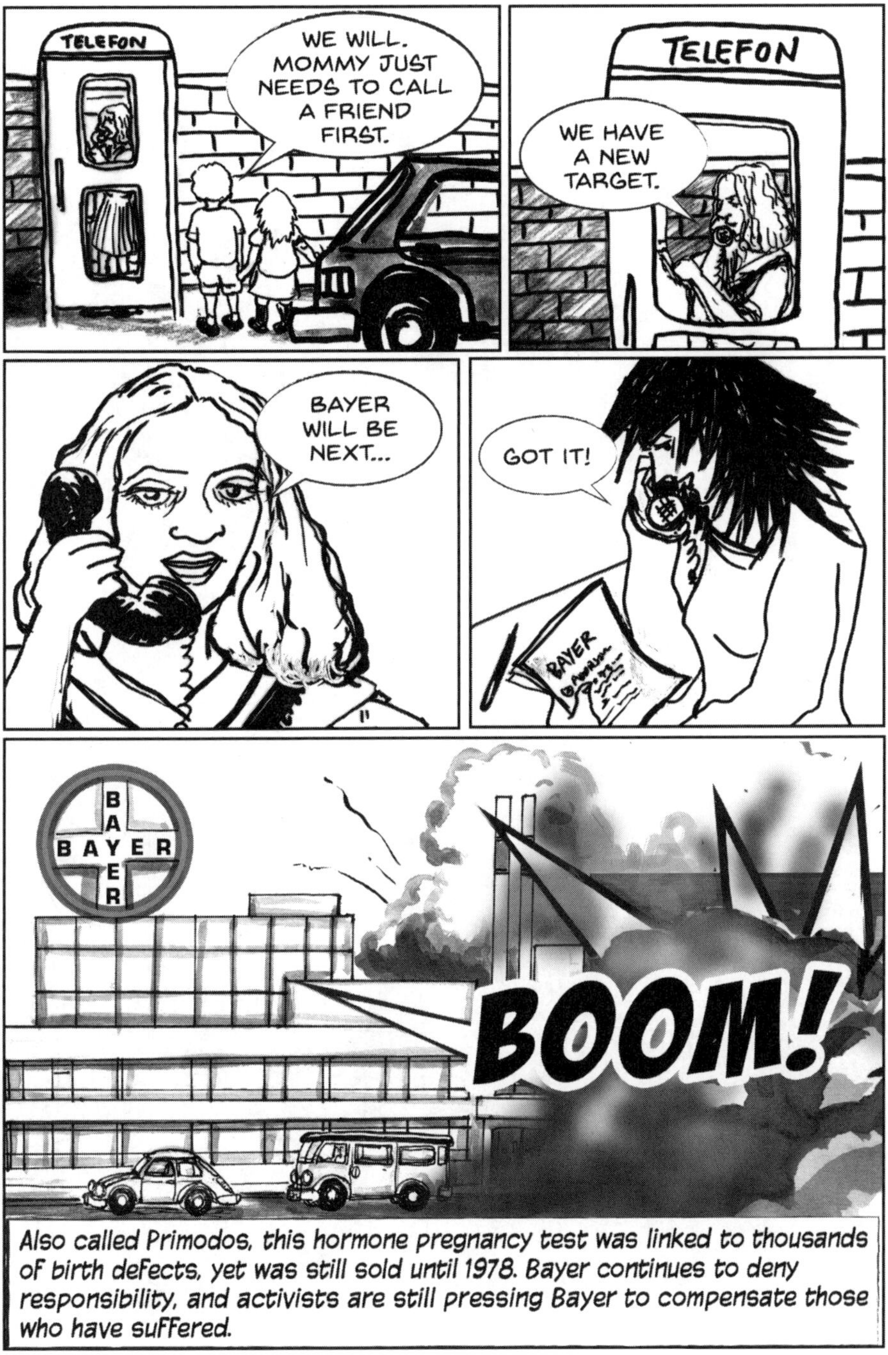
TELEFON
WE WILL. MOMMY JUST NEEDS TO CALL A FRIEND FIRST.
TELEFON
WE HAVE A NEW TARGET.
BAYER WILL BE NEXT...
GOT IT!
BAYER
BAYER
BOOM!
Also called Primodos, this hormone pregnancy test was linked to thousands of birth defects, yet was still sold until 1978. Bayer continues to deny responsibility, and activists are still pressing Bayer to compensate those who have suffered.

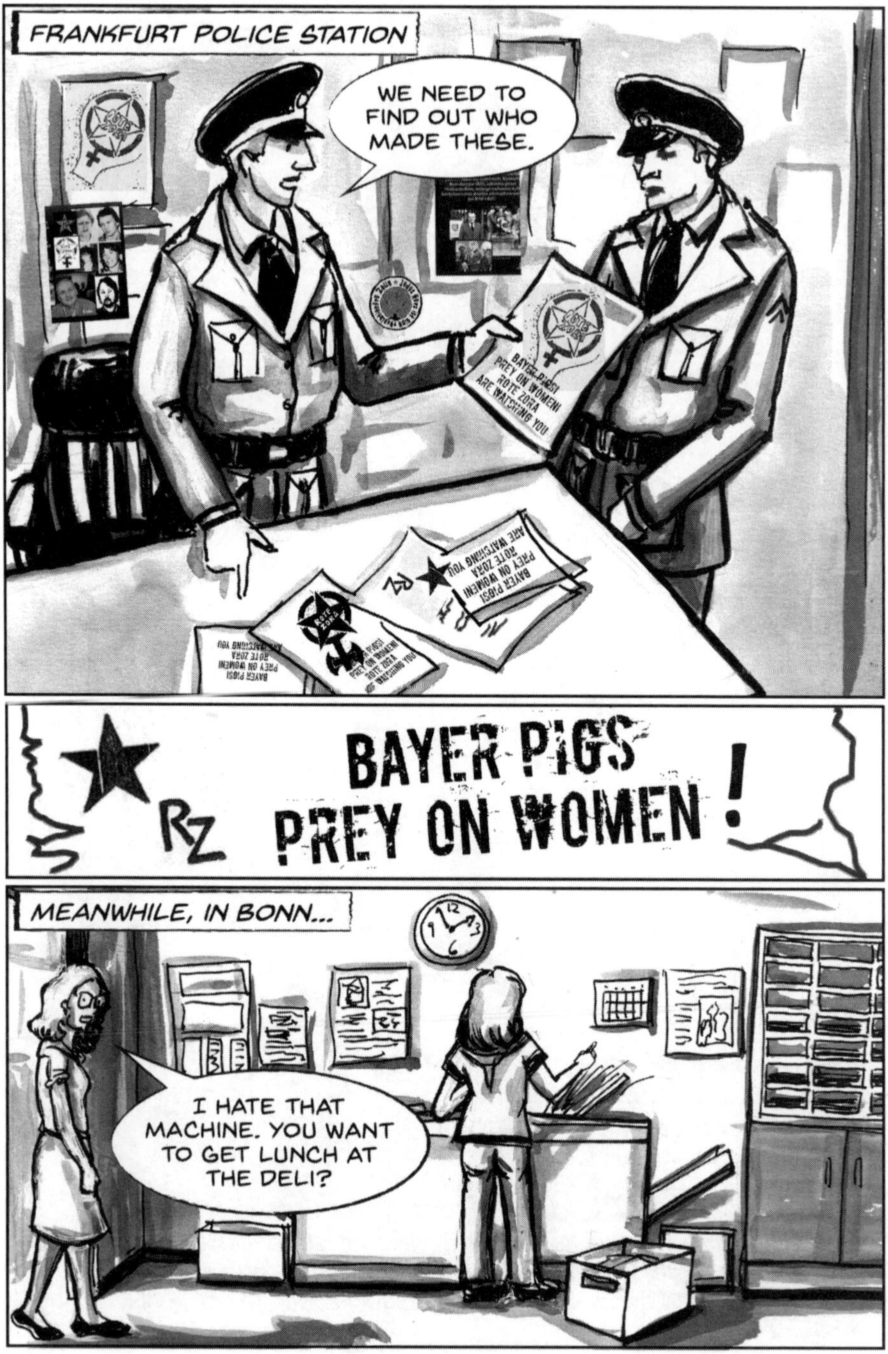
FRANKFURT POLICE STATION
WE NEED TO FIND OUT WHO MADE THESE.
BAYER PIGS! PREY ON WOMEN! ROTE ZORA ARE WATCHING YOU
RZ
BAYER PIGS PREY ON WOMEN!
MEANWHILE, IN BONN...
I HATE THAT MACHINE. YOU WANT TO GET LUNCH AT THE DELI?

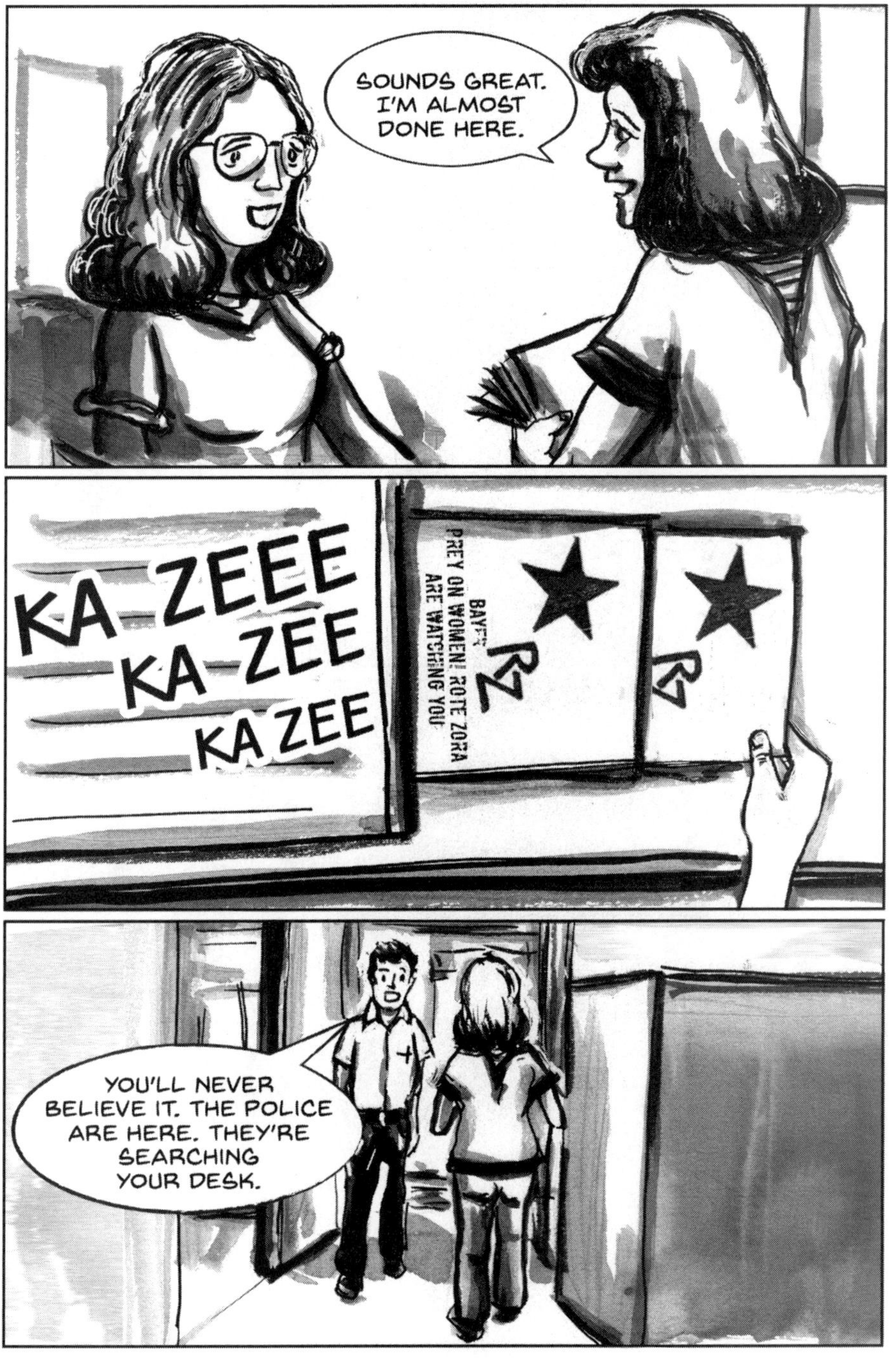
SOUNDS GREAT. I'M ALMOST DONE HERE.
KA ZEEE
KA ZEE
KA ZEE
RZ
PREY ON WOMEN! ROTE ZORA
ARE WATCHING YOU
YOU'LL NEVER BELIEVE IT. THE POLICE ARE HERE. THEY'RE SEARCHING YOUR DESK.

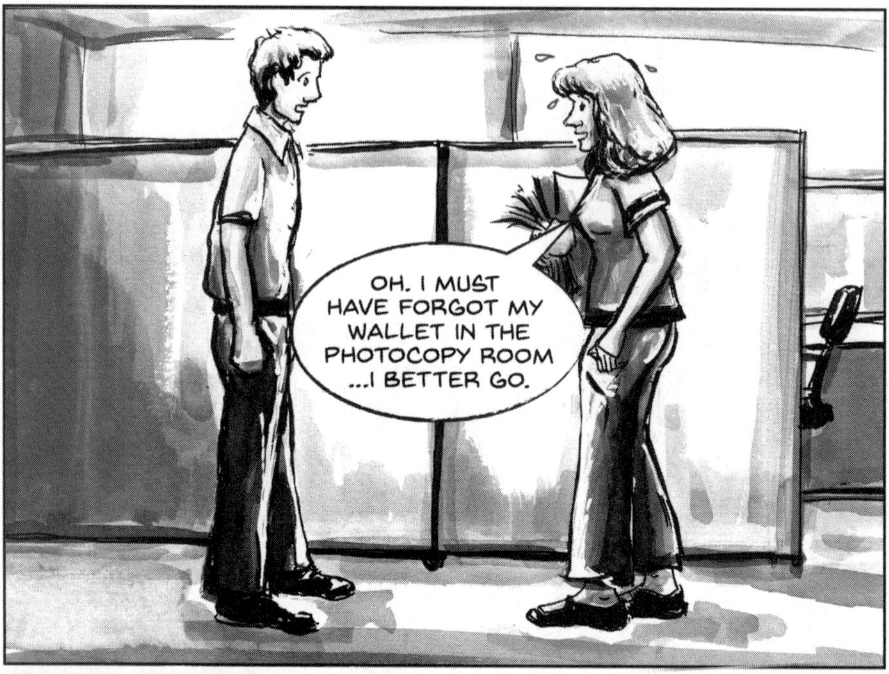
OH. I MUST HAVE FORGOT MY WALLET IN THE PHOTOCOPY ROOM ...I BETTER GO.

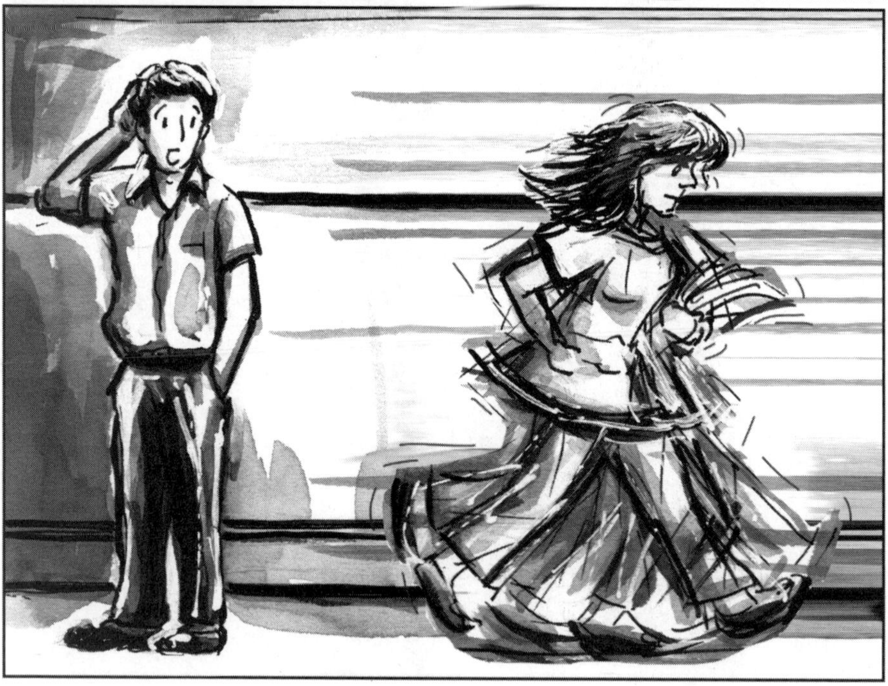

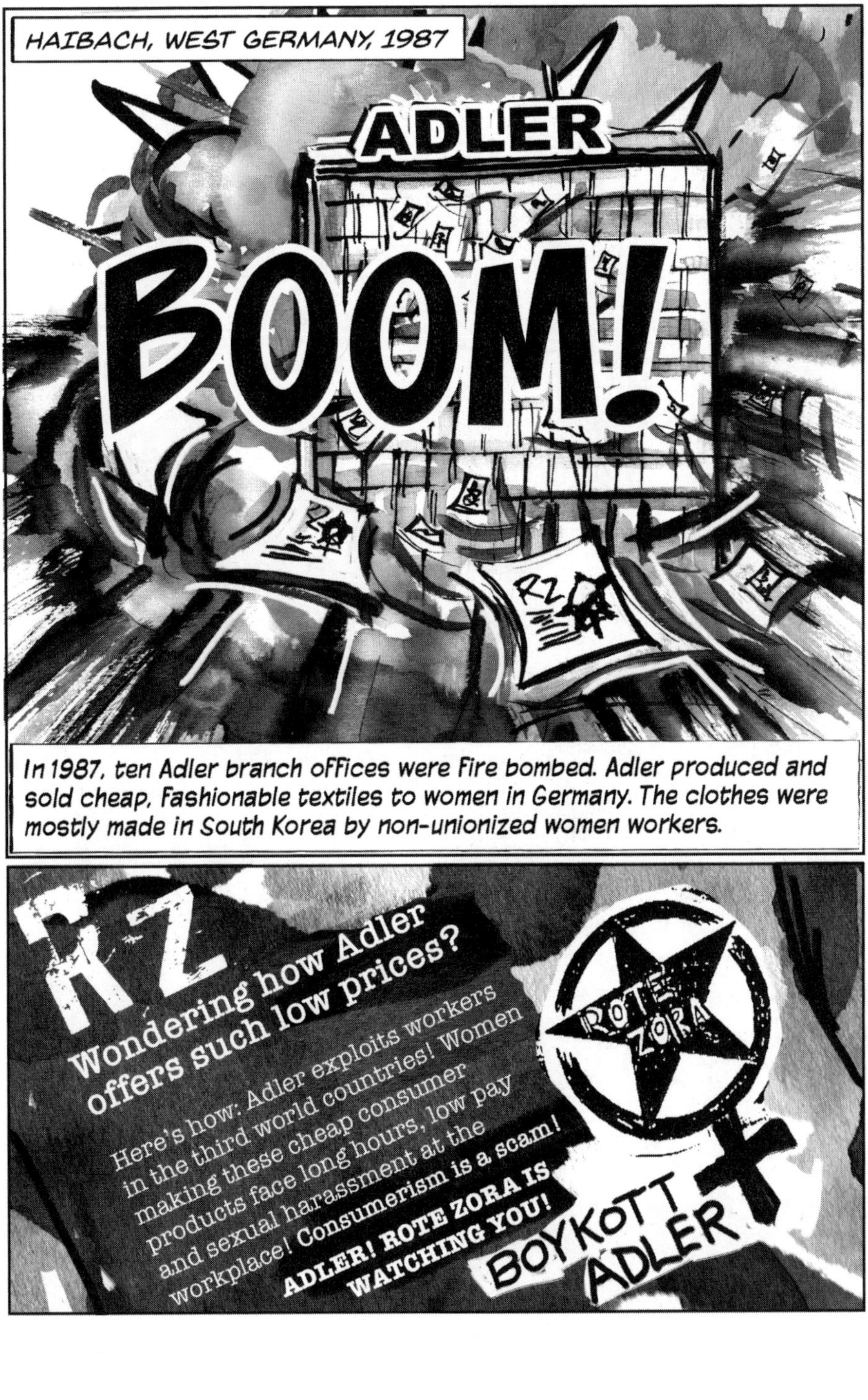
HAIBACH, WEST GERMANY, 1987
ADLER
BOOM!
In 1987, ten Adler branch offices were fire bombed. Adler produced and sold cheap, fashionable textiles to women in Germany. The clothes were mostly made in South Korea by non-unionized women workers.
RZ
Wondering how Adler offers such low prices?
Here's how: Adler exploits workers in the third world countries! Women making these cheap consumer products face long hours, low pay and sexual harassment at the workplace! Consumerism is a scam!
ADLER! ROTE ZORA IS WATCHING YOU!
ROTE ZORA
BOYKOTT ADLER

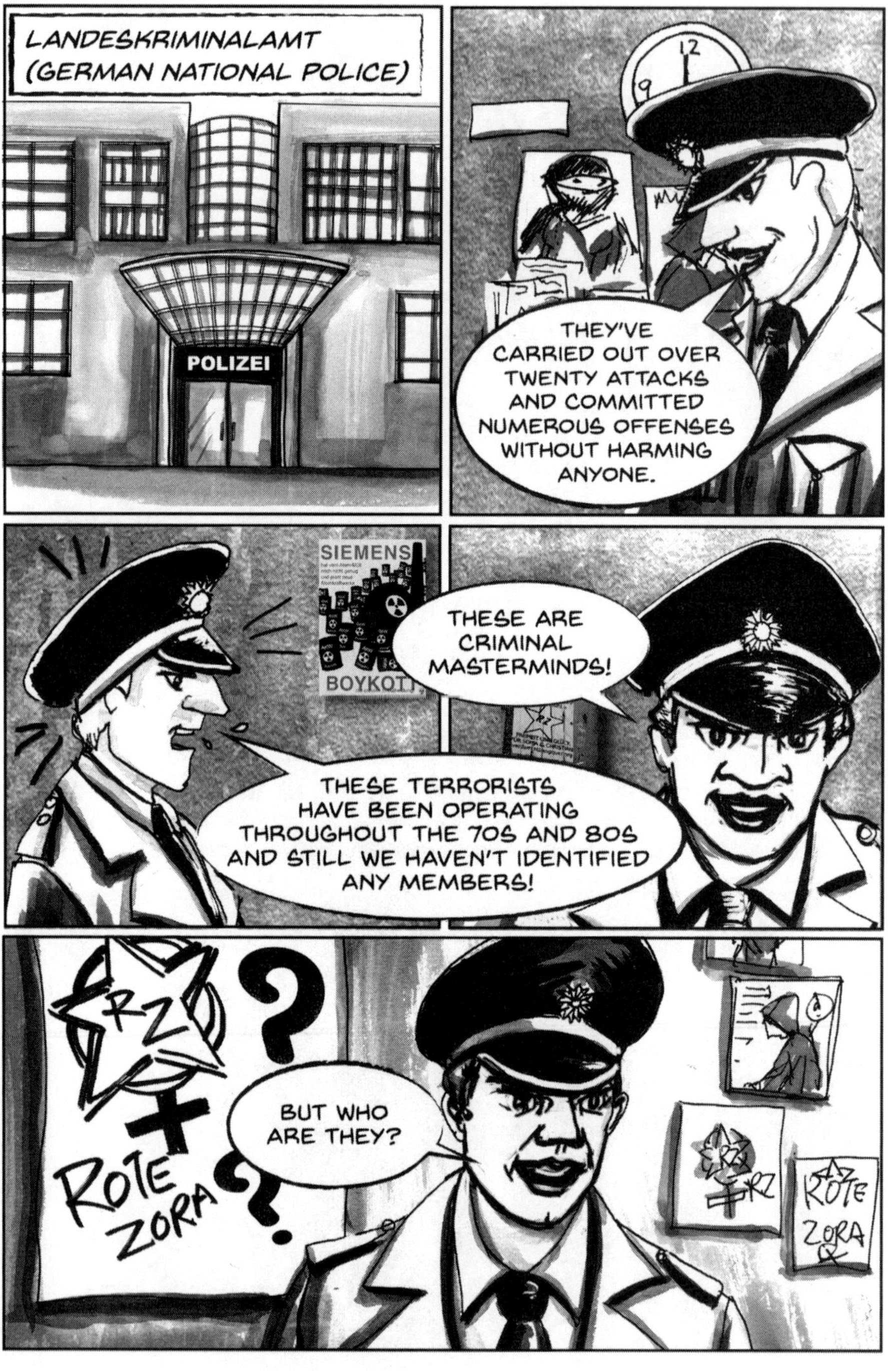
LANDESKRIMINALAMT (GERMAN NATIONAL POLICE)
POLIZEI
THEY'VE CARRIED OUT OVER TWENTY ATTACKS AND COMMITTED NUMEROUS OFFENSES WITHOUT HARMING ANYONE.
SIEMENS
BOYKOTT
THESE ARE CRIMINAL MASTERMINDS!
THESE TERRORISTS HAVE BEEN OPERATING THROUGHOUT THE 70S AND 80S AND STILL WE HAVEN'T IDENTIFIED ANY MEMBERS!
RZ
ROTE ZORA
BUT WHO ARE THEY?
RZ
ROTE ZORA

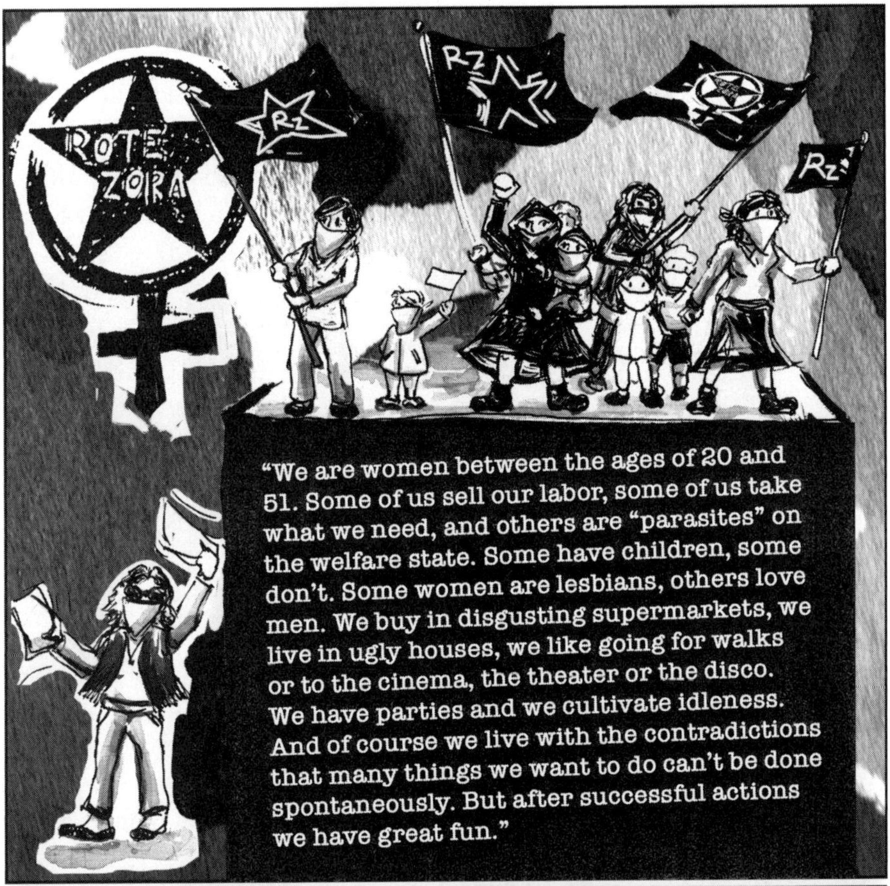
ROTE ZORA
RZ
RZ
RZ
"We are women between the ages of 20 and 51. Some of us sell our labor, some of us take what we need, and others are "parasites" on the welfare state. Some have children, some don't. Some women are lesbians, others love men. We buy in disgusting supermarkets, we live in ugly houses, we like going for walks or to the cinema, the theater or the disco. We have parties and we cultivate idleness. And of course we live with the contradictions that many things we want to do can't be done spontaneously. But after successful actions we have great fun."

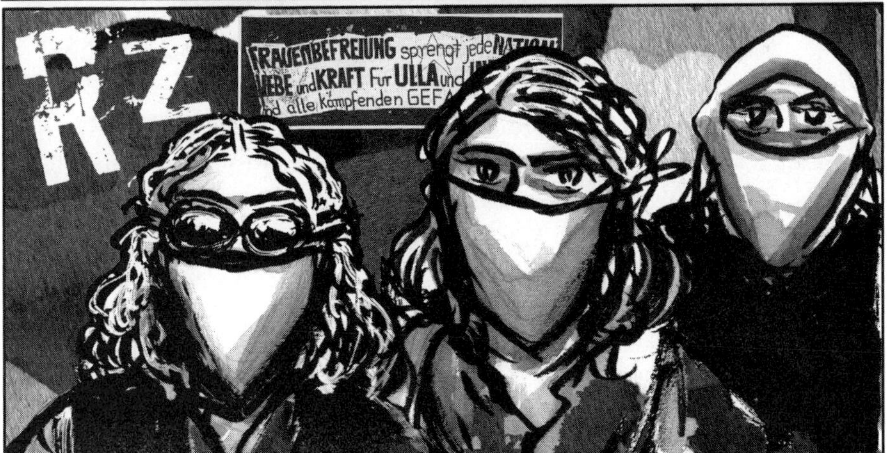
RZ
FRAUENBEFREIUNG sprengt jede
und KRAFT Fur ULLA und
alle kämpfenden

With their slogans of *Rapists Watch Out!* and anti-capitalist, anti-patriarchy politics, Rote Zora was unabashedly militant. Their dream was rapists, misogynists, and porn producers would be afraid that they would be tracked down and humiliated by "small bands of women everywhere." They said that a porn shop should burn every day and that all their actions, taken together over time, would contribute to a social revolution that would overturn global capitalism and patriarchy.

Rote Zora was associated with other violent revolutionary cell groups operating at the same time in Europe; but unlike the other revolutionary cells Rote Zora strategically targeted only property and never killed or harmed people. The members published flyers and small newspapers to disseminate their political views, and they gave a few interviews to supportive journalists. They stated that their property violence was insignificant in comparison to domestic violence against women in Germany. They announced that they operated in solidarity with women in poor countries who were exploited producing consumer goods for wealthier countries; Rote Zora believed that by attacking icons of capitalism they were defending the rights of poor women around the world. This expression of a preference for solidarity over philanthropy resonates with anarchist principles, and is an example of transnational feminist organizing.

Along with attacks on pharmaceutical companies and clothing manufacturers, the women of Rote Zora set fire to cars belonging to landlords they deemed exploitative, printed pirated bus tickets and gave them out to strangers, and bombed shops that sold pornography. Their acts represented a wide-ranging attack on capitalist patriarchy.

Rote Zora members operated in secret, underground, and for the most part carried out their actions without being detected. There is still very little published about Rote Zora. In 2007, Adrienne Gershäuser received a suspended two-year sentence for attempted bombings carried out in 1986 and 1987. To this day, most former Rote Zora members remain underground and are unrecognized.

Reflecting Western feminist concerns of the time, Rote Zora targeted shops that sold pornography they felt denigrated women, as well as corporations and institutions that they believed stood in the way of women's reproductive freedom. Their first action was the bombing of the West German Supreme Court in Berlin to protest legislation that limited women's access to abortion. In total, Rote Zora was responsible for forty-five attacks, none of which caused bodily harm. In 1995 Rote Zora disbanded, and today they are mostly forgotten in the reunited Germany.

Violent pornography is in wider circulation now than it was in the 1970s and 1980s. Does this mean that Rote Zora failed, or does it mean that feminism missed an opportunity to intervene in rape culture in those decades? What can we do now? We hope that readers will ask these and more questions about Rote Zora. Readers might also look into Canada's Abortion Caravan, a reproductive rights direct action group formed in 1970, and the Bolivian anarcha-feminist group Mujeres Creando.

Discussion Questions

1 What targets did Rote Zora choose, and why? What actions did they carry out against these targets?
2 How were the women of Rote Zora able to conceal their identities and remain a secret organization?
3 How did Rote Zora communicate their feminist ideology, and how do these methods of communication compare to those of other collective feminist resistance groups discussed in this book?

Research Questions and Activities

1 During the 1970s, the Red Army Faction (RAF) in Germany was an active underground guerrilla movement. Research the tactics and ideology of the RAF and compare them to those of Rote Zora.
2 In the age of the internet, how do feminists today think about pornography, and what critiques of pornography do they put forward?

3 Rote Zora used anonymous bombings as key strategic actions. While they were careful to never hurt or kill people during their bombings, they did destroy buildings, cars, and newspaper kiosks. How does their violence compare with other violent terrorist actions in Europe in the 1970s, 1980s, and 1990s?

Further Reading

Dark Star Collective, ed. *Quiet Rumours: An Anarcha-Feminist Reader.* Washington, DC: AK Press, 2012.

Deric, Shannon. "Articulating a Contemporary Anarcha-Feminism." *Theory in Action* 2.3 (July 2009): 58–74.

Mair, Kimberly. *Guerrilla Aesthetics: Art, Memory, and the West German Urban Guerrilla.* Montreal: McGill-Queen's University Press, 2016.

HARSHA WALIA

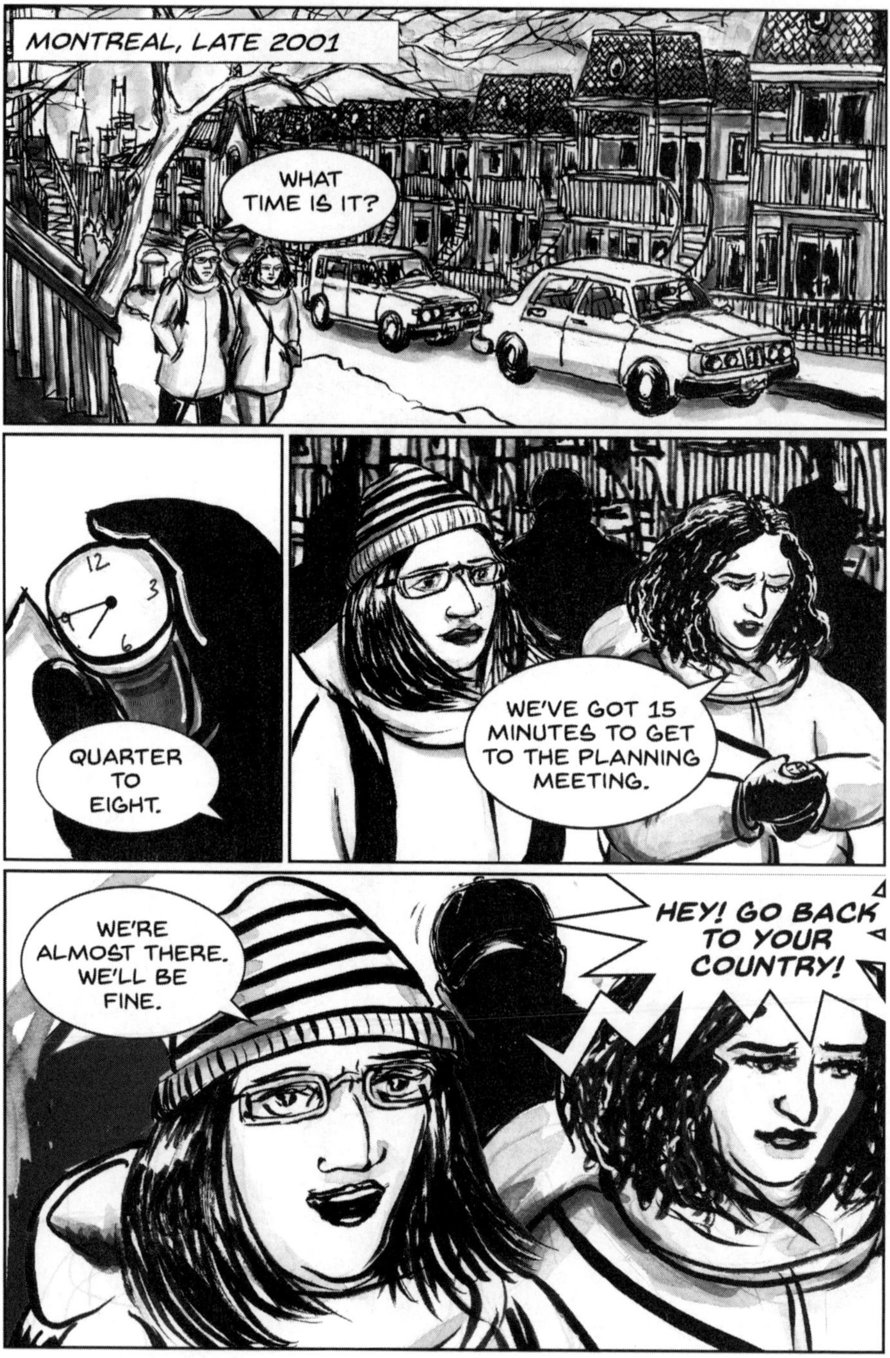
MONTREAL, LATE 2001
WHAT TIME IS IT?
12 3 9 6
QUARTER TO EIGHT.
WE'VE GOT 15 MINUTES TO GET TO THE PLANNING MEETING.
WE'RE ALMOST THERE. WE'LL BE FINE.
HEY! GO BACK TO YOUR COUNTRY!

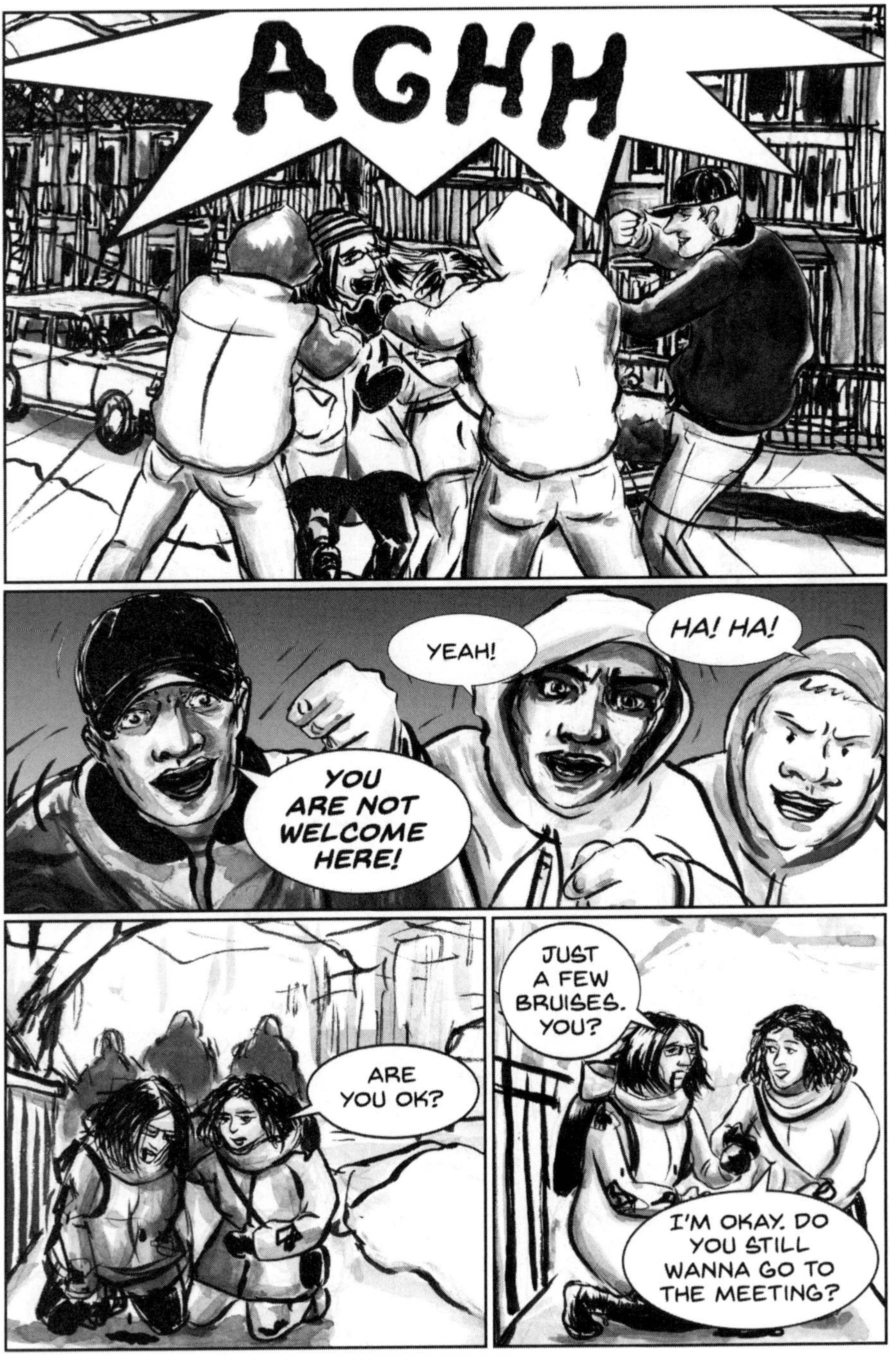
AGHH
YEAH!
HA! HA!
YOU ARE NOT WELCOME HERE!
ARE YOU OK?
JUST A FEW BRUISES. YOU?
I'M OKAY. DO YOU STILL WANNA GO TO THE MEETING?

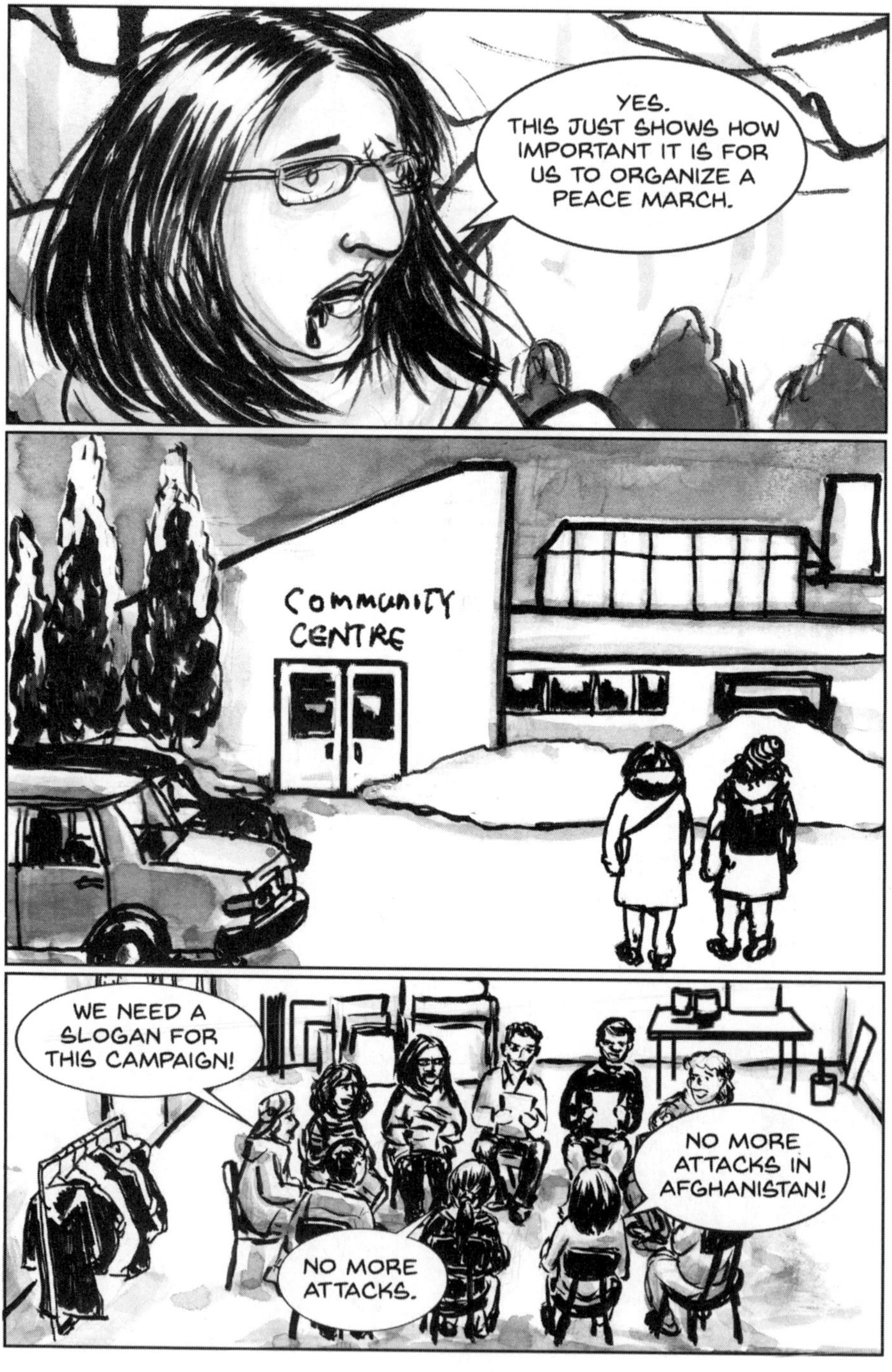
YES. THIS JUST SHOWS HOW IMPORTANT IT IS FOR US TO ORGANIZE A PEACE MARCH.
COMMUNITY CENTRE
WE NEED A SLOGAN FOR THIS CAMPAIGN!
NO MORE ATTACKS IN AFGHANISTAN!
NO MORE ATTACKS.

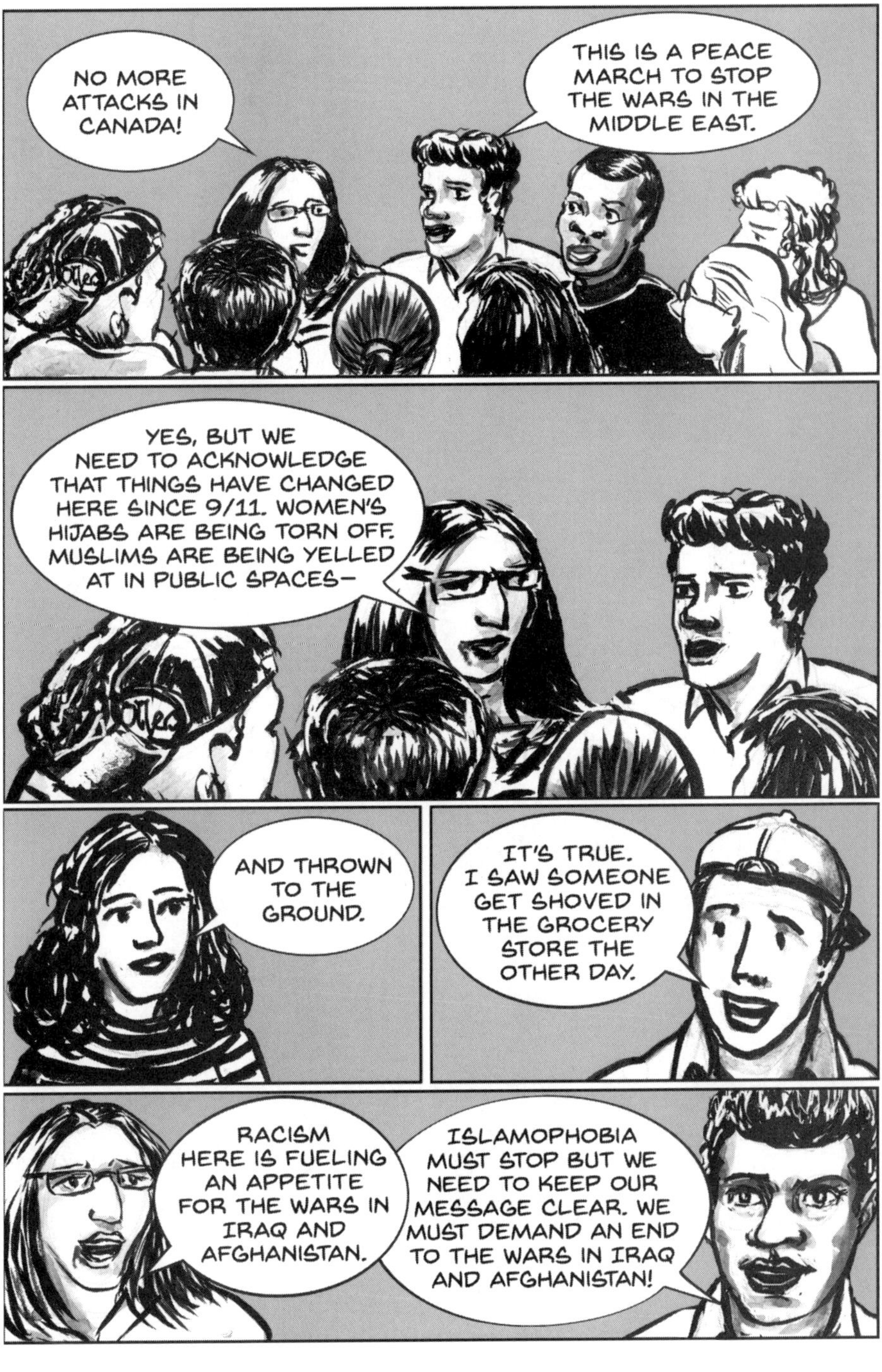
NO MORE ATTACKS IN CANADA!
THIS IS A PEACE MARCH TO STOP THE WARS IN THE MIDDLE EAST.
YES, BUT WE NEED TO ACKNOWLEDGE THAT THINGS HAVE CHANGED HERE SINCE 9/11. WOMEN'S HIJABS ARE BEING TORN OFF. MUSLIMS ARE BEING YELLED AT IN PUBLIC SPACES—
AND THROWN TO THE GROUND.
IT'S TRUE. I SAW SOMEONE GET SHOVED IN THE GROCERY STORE THE OTHER DAY.
RACISM HERE IS FUELING AN APPETITE FOR THE WARS IN IRAQ AND AFGHANISTAN.
ISLAMOPHOBIA MUST STOP BUT WE NEED TO KEEP OUR MESSAGE CLEAR. WE MUST DEMAND AN END TO THE WARS IN IRAQ AND AFGHANISTAN!

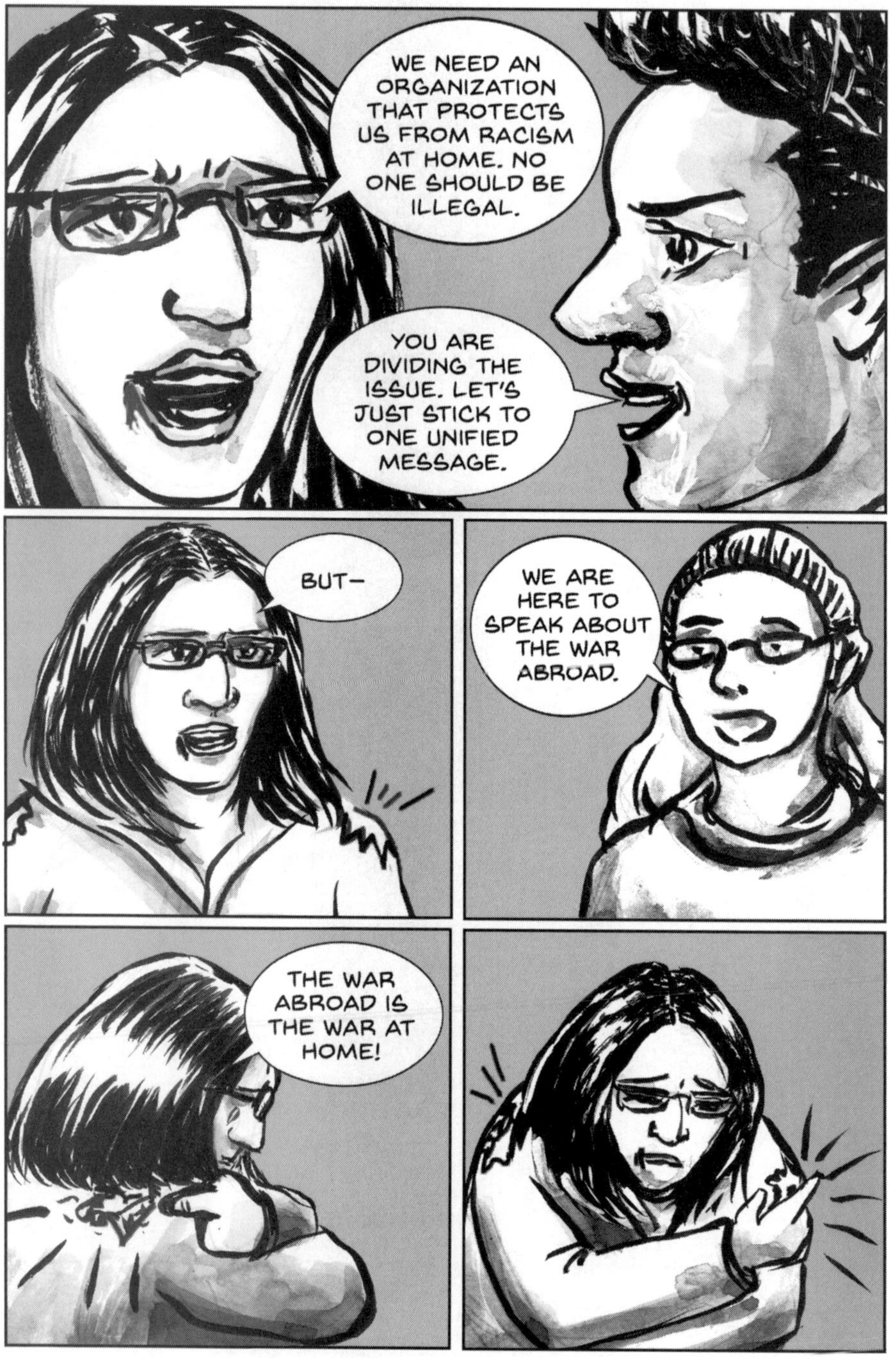
WE NEED AN ORGANIZATION THAT PROTECTS US FROM RACISM AT HOME. NO ONE SHOULD BE ILLEGAL.
YOU ARE DIVIDING THE ISSUE. LET'S JUST STICK TO ONE UNIFIED MESSAGE.
BUT–
WE ARE HERE TO SPEAK ABOUT THE WAR ABROAD.
THE WAR ABROAD IS THE WAR AT HOME!

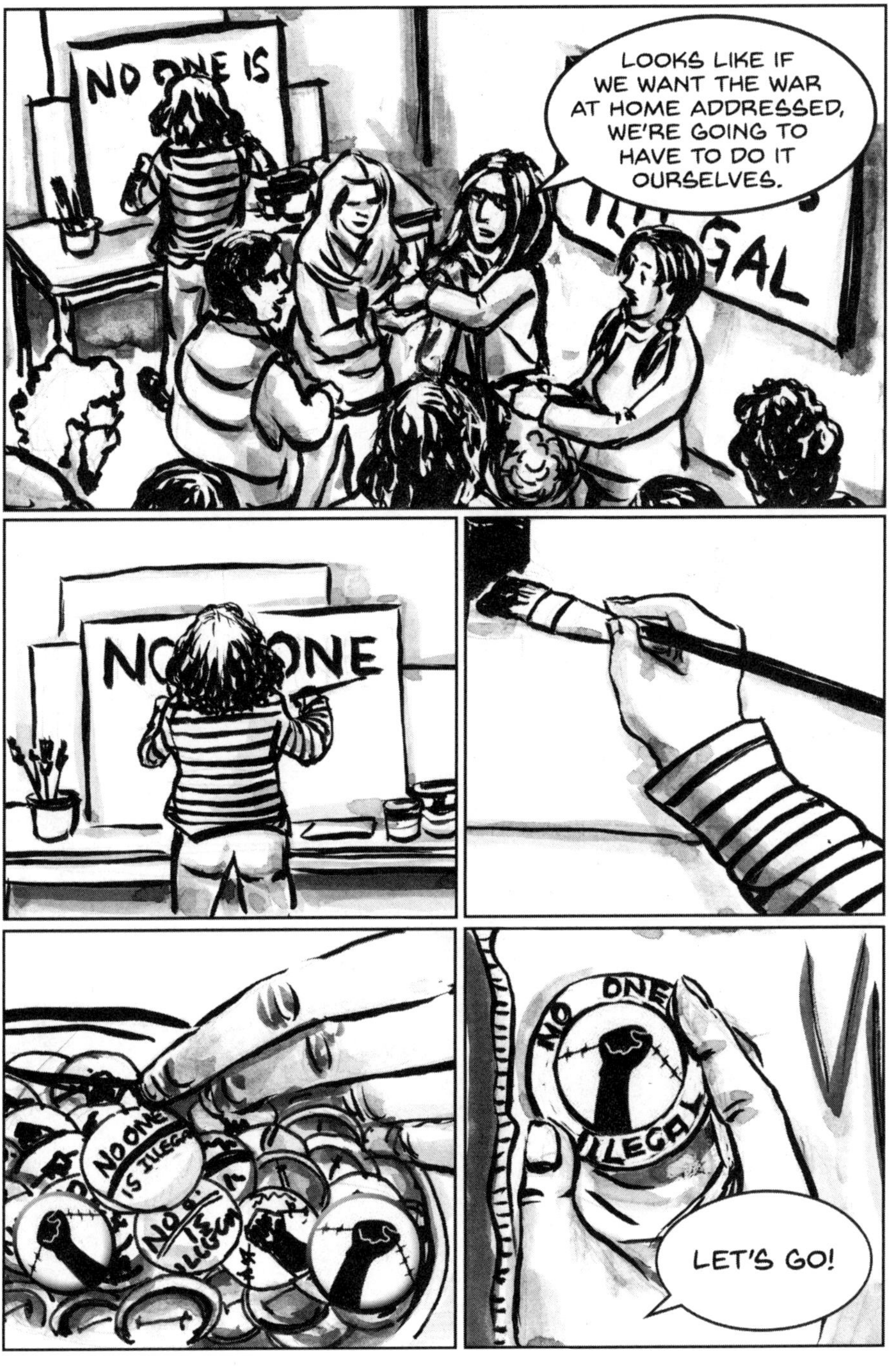
LOOKS LIKE IF WE WANT THE WAR AT HOME ADDRESSED, WE'RE GOING TO HAVE TO DO IT OURSELVES.
LET'S GO!

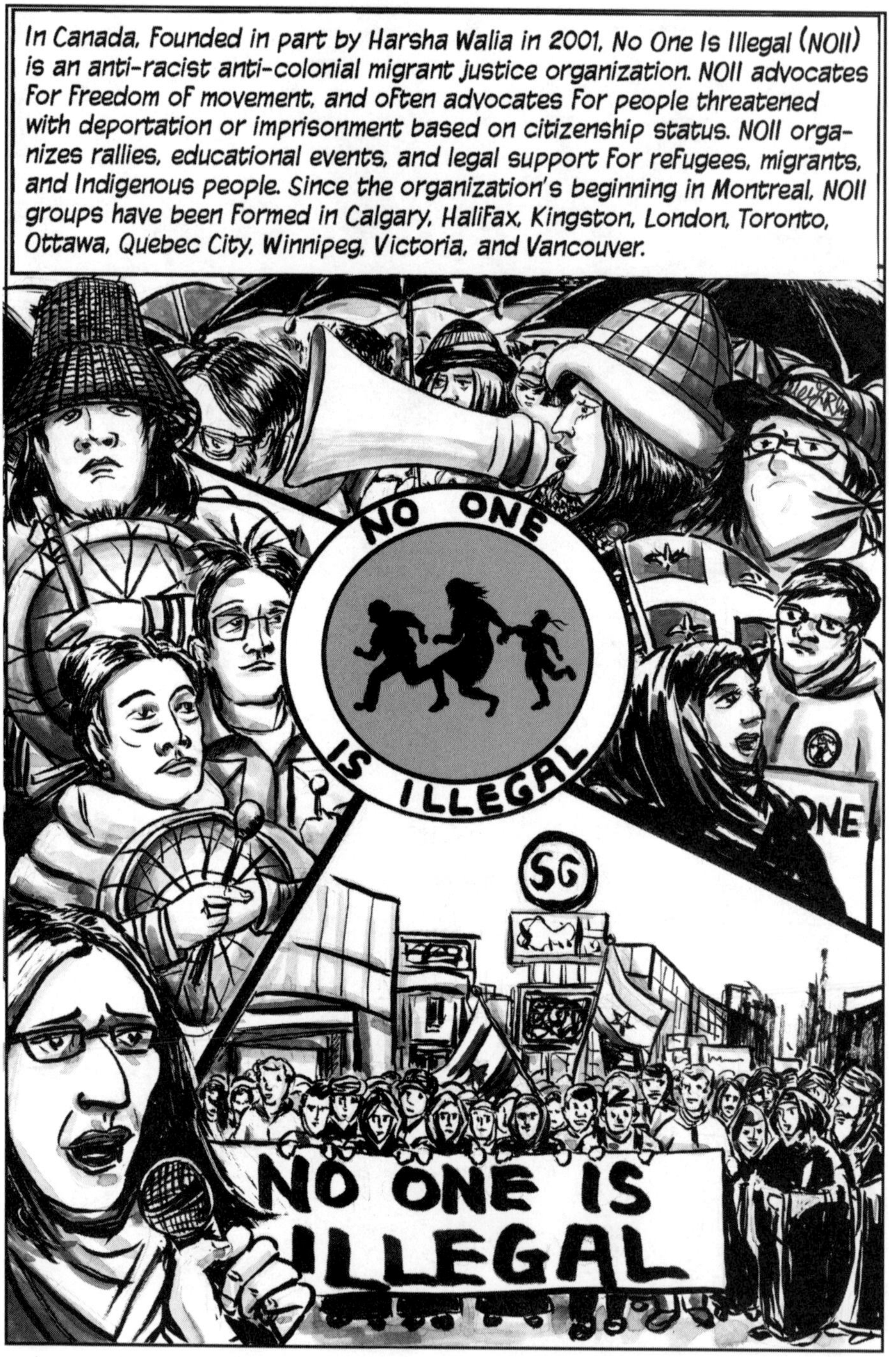
In Canada, Founded in part by Harsha Walia in 2001, No One Is Illegal (NOII) is an anti-racist anti-colonial migrant justice organization. NOII advocates For Freedom oF movement, and often advocates For people threatened with deportation or imprisonment based on citizenship status. NOII organizes rallies, educational events, and legal support For reFugees, migrants, and Indigenous people. Since the organization's beginning in Montreal, NOII groups have been Formed in Calgary, HaliFax, Kingston, London, Toronto, Ottawa, Quebec City, Winnipeg, Victoria, and Vancouver.
NO ONE IS ILLEGAL
ONE
SG
NO ONE IS ILLEGAL

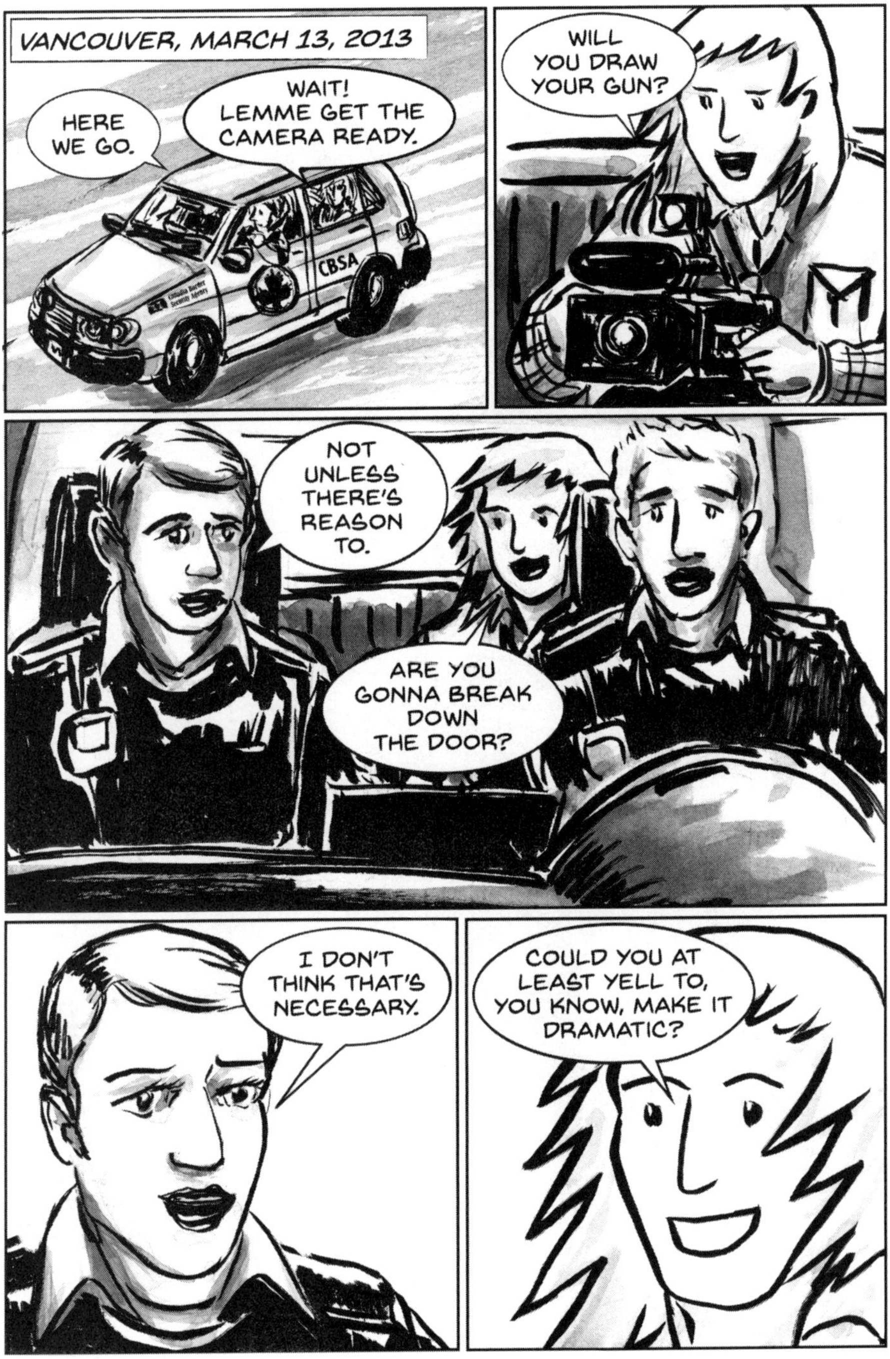
VANCOUVER, MARCH 13, 2013
HERE WE GO.
WAIT! LEMME GET THE CAMERA READY.
CBSA
WILL YOU DRAW YOUR GUN?
NOT UNLESS THERE'S REASON TO.
ARE YOU GONNA BREAK DOWN THE DOOR?
I DON'T THINK THAT'S NECESSARY.
COULD YOU AT LEAST YELL TO, YOU KNOW, MAKE IT DRAMATIC?

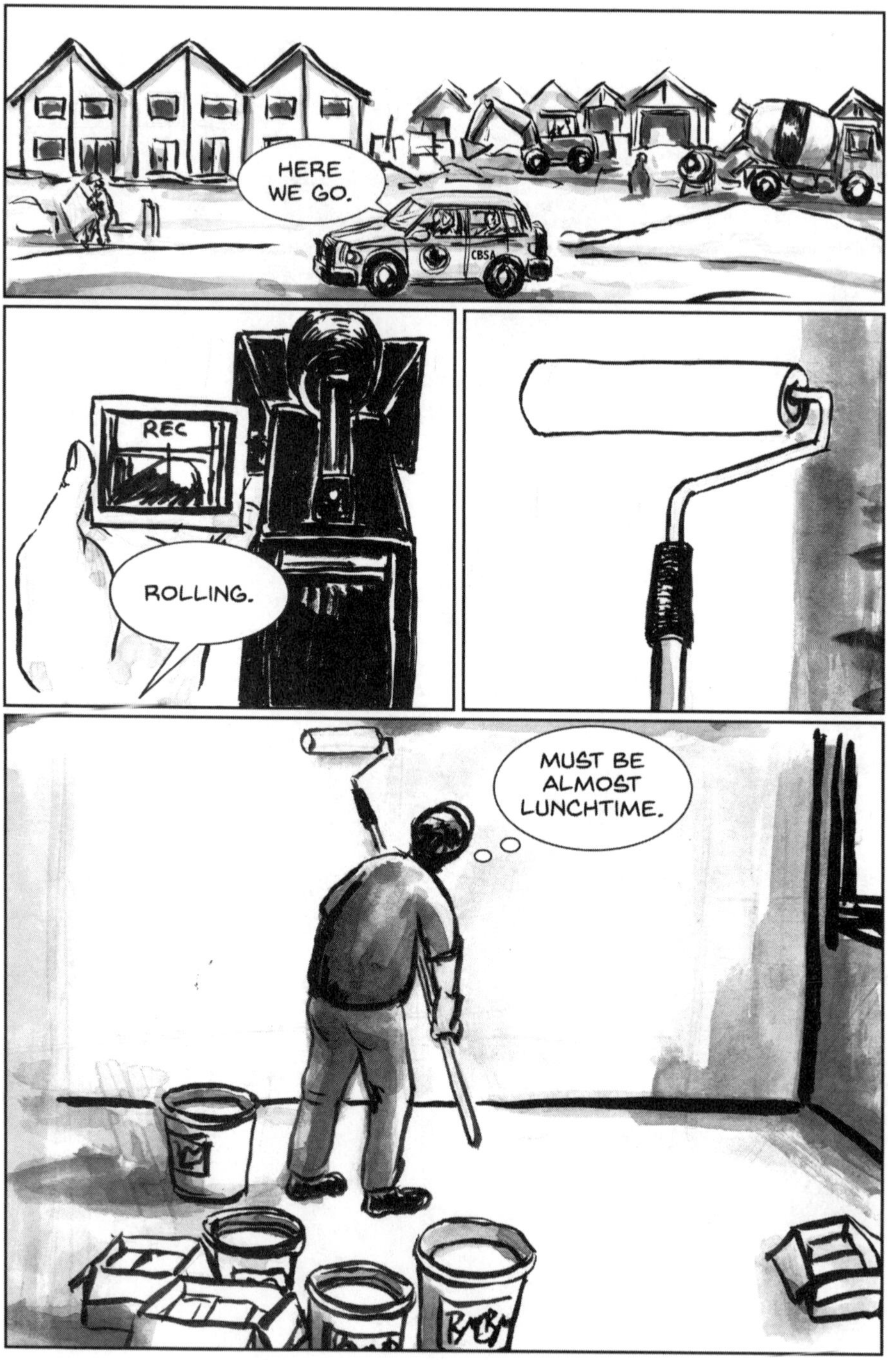
HERE WE GO.
CBSA
REC
ROLLING.
MUST BE ALMOST LUNCHTIME.

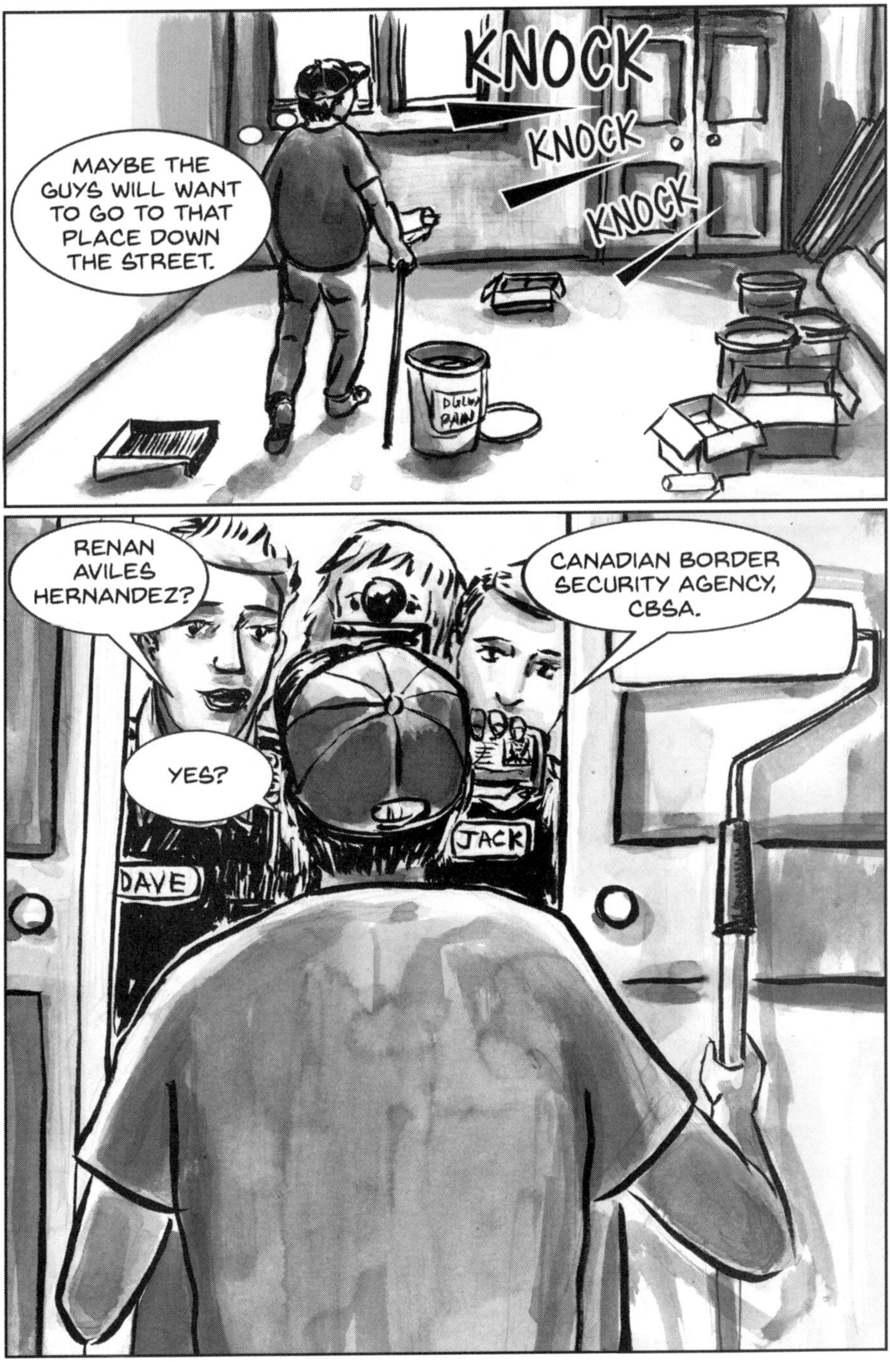
MAYBE THE GUYS WILL WANT TO GO TO THAT PLACE DOWN THE STREET.
KNOCK
KNOCK
KNOCK
RENAN AVILES HERNANDEZ?
CANADIAN BORDER SECURITY AGENCY, CBSA.
YES?
JACK
DAVE

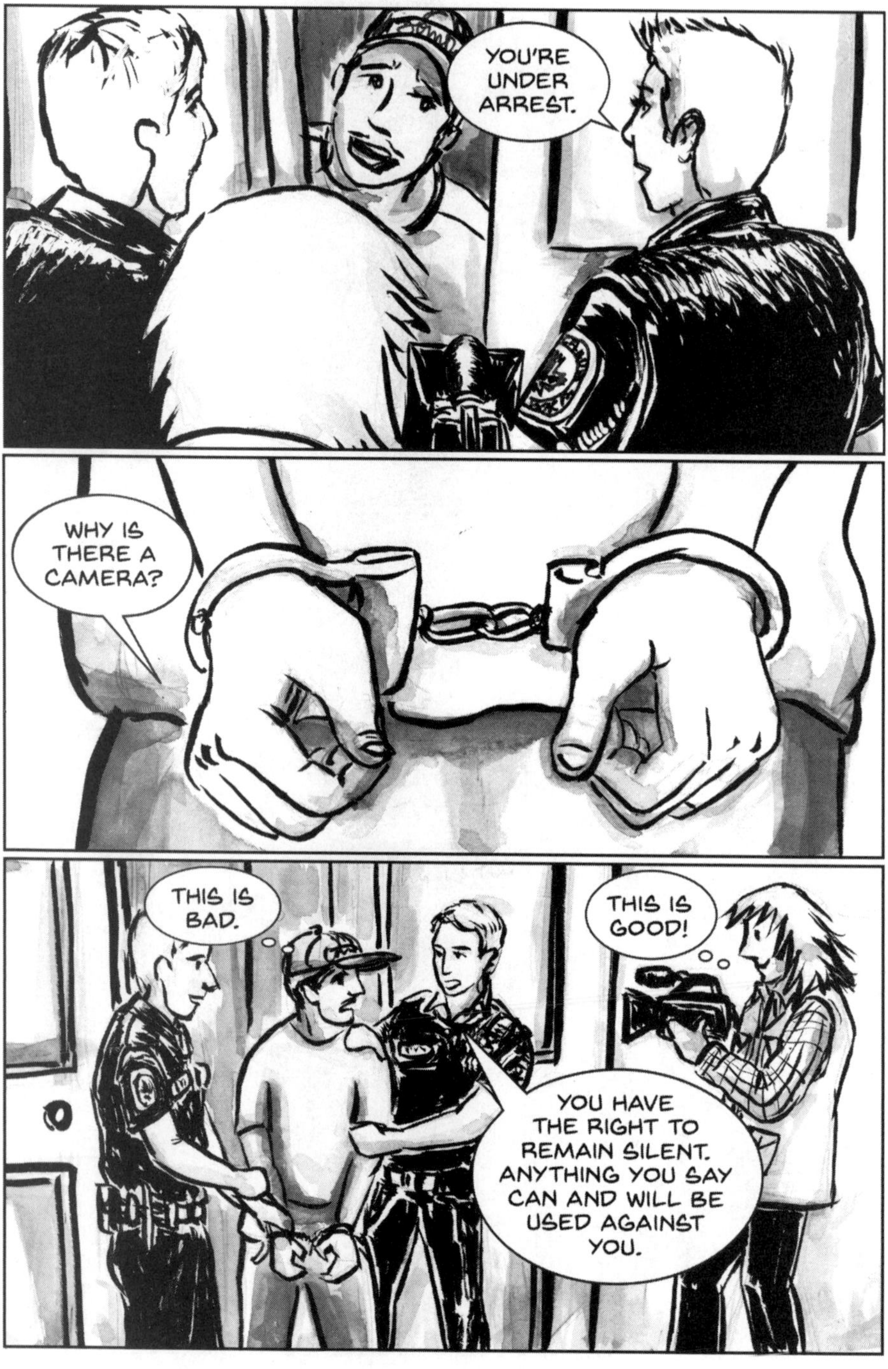
YOU'RE UNDER ARREST.
WHY IS THERE A CAMERA?
THIS IS BAD.
THIS IS GOOD!
YOU HAVE THE RIGHT TO REMAIN SILENT. ANYTHING YOU SAY CAN AND WILL BE USED AGAINST YOU.

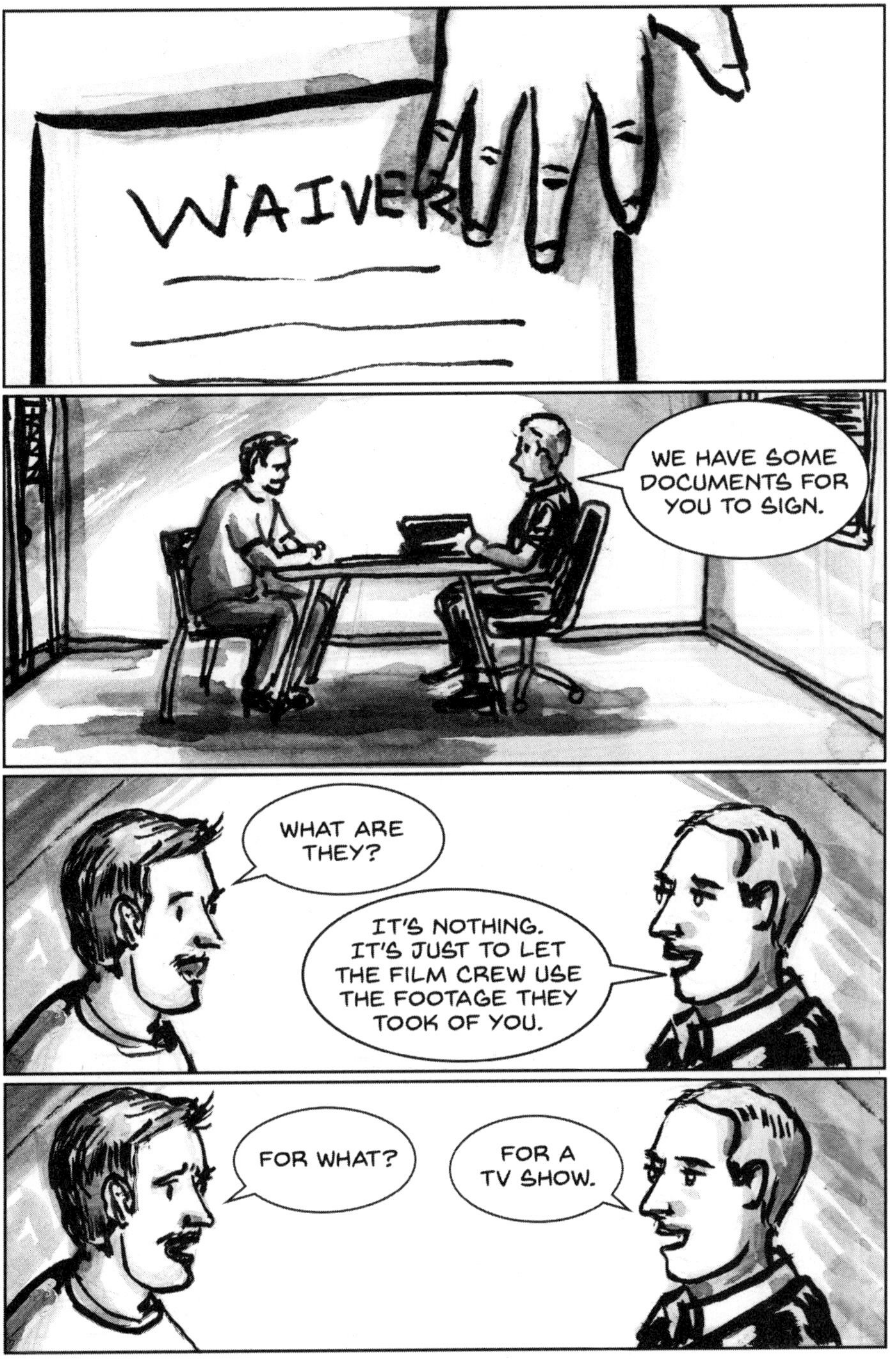
WAIVER
WE HAVE SOME DOCUMENTS FOR YOU TO SIGN.
WHAT ARE THEY?
IT'S NOTHING. IT'S JUST TO LET THE FILM CREW USE THE FOOTAGE THEY TOOK OF YOU.
FOR WHAT?
FOR A TV SHOW.

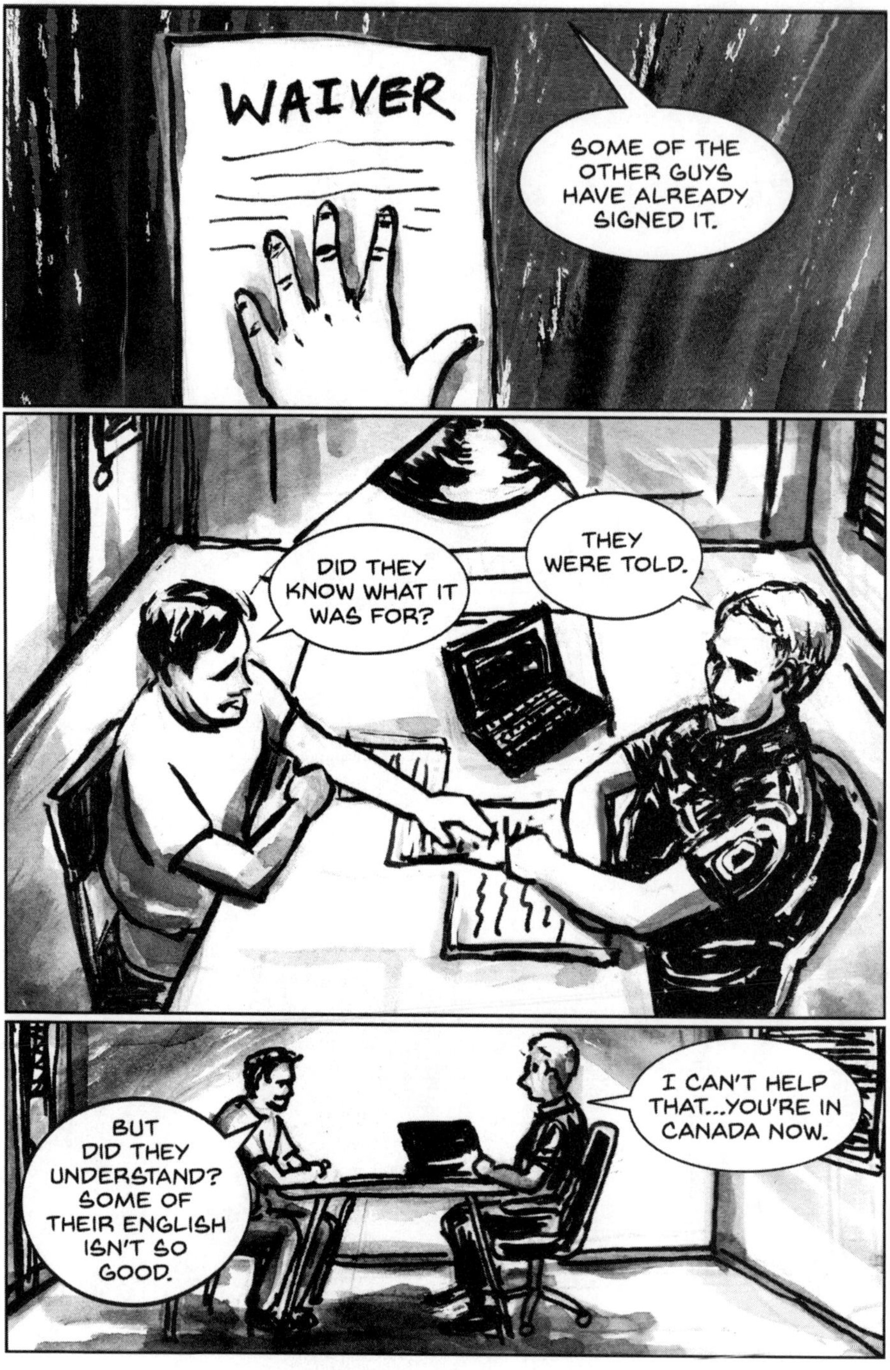
WAIVER
SOME OF THE OTHER GUYS HAVE ALREADY SIGNED IT.
DID THEY KNOW WHAT IT WAS FOR?
THEY WERE TOLD.
BUT DID THEY UNDERSTAND? SOME OF THEIR ENGLISH ISN'T SO GOOD.
I CAN'T HELP THAT...YOU'RE IN CANADA NOW.

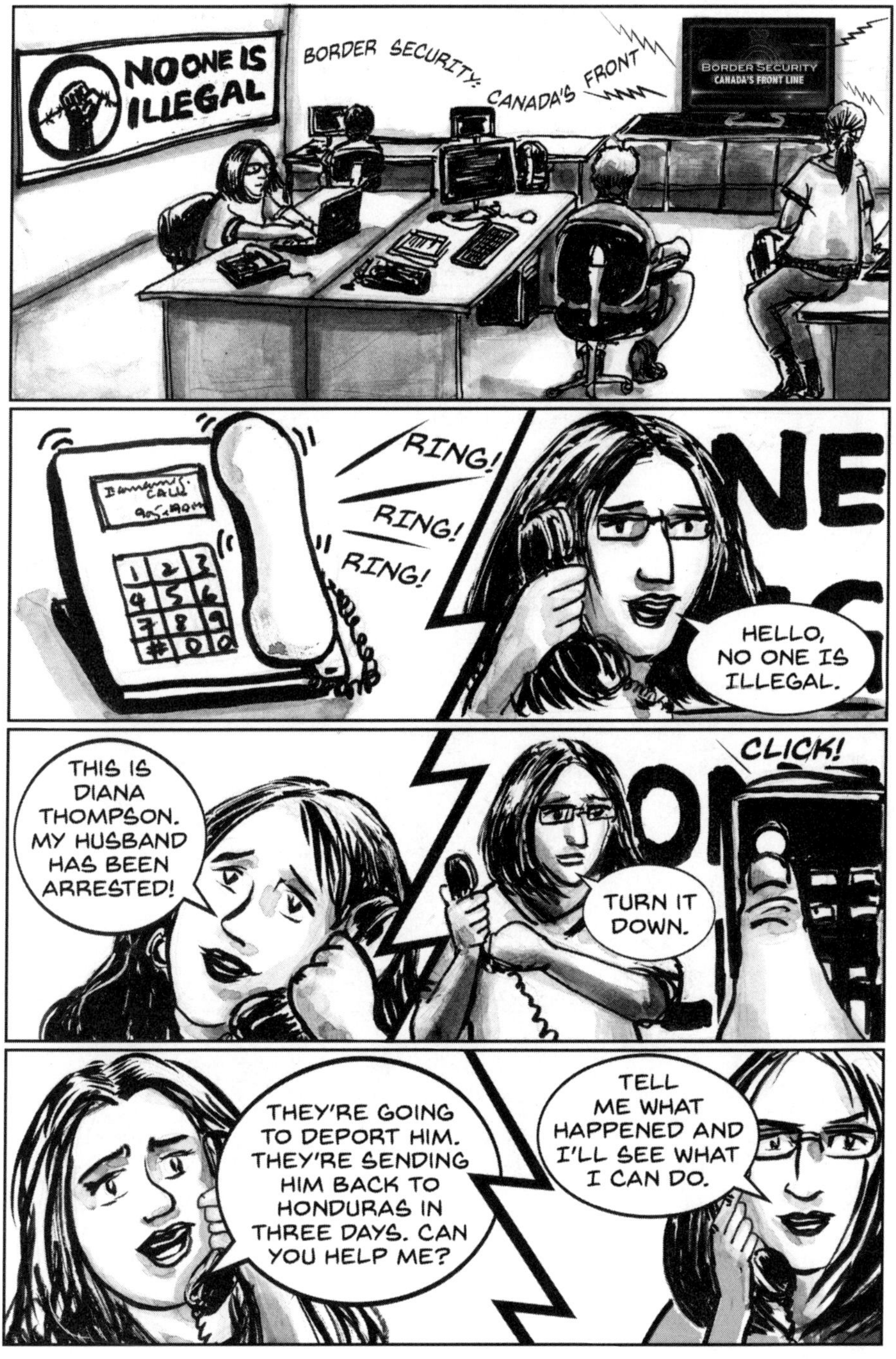
NO ONE IS ILLEGAL
BORDER SECURITY: CANADA'S FRONT
BORDER SECURITY
CANADA'S FRONT LINE
RING!
RING!
RING!
HELLO, NO ONE IS ILLEGAL.
THIS IS DIANA THOMPSON. MY HUSBAND HAS BEEN ARRESTED!
CLICK!
TURN IT DOWN.
THEY'RE GOING TO DEPORT HIM. THEY'RE SENDING HIM BACK TO HONDURAS IN THREE DAYS. CAN YOU HELP ME?
TELL ME WHAT HAPPENED AND I'LL SEE WHAT I CAN DO.

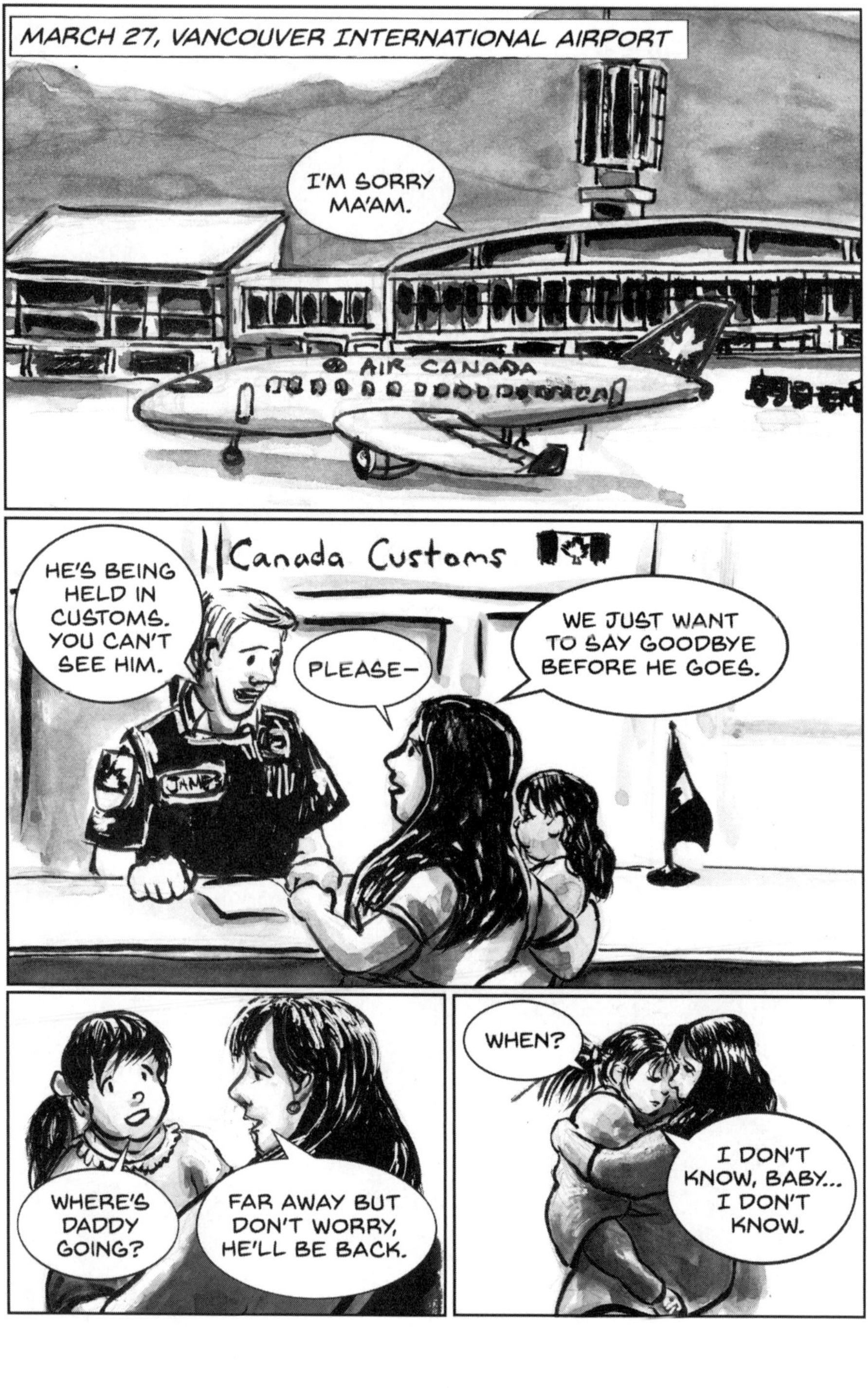

MARCH 27, VANCOUVER INTERNATIONAL AIRPORT
I'M SORRY MA'AM.
AIR CANADA
Canada Customs
HE'S BEING HELD IN CUSTOMS. YOU CAN'T SEE HIM.
PLEASE-
WE JUST WANT TO SAY GOODBYE BEFORE HE GOES.
WHERE'S DADDY GOING?
FAR AWAY BUT DON'T WORRY, HE'LL BE BACK.
WHEN?
I DON'T KNOW, BABY... I DON'T KNOW.

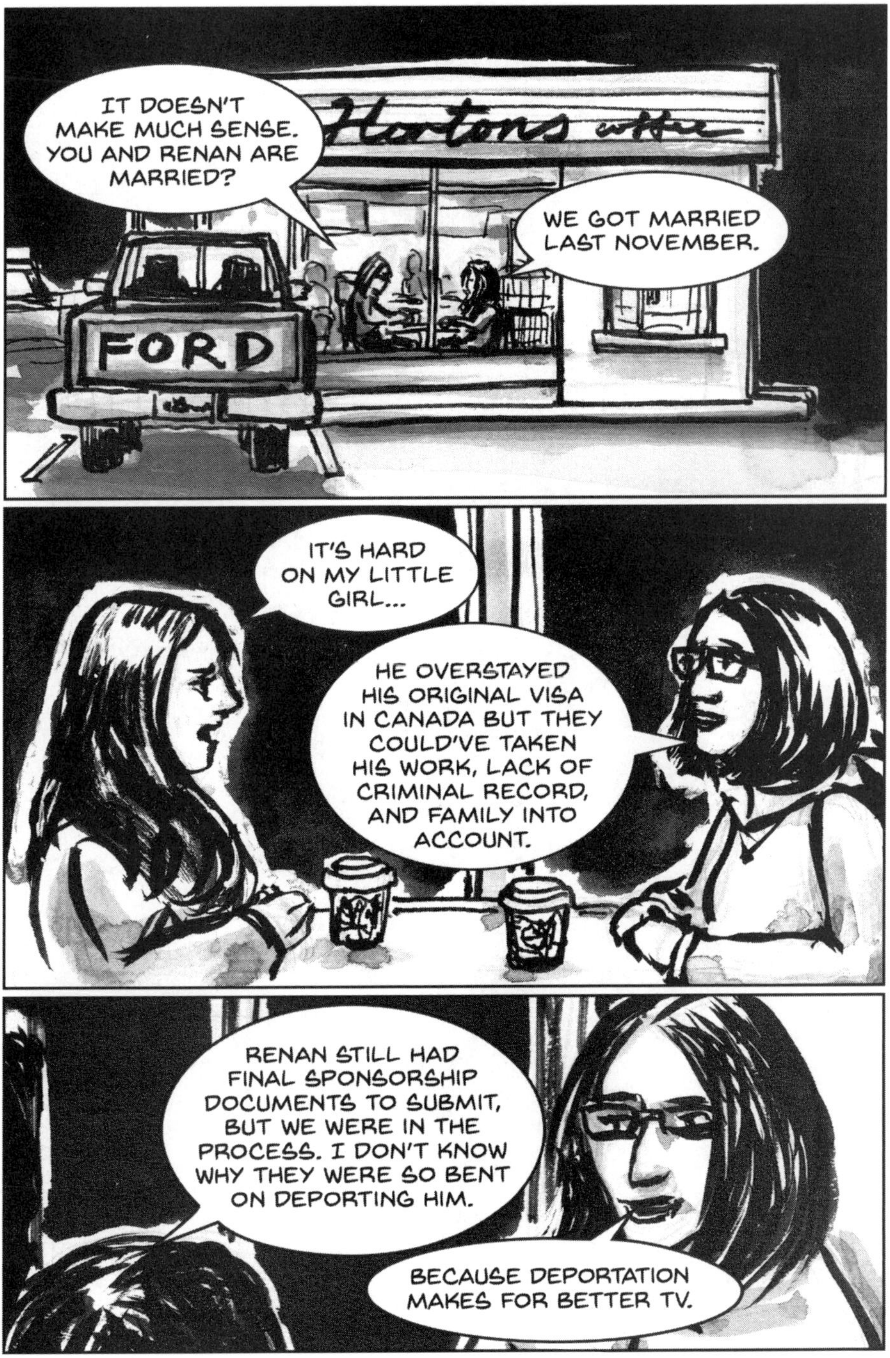
IT DOESN'T MAKE MUCH SENSE. YOU AND RENAN ARE MARRIED?
WE GOT MARRIED LAST NOVEMBER.
FORD
IT'S HARD ON MY LITTLE GIRL...
HE OVERSTAYED HIS ORIGINAL VISA IN CANADA BUT THEY COULD'VE TAKEN HIS WORK, LACK OF CRIMINAL RECORD, AND FAMILY INTO ACCOUNT.
RENAN STILL HAD FINAL SPONSORSHIP DOCUMENTS TO SUBMIT, BUT WE WERE IN THE PROCESS. I DON'T KNOW WHY THEY WERE SO BENT ON DEPORTING HIM.
BECAUSE DEPORTATION MAKES FOR BETTER TV.

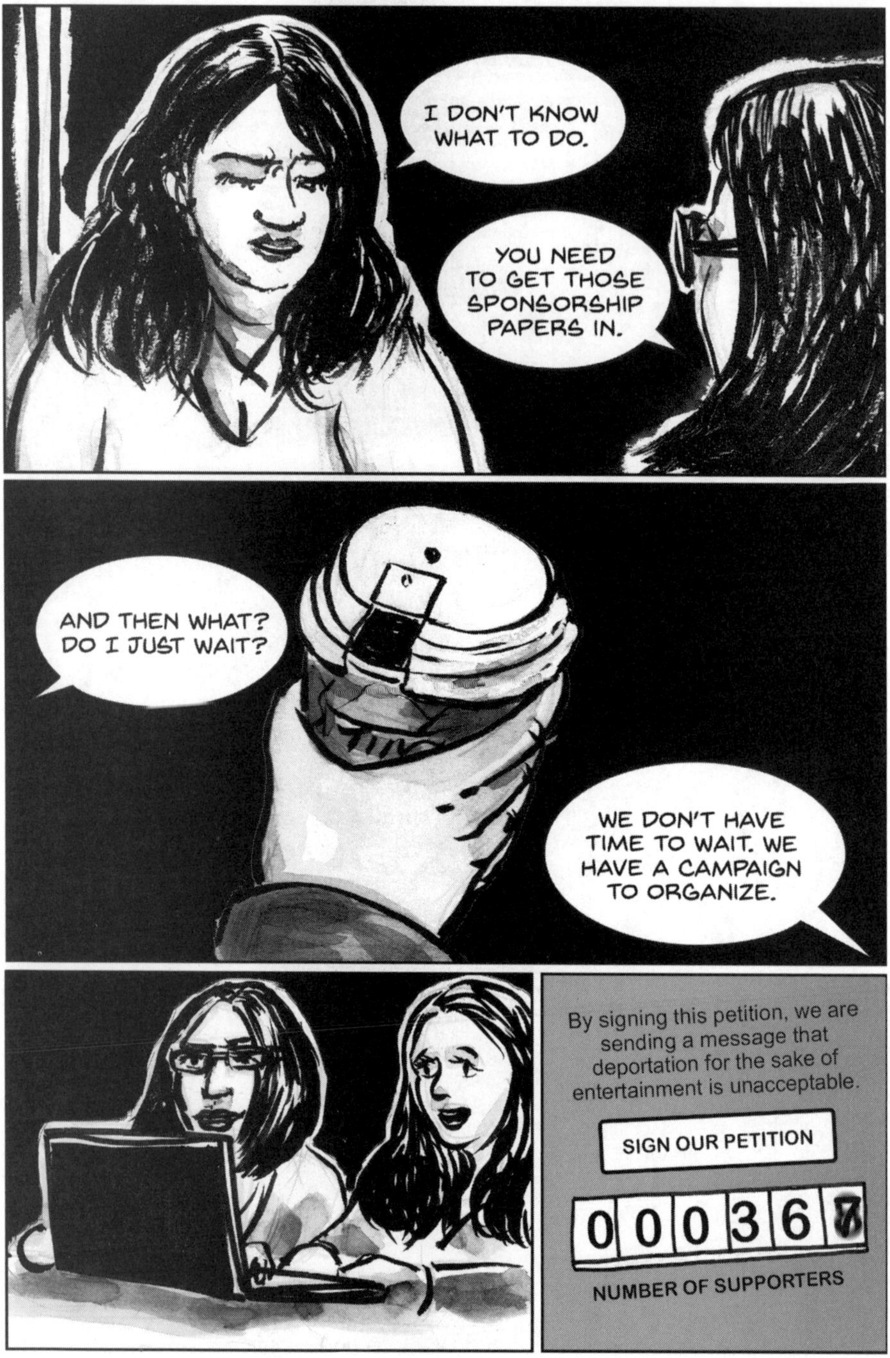
I DON'T KNOW WHAT TO DO.
YOU NEED TO GET THOSE SPONSORSHIP PAPERS IN.
AND THEN WHAT? DO I JUST WAIT?
WE DON'T HAVE TIME TO WAIT. WE HAVE A CAMPAIGN TO ORGANIZE.
By signing this petition, we are sending a message that deportation for the sake of entertainment is unacceptable.
SIGN OUR PETITION
000367
NUMBER OF SUPPORTERS

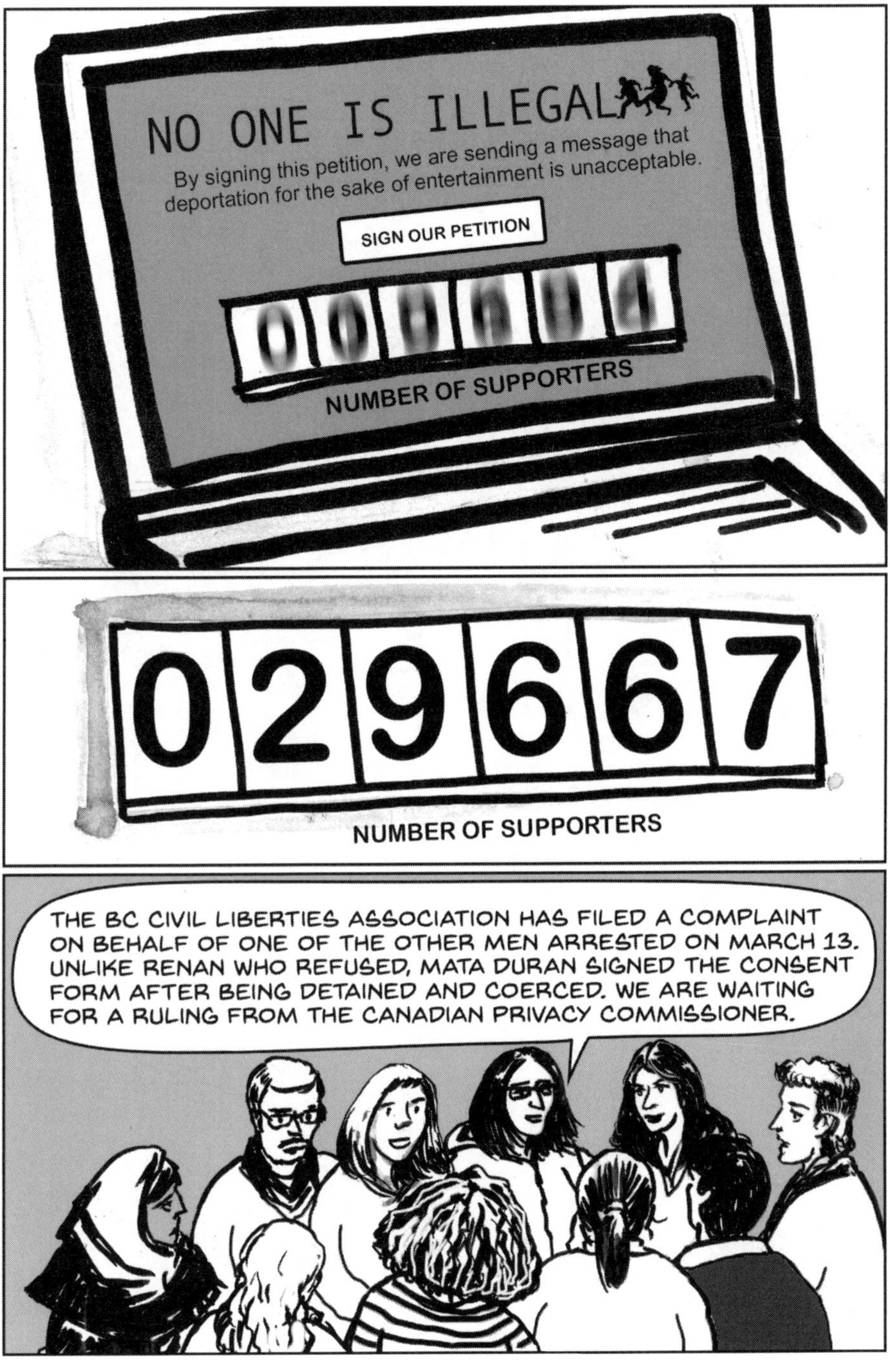
NO ONE IS ILLEGAL
By signing this petition, we are sending a message that deportation for the sake of entertainment is unacceptable.
SIGN OUR PETITION
NUMBER OF SUPPORTERS
029667
NUMBER OF SUPPORTERS
THE BC CIVIL LIBERTIES ASSOCIATION HAS FILED A COMPLAINT ON BEHALF OF ONE OF THE OTHER MEN ARRESTED ON MARCH 13. UNLIKE RENAN WHO REFUSED, MATA DURAN SIGNED THE CONSENT FORM AFTER BEING DETAINED AND COERCED. WE ARE WAITING FOR A RULING FROM THE CANADIAN PRIVACY COMMISSIONER.

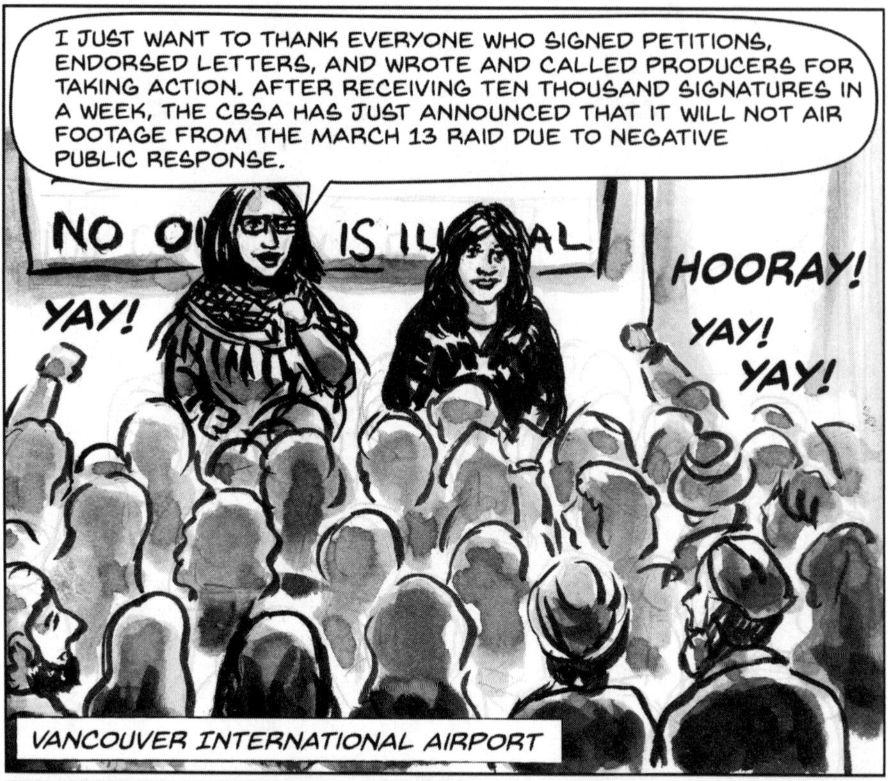
I JUST WANT TO THANK EVERYONE WHO SIGNED PETITIONS, ENDORSED LETTERS, AND WROTE AND CALLED PRODUCERS FOR TAKING ACTION. AFTER RECEIVING TEN THOUSAND SIGNATURES IN A WEEK, THE CBSA HAS JUST ANNOUNCED THAT IT WILL NOT AIR FOOTAGE FROM THE MARCH 13 RAID DUE TO NEGATIVE PUBLIC RESPONSE.
YAY!
HOORAY!
YAY!
YAY!
VANCOUVER INTERNATIONAL AIRPORT

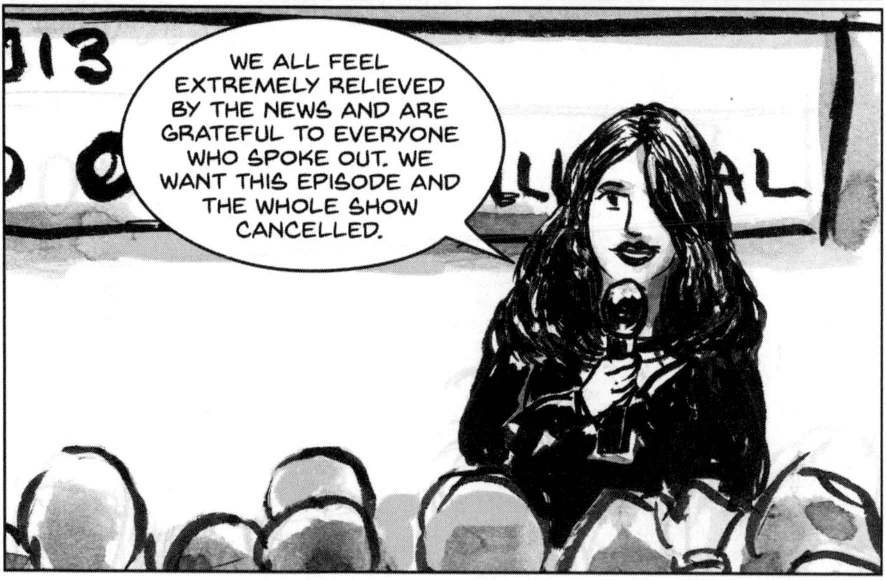
WE ALL FEEL EXTREMELY RELIEVED BY THE NEWS AND ARE GRATEFUL TO EVERYONE WHO SPOKE OUT. WE WANT THIS EPISODE AND THE WHOLE SHOW CANCELLED.

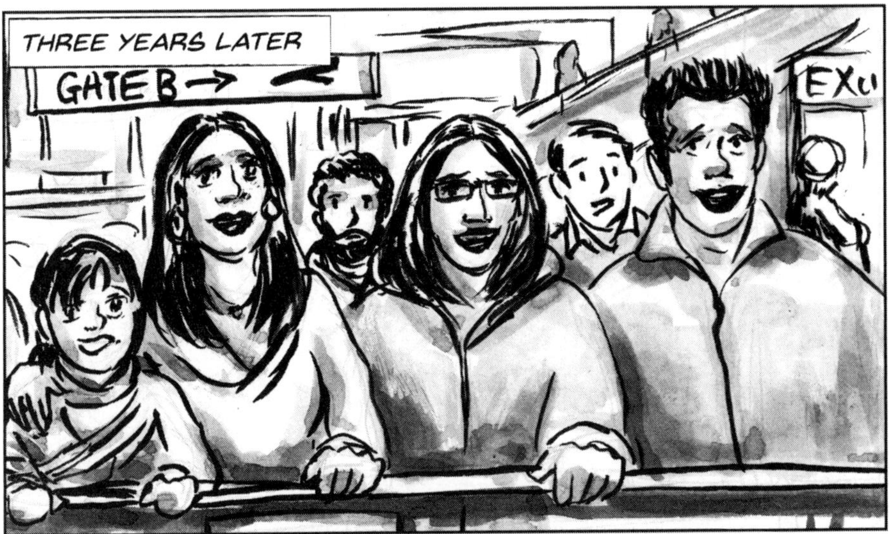
THREE YEARS LATER
GATE B →

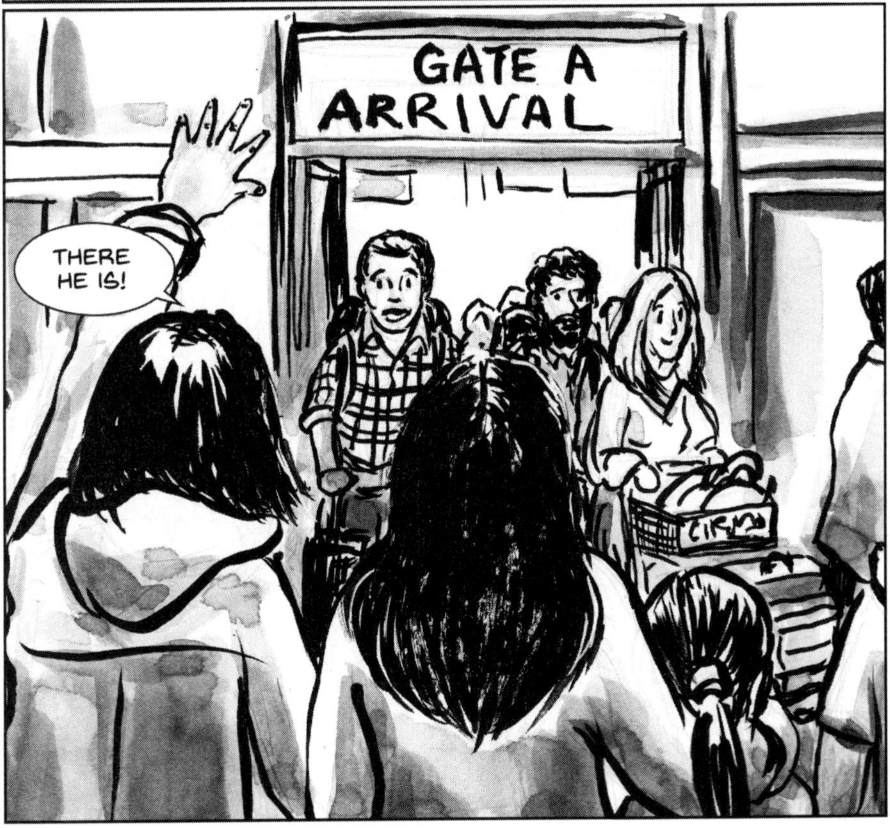
GATE A
ARRIVAL
THERE HE IS!

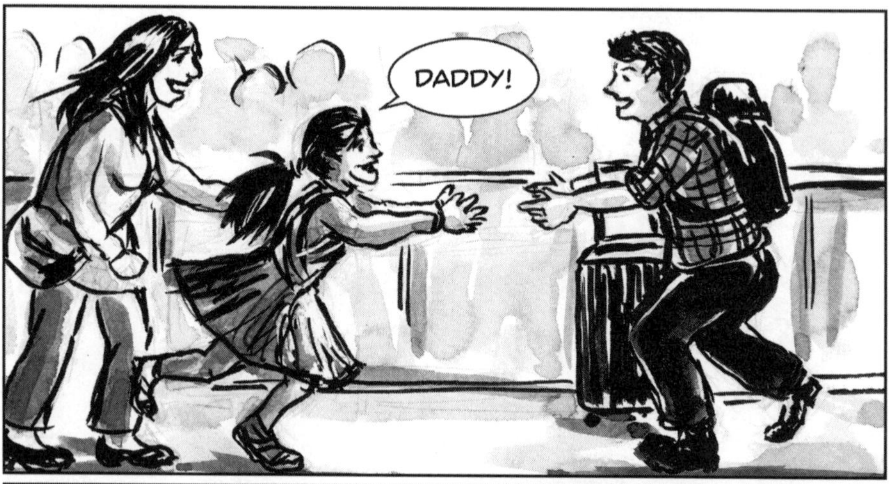
DADDY!

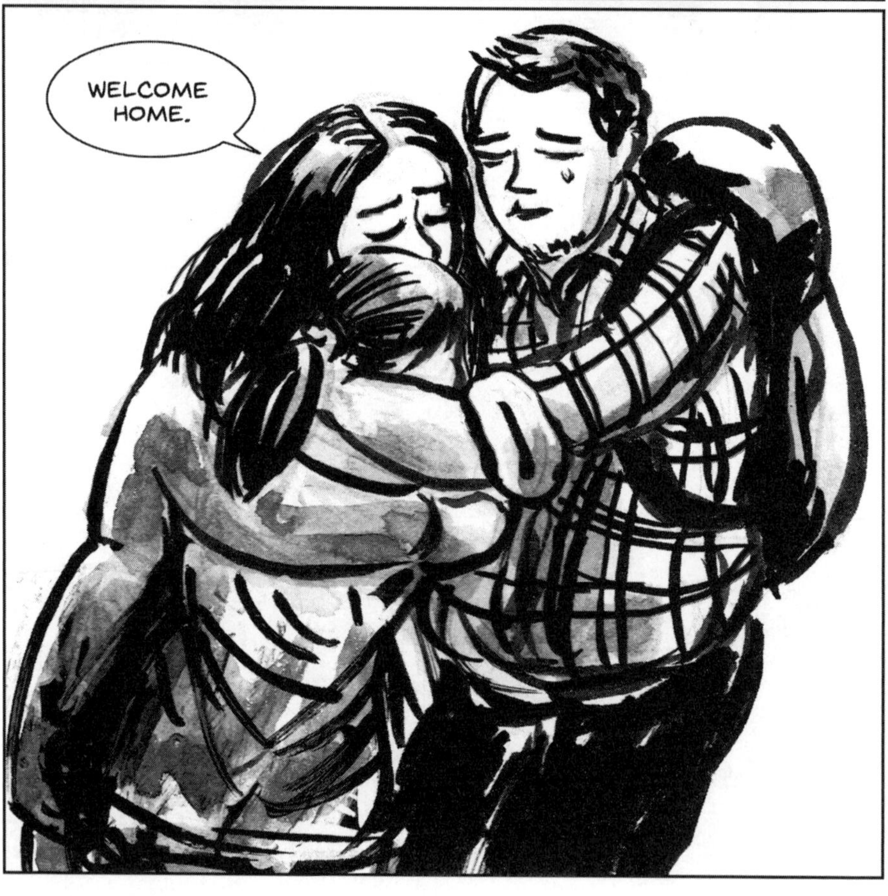
WELCOME HOME.

Harsha Walia was less than twenty years old when she and a group of fellow activists in Montreal started the anti-racist group that became Canada's No One Is Illegal (NOII). In the context of the early 2000s anti-globalization peace movement, Walia and her friends called for action against racism and Islamophobia at home in Canada; they were met with resistance from fellow activists who didn't share Walia's more holistic, fundamental view of the issues. Now active in Canada in seven cities, NOII has supported thousands of people in their struggle for justice in the immigration, border control, and citizenship systems. Their struggle is for the right to remain, the right to leave, and the right to return; Harsha Walia and NOII argue that the right to mobility without harassment is a fundamental freedom.

Today, people moving across borders face increased surveillance, questioning, and sometimes dehumanizing treatment. Intersectional feminist analysis considers ways in which people experience multiple, overlapping, and intersecting oppressions and privileges. People who cross borders often have their oppressions and privileges magnified by way of their passport; gender, racialization, ethnicity, and citizenship are scrutinized, and from this scrutiny a state may assign or withhold an element or degree of freedom and dignity. Advocacy at borders is intersectional advocacy in a place meant to symbolize state power.

For Walia, feminist work is a constant ethical practice of questioning her own relationship to power. The questions Walia brings to social justice organizing create an atmosphere moving towards kinship, community, and inclusivity, and moving away from rigidity and exclusion. That means that NOII advocates for the rights of migrant workers, refugees, and Indigenous people in their respective struggles for mobility and justice within the structure of the state.

Since 2005 Walia has been working at the Vancouver Downtown Eastside Women's Centre, an urban service hub that assists more than 500 people a day. Feminist activism is her daily practice. In her work at the Women's Centre, her organizing for NOII, and in her academic writing, Walia expresses her interest in contradictions. Social justice movements exist in the societies they struggle to change, and even a feminist anti-racist organization needs to reflect on its own structure.

White supremacy and patriarchy, Walia says, are not abstract, but are forms of direct oppression that combine and compound contradictions, and their presence is evident even within activist communities as a type of collateral damage, sometimes referred to as *lateral violence*. Just as Walia's critique of the anti-globalization movement led to the formation of NOII, ongoing critique of activist movements can lead to more inclusive, more imaginative ways of building a better world. Dating back to the time of her early work in Montreal in 2001, Harsha Walia's habit of questioning her own movement, calling for a smarter, more resilient, and more inclusive vision, continues today.

Discussion Questions

1 What different kinds of organizing and resistance actions did Harsha Walia take part in?
2 How did the other peace group activists in Montreal react when Harsha Walia and her friend tried to convince them to address racism in Canada? Why do you think they reacted in such a way?
3 What did the reality TV show on law enforcement try to film, and why? How did Harsha Walia and NOII react to the show, and what was the outcome of this reaction?

Research Questions and Activities

1 Research the anti-globalization movement of the early 2000s. Consider the record of involvement and influence of feminist, anti-fascist, and anti-racist organizers in that movement, and compare it to news coverage or other information you find about social justice organizing today.

2 Lateral violence is harassment and violence between peers who should otherwise be aligned against other oppressive structures. It is difficult to address because the actors are supposed to be on the same side. Find research about lateral violence in anti-racist and feminist organizing. What are some of the recommended strategies for resolving lateral violence, and why do you think they are necessary to feminist anti-racist activism?

3 Are there people in your community who are criminalized because of their citizenship status? Find out which organizations provide support for immigrants, refugees, or migrants, and compare their support to the kind of supports NOII provides. You can find out more about NOII online.

Further Reading

Anzaldua, Gloria. *Borderlands: The New Mestiza*. San Francisco: Aunt Lute Books, 2012.

Stierl, Maurice. "'No One Is Illegal!' Resistance and the Politics of Discomfort." *Globalizations* 9.3 (June 2012): 425–38.

Walia, Harsha. *Undoing Border Imperialism*. Washington, DC: AK Press, 2013.

CONCLUSION

The stories you have read in this book are but short vignettes of resistance. As this book goes to print, we continue to learn about women, men, and non-binary people around the world organizing for justice. Non-binary people continue to struggle to access justice and freedom at borders, in the courts, and in schools. The backlash to feminism takes on new forms on the internet and in popular culture. While intersectional feminist analysis is taught in many classrooms around the world, there is a growing movement to re-entrench binary gender roles and strict, oppressive rules of gender behavior. In Canada and the United States, conservative politicians are cancelling progressive sex education and replacing it with abstinence-only education, without providing information about consent and same-sex relationships. And even in the wake of the #MeToo movement, women standing up against workplace sexual harassment in business, academia, and film are still not always believed, and often face ridicule. Migrant women continue to struggle against poverty, racism, and violence. Parents advocating for their transgender children at schools often face vitriolic remarks in person and online. These are only some examples of progressive movements being under attack from sexist, racist, ableist, homophobic, transphobic forces of oppression.

Backlash to advancements for gender equality is nothing new. When black women in the United States organized for their rights in the late 1800s, when suffragettes organized for the right to vote, and when Indigenous women in Canada protested against murdered and missing Indigenous women there were angry responses. And yet, backlash to feminist justice comes largely from fear. Some people are afraid that if one group has rights, another group loses rights; this politics of scarcity is unfounded, but is emotionally convincing. This panicked and illogical notion that liberation is a finite resource is circulated every time a group advocates for rights and freedom. Those of us who struggle for liberation, who stand up for justice and equality know that when it comes to the right to vote, the right to security and safety, the right to fair pay, and the right to freedom of movement, there is enough liberation for all of us.

The other fear that fuels backlash is the fear of social instability. For example, anti-feminists have long argued that if women wear pants, go to work, gain access to birth control, gain the right to become lawyers, and so on, then men will lose hold of their masculinity and the entire system of family and nation will become undone. The gender order is held up as unassailable and an essential social structure, and the backlash movement against feminism positions itself as a defender of social stability. In this case, the fear of social change is not entirely unfounded. Gender and sexuality freedom does indeed lead to a different type of family and a different nation. It creates new relationships and communities, but with the goal of addressing and reducing sources of division and anger. Feminist liberation has led to more inclusivity and personal fulfillment inside and outside the family. Same-sex and single-parent families are just as loving and dedicated as traditional families, and access to birth control and reproductive health leads to healthier, more prosperous communities.

Yet the fear of change is real and the backlash to feminist organizing can be frightening. The authors of this book are not naive; we acknowledge the courage and heart it takes to be part of social justice organizing in the early twenty-first century. In your own classroom, find out who among you has been part of community organizing. Find out who has experienced racism, ableism, sexism, or homophobia. Find out what skills you have that could contribute to greater solidarity – it could be as simple as starting an anti-racist feminist conversation group. Once you start talking and listening, you may find your capacity to resist oppression is greater as part of a group than on your own. Together you can plan and enact your own feminist resistance actions.

We offer this book in solidarity. The stories told here are varied, and some demonstrate forms of resistance that may extend beyond those forms of legal, peaceful organizing you may wish to organize. Pay attention to the relationships built by the activists represented in this book. Ultimately, political change occurs through relationships. In future research about feminist resistance, the process of moving a dream to action should be studied as a process of collective imagination and the communication of that imagined dream. Through collective political action, as well as through music, videos, social media, literature, books, and the arts, feminists share solidarity and dreams for a better world.

GLOSSARY

Capitalism: A system in which production, trade, industry, labor, and wealth are controlled and owned by private interests rather than by the state.

Colonialism: Systematic, forced occupation of an already occupied place or territory for the purpose of economic exploitation of the resources and people of the place or territory, with profit flowing to the colonial center rather than to the original inhabitants of the place or territory.

Decolonization: The process of undoing colonial economic, cultural, political, geographic, legal, and cultural authority over a colonized people and land.

Direct action: Organized collective social resistance that directly and publicly confronts a location, agent, or event of oppression. Protest, marches, boycotts, blockades, and rallies are examples of direct action.

Feminist resistance: The process of taking a radically imaginative feminist vision and working to put it into action in contemporary society.

Gender expression: The representation or communication of gender identity.

Gender identity: Culturally located, individually expressed, relational identity position based on masculinity, femininity, or other genders.

Grassroots: Organizing for social change that begins with and is informed by, led by, and created for people living directly with the consequences of the effects of that social change.

Heteronormativity: The expectation, expressed in media, science, cultural messages, and individual encounters, that people be heterosexual (i.e., "straight"), will perform straight normative gender roles, and will strive to succeed in these straight normative expectations.

Intersectional feminism: A form of feminism that recognizes overlapping, mutually reinforcing, and uniquely configured oppressions and privileges such as race, class, sexuality, age, and ability, and thus calls for appropriately thoughtful and flexible feminist analysis and activism.

Lateral violence: Harassment and/or violence between peers who should otherwise be aligned against other oppressive structures.

Neoliberalism: An economic and social philosophy in which the deregulation of trade, privatization of state assets, and reduction of social welfare and support programs are seen as morally good. Property rights and the freedom of market trade are valued above individual or community rights and freedoms.

Non-binary gender identity: A gender identity that is fluid, or that takes a third position that may include some alignment with feminine and masculine identity, or that takes on a creative gender identity unique to the individual.

Oppression: Systematic or individual disempowerment of a group of people or individuals. This may involve limiting the freedom and access of a group of people based on an externally stereotyped identity, or it may involve individual attacks on people based on their real or assumed membership with a stereotyped group identity.

Propaganda of the deed: Specific political action meant to be exemplary to others and serve as a catalyst for revolution.

Queer: A term once used as a slur against gay or lesbian men and women, now mostly used as either a celebratory term for the LGBTQIIA community or to describe a gender or sexual identity that is non-conforming in regard to heteronormative binary standards.

Racialization: The process through which a group of people may be categorized as *other* than the group doing the categorizing, and then treated inequitably. This racialized group differentiation may be based on perceptions of shared religion, ethnicity, appearance, language, or culture.

Radical inclusion: The process by which diverse groups – some of which are often excluded from political action (such as people with disabilities, the incarcerated, and the very young) – come together over time to contribute to social change.

Rape culture: Cultural practices that make light of, celebrate, or accommodate non-consensual sexual activity, sometimes by mocking and humiliating women and queer people, and sometimes by assuming that men are naturally libidinous, violent, and not responsible for their sexual behavior.

Resistance: A position and practice that does not acquiesce to political or social expectations, norms, rules, or structures. Resistance may be personal or collective and is expressed through a range of actions, including art, speech, direct action, electoral intervention, education, violence, solidarity, and civil disobedience.

Settler colonialism: Colonialism in which the colonizing forces live permanently on and extract wealth from the colonized people's land and seek to eradicate and replace Indigenous culture and values with settler culture and values.

Solidarity: Shared strength between people working together, directly, for liberation from oppression.

Transnational feminism: Feminist practice that learns from and listens to the knowledge and capacity of feminists living in every part of the world, especially activists living in places currently colonized economically, politically, or otherwise by Western nations.

White supremacy: The inherent belief that white people and white culture are superior, and that the culture of people of color is inferior and in need of white control.

BIBLIOGRAPHY

Agoramoorthy, Govindasamy, and Minna Hsu. "Living on the Societal Edge: India's Transgender Realities." *Journal of Religion & Health* 54.4 (Aug. 2015): 1451–59.

Ahmed, Sara. "Embodying Diversity: Problems and Paradoxes for Black Feminists." *Race, Ethnicity & Education* 12.1 (March 2009): 41–52.

Ahmed, Sara. *Willful Subjects*. Durham: Duke University Press, 2014.

bandele, asha. "Kathleen Cleaver." *Essence* 34.10 (2004): 198. Academic Search Complete. Web. 11 April 2016.

Bloom, Joshua. *Black against Empire: The History and Politics of the Black Panther Party*. Berkeley: University of California Press, 2014.

Carastathis, Anna. "Identity Categories as Potential Coalitions." *Signs: Journal of Women in Culture & Society* 38.4 (Summer 2013): 941–65.

Ciszek, Erica L. "Activist Strategic Communication for Social Change: A Transnational Case Study of Lesbian, Gay, Bisexual, and Transgender Activism." *Journal of Communication* 67.5 (Oct. 2017): 702–18.

Crenhsaw, Kimberlé Williams. "Mapping the Margins: Intersectionality, Identity Politics, and Violence against Women of Color." *Stanford Law Review* 43 (1991).

Crenshaw, Kimberlé Williams. "Race Liberalism and the Deradicalization of Racial Reform." *Harvard Law Review* 130.9 (Oct. 2017): 2298–319.

Dark Star Collective, ed. *Quiet Rumours: An Anarcha-Feminist Reader*. Washington, DC: AK Press, 2012.

Davis, Angela. *The Angela Davis Reader*. Ed. Joy James. Oxford: Blackwell Publishing, 1998.

Gessen, Masha. *Words Will Break Cement: The Passion of Pussy Riot*. New York: Riverhead Books, 2013.

Hagen, Whitney B., Stephanie M. Hoover, and Susan L. Morrow. "A Grounded Theory of Sexual Minority Women and Transgender Individuals' Social Justice Activism." *Journal of Homosexuality* 65.7 (July 2018): 833–59.

hooks, bell. *Feminism Is for Everybody: Passionate Politics*. Cambridge, MA: Southend Press, 2000.

Khan-Cullors, Patrisse, and asha bandele. *When They Call You a Terrorist: A Black Lives Matter Memoir*. New York: St. Martin's Press, 2017.

Milstein, Cindy, ed. *Taking Sides: Revolutionary Solidarity and the Poverty of Liberalism*. Washington, DC: AK Press, 2015.

Perera, Suvendrini, and Sherene H. Razack, eds. *At the Limits of Justice: Women of Colour on Terror*. Toronto: University of Toronto Press, 2014.

Platt, Tony. "Interview with Angela Davis." *Social Justice* 40.1–2 (Jan. 2013).

Rohrer, Judy. "'We Say Code Pink': Feminist Direct Action and the 'War on Terror.'" *Feminism and War: Confronting U.S. Imperialism*, Chandra T. Mohanty, Minnie Bruce Pratt, and Robin Riley, eds. London: Zed Press, 2008, 224–31.

Shakur, Assata. *Assata: An Autobiography*. Chicago: Lawrence Hill Books, 2001.

"'Stay Outraged': A Conversation with Masha Gessen." *World Policy Journal* 34.1 (Spring 2017): 55–59.

Taylor, Keeanga-Yamahtta, ed. *How We Get Free: Black Feminism and the Combahee River Collective*. Chicago: Haymarket Books, 2017.

Walia, Harsha. "Transient Servitude: Migrant Labour in Canada and the Apartheid of Citizenship." *Race & Class* 52.1 (July 2010): 71–84.

Walia, Harsha. *Undoing Border Imperialism*. Washington, DC: AK Press, 2013.

Wiedlack, Katharina. "Pussy Riot and the Western Gaze: Punk Music, Solidarity and the Production of Similarity and Difference." *Popular Music & Society* 39.4 (Oct. 2016): 410–22.